IRISH LONDON DURING THE TROUBLES

First published in 2012 by Irish Academic Press

8 Chapel Lane,
Sallins,
Co. Kildare, Ireland

920 NE 58th Avenue, Suite 300
Portland, Oregon,
97213-3786, USA

© Seán Sorohan 2012

www.iap.ie

British Library Cataloguing in Publication Data

Sorohan, Sean.
 Irish London during The Troubles.
 1. Irish—England—London—History—20th century.
 2. Irish—England—London—Attitudes. 3. Children of
 immigrants—England—London—History—20th century.
 4. Children of immigrants—England—London—Attitudes.
 5. Northern Ireland—History—1969-1994.
 I. Title
 305.8′91620421-dc23

ISBN 978 0 7165 3102 9 (cloth)
ISBN 978 0 7165 3103 6 (paper)
ISBN 978 0 7165 3204 0 (Ebook)

Library of Congress Cataloging-in-Publication Data
An entry can be found on request

Printed and bound by SPRINT-Print, Rathcoole, Co. Dublin

In memory of John Sorohan,
my grandad

Contents

List of Plates

1. First Holy Communion, mid 60s
2. Second-generation children on the boat to Ireland for the summer, 60s
3. Second-generation boy on his uncle's farm in Ireland in the summer, 60s
4. Catholic high school in north London, late 70s
5. Second-generation dancers, 1980
6. Second-generation dancers, 60s
7. First Holy Communion, 60s
8. Big Tom (famous country and western singer very popular at the Galtymore)
9. Irishmen in an Irish pub with the Sam Maguire trophy (the All-Ireland winning Kerry team were visiting London)
10. Second-generation in Ireland in the summer
11. Second-generation in Ireland in the summer
12. Garryowen Gaelic football team, 1964

Acknowledgements

I was born in London and am third-generation Irish with four Irish-born grandparents. One of my earliest memories is set in the 'mother and child' room at our local Catholic church. The catechist asked if there were any children who were not from England. I remember enthusiastically putting my hand up and proudly proclaiming that I was from Ireland. At 4 years old I was so stumped at the catechist's reply – 'Do you know if you came here by boat or by aeroplane?' – that I ran over to my mum and asked if I had said the right thing. The reply was: 'Yes, you are Irish *and* English.'

The ensuing identity crisis over the next two decades eventually led to this book, which is an exploration of the London Irish world into which I was born. Through interviews with Irish people in London it explores the Irish emigrant community of the 1960s to 1980s in the English capital, particularly the north-west part of the city; the experiences of those emigrants during the period of the Troubles in Northern Ireland; and the ways in which the second-generation Irish visualize and express their own identities.

This work began life as a Masters dissertation at Queen's University Belfast and thus I would like to thank the history department there and particularly Professor Sean O'Connell, who was my supervisor. Thank you to the interviewees for the time that they kindly gave up, and to those who helped me find suitable candidates for interview. Thanks also to Michael Cahillane, for giving me permission to use his painting on the cover of this book. *Crownhill All-Ireland* depicts a group of the London Irish attempting to pick up radio coverage of the All-Ireland final.

Thank you to my family, especially my grandparents, for being the inspiration behind this book.

Finally, thank you, Siobhán, for your love and support.

Introduction

Leaving Ireland has always been an emotive topic, from the 'emigrant wakes' that bade farewell to those heading for America in the nineteenth century to the myriad songs of leaving and longing for home that populate the canon of Irish ballads. In recent times the death of the fabled Celtic Tiger has caused emigration to weigh heavily once again on Irish minds. Since 2011 *The Irish Times* has been running a section of its website named 'Generation Emigration', in which fierce debates about motivations for emigration and the state of Ireland run alongside stories of how emigrants are settling in their adopted homes and more nostalgic comments about missing Ireland on St Patrick's Day.[1] This book focuses on a part of another 'Generation Emigration', that which left Ireland for London on an enormous scale in the two decades following the Second World War. They did not have the comment boards of websites to relay their experiences but listening to them talk through their memories can illuminate the history of London's largest ethnic minority.[2] Through interviews with twenty-four emigrants who left Ireland from shortly after the war up until the early 1970s (and two slightly later), eleven London-born second-generation Irish and three priests who ministered to them, this book looks to bring alive the experiences of Irish London.

Whether the Irish throughout Britain have formed coherent ethnic communities, their involvement in political movements, the extent to which they were victims of anti-Irish feeling and the durability of ethnic identity through generations have formed the major topics of discussion in historical literature.[3] There has been little agreement on these matters for the nineteenth and early twentieth centuries, with some, such as Fitzpatrick, dismissing the idea of any strong sense of community, but others, such as Lees, Fielding and Belchem, portraying strong Irish communities that eventually gave way but left a residue of a distinctive identity across generations in London, Manchester and Liverpool.[4] Nevertheless, in spite of differences in terms of how swift the process was, it is generally accepted that Irish Catholics have historically 'disappeared' into, or at most made up a distinctive subculture within, the British working class. There have also been differences of opinion on the degree to which anti-Irishness affected emigrants and whether to classify it as 'racism' or simply national prejudice, although it is relatively well accepted that there were periods of anti-Irish and anti-Catholic sentiment in Britain.[5] The matters of political involvement and to what extent an Irish identification bridged the generation gap have varied from place to place. Whereas the Liverpool Irish continued to elect an Irish nationalist MP, T.P. O'Connor, for decades in the late nineteenth and early twentieth centuries, the London Irish of the same period organized themselves politically only intermittently and rarely on any significant scale.[6] This book is primarily an historical portrait of the Irish presence in London and thus is focused on these aspects that have informed historical debate. Nevertheless, being a study of the experiences and identities of people who are still living, it inevitably touches on the research of those in other academic fields. Sociologists, psychologists and researchers of popular culture have all focused on issues of racism and discrimination within contemporary Britain, identity formation among the second-generation and the social issues of health and socio-economic mobility, all of which are encountered in this work.[7]

Among historians, Delaney was the first to analyse in detail the experiences of the post-Second World War influx of Irish into Britain, taking the story to 1969.[8] Moran has recently published a history of the Irish in Birmingham that spans the period covered by this work, offering a Midlands perspective on some of the themes that will be explored, and McGowan has approached the Irish in Leeds through an oral history methodology in much the same way as this work approaches their compatriots in London.[9] This work therefore treads new ground for historians, as it is primarily concerned with the time period after that of Delaney and has a geographical focus different to existing studies. Delaney and McGowan follow a trend with which sociologists have often persisted, that of excluding Northern Irish Catholics from their analyses. While this makes good sense for empirical research purposes, where numbers from Northern Ireland are hard to come by, it was not logical to omit them from this work. Catholics from Northern Ireland, while they had their differences in terms of the milieu they were brought up in and the educational system they came through, largely became part of the great body of the Irish in London, involving themselves in all the same spheres of

Irishness, such as the Gaelic Athletic Association (GAA), county associations, the Catholic Church and Irish dance halls, that their co-religionists from the Republic did. In addition, a study that covers the Irish in Britain during the 1970s cannot ignore the Troubles and thus should not ignore those most personally affected by it. This study does, however, omit Northern Irish Protestants, although they have been included in the demographic figures, due to the lack of any statistics of immigrants broken down by religion, and 'Irish' has been used synonymously with 'Irish Catholic' throughout. While they have shared many similar experiences of emigration to their Catholic counterparts, it is felt that their stories are fundamentally different because they came from a community that shared a religion and, nominally at least, a national identity with the indigenous population of Britain. This omission seemed justified when carrying out the research because Northern Irish Protestants featured very rarely in narratives of Irish lives in London among the Catholic-background interviewees.

The main focus of Chapter 1 is to ask whether the post-war Irish could be said to have formed a coherent 'ethnic community' within the English capital. It explores the spheres through which Irish people interacted and the divisions among them. Chapter 2 wades into territory previously largely inhabited by sociologists and political polemicists, the effects of the Northern Ireland Troubles on the Irish in London. It questions how far the alleged suppression of the political voice of the Irish people by the forces of the British state is true and to what extent the revival of 'visceral anti-Irish prejudices' among the British population was felt by the Irish in London.[10] Chapter 3 looks to the children of the post-war generation, analysing how the ethno-religious structures inhabited by the Irish affected their childhoods and how they have visualized and expressed their own identities throughout their lives. The epilogue to this work brings out some of the changes among the Irish in London in the 1980s, when a conducive local government authority, a mature second-generation and new emigrants combined to expand the cultural horizons and change the political landscape of Irish London. One of the main themes that struck me during research for this book is that while much of what has been written about the Irish in Britain has been problem-centred, whether it be about anti-Irish racism, alcoholism, mental health or the poor working conditions of the building trade, many of the interviewees were very positive about their lives in London. It is hoped that one of the contributions of this book will be to show that, for most, the craic was indeed good in Cricklewood.

METHODOLOGY AND SOURCES

This work is largely based on oral testimony. A sampling technique was considered unnecessary; it was more important to achieve a selection of people representing different strands among the Irish in London. Thus I have spoken with a wide variety of people: male and female; from across social classes and educational backgrounds; from Northern Ireland and the Republic; urban and rural backgrounds; some involved in Irish community activity and others not; clergy and laity; some politically active and others with no political interest.[11] Emails and letters to Irish organizations and people, an advert on a social networking site, chance meetings and personal contacts all provided candidates for interviews. In two cases the interviewees had never lived in London itself but lived relatively close by and had worked or socialized in London during their lives. As such, the sample is not a representative cross section of the Irish population of London and some biases in the sample exist. Simply by chance, those from Northern Ireland are over-represented, as are second-generation interviewees with two Irish-born parents, something that in itself is interesting, as the difficulties I had in finding interviewees of 'mixed' parentage highlighted the strength of Irish connections in London. Among all interviewees there is also a notable bias towards north-west London, mostly due to the fact that it represents the greatest area of Irish settlement in London. The interviews were not rigid, varying greatly in time and content. The preference was for a life-story approach, allowing themes to come out in narrative without prompting. However, there was an interview schedule of questions that were of particular interest that were asked if the topic was not covered in a life story, some of which were asked of all interviewees and others that were interviewee-specific.

It is understood that oral history can be fraught with danger if one does not recognize the problems of memories fading with time and the testimony of the past being filtered through later experiences and current-day views.[12] Particularly in cases where interviewees have been asked to recall opinions, statements may be significantly affected by these pitfalls. When this is felt to be the case, statements have either not been used or have been flagged in the text. In addition to my own interviews, five volumes of interviews with Irish people in Britain, two of which are made up of only women and one that focuses on London, have been utilized.[13] Four interviews in the British Library Sound Archive were also consulted, as well as some transcripts in the HISTORYtalk archive in Kensington. By far the most significant among documentary sources is *The Irish Post*, the first successful newspaper aimed at the Irish in Britain, which was launched in 1970. The Irish in Britain Archive, based at London Metropolitan University, provided a wide range of additional primary sources, including leaflets of political groups, minutes from the meetings of some Irish organizations and pamphlets from community events. Memoirs, such as MacAmhlaigh's *Diary of an Irish Navvy*, have been utilized for information on the first-generation.[14] Second-generation memoirs, in particular Walsh's *Falling Angels* and Mangan's *Me and Mine*, formed key sources for Chapter 3.[15]

A DEMOGRAPHIC PICTURE OF IRISH LONDON

Since 1700 around eight million people have emigrated from Ireland, with five million of these leaving from 1800 to 1870.[16] While it is now accepted that emigration became a significant feature of Irish life before the Great Famine of 1845–50, the decade after the potato blight, which saw over 1,500,000 leaving Ireland, was at the very least a wholesale change in the scale of the trend.[17] Due to continuing emigration and the deaths of over one million from starvation and disease, from 1841 to 1891 the population of Ireland declined from over eight million to just over four million.[18] It was this phenomenon that first created major settlements of Irish people throughout the world. Among these, it is the Irish who sailed for America who have garnered the most attention, both from scholars and in the national imagination. This is perhaps understandable considering the huge scale on which the Irish left for the States in the nineteenth century, with the USA receiving perhaps six times as many emigrants as Britain in the last quarter of the century.[19] However, the Irish population in Britain has always been significant in absolute terms. Even before the famine years, in 1841, the Irish-born in Britain numbered 415,000. Peaking at over 800,000 in 1881, the population remained over 600,000 for the rest of the century.[20] The north-west of England and Scotland are often thought of as the areas which experienced the greatest impact from nineteenth-century immigration. Certainly, in terms of percentage of population, Liverpool and Glasgow were the most heavily Irish – in 1851, 22 per cent of the former's population was Irish-born, as was 17 per cent of the latter's. Yet the greatest numbers of Irish people in any one city since the famine has consistently been

London.[21] In the first decades of the twentieth century, emigration remained a feature of Irish life but to a smaller degree than previously. Thus, the Irish-born population of Britain began to fall and reached about half a million in 1931.[22]

What is commonly referred to as the 'second wave' of emigration from Ireland to Britain, the first being the post-famine decades, began in the mid-1930s and accelerated in the post-war years. From 1946 to 1971, net emigration from the Republic of Ireland was around 640,000 people. An estimated 80 per cent of these went to Britain, due primarily to its booming post-war economy and restrictions on entry to the USA.[23] The total number of those born on the island of Ireland living in Britain rocketed to 960,000 in 1971.[24] Seventy-five per cent of the Republic of Ireland-born (hereafter ROI-born) in 1971 had emigrated since 1940, showing the enormous impact of this phase of emigration.[25] Over the decade 1961–71, economic development in Ireland saw emigration begin to slow, and throughout the 1970s return migration to Ireland outweighed those leaving for Britain. Thus, by 1981 the Irish population of Britain had fallen to 850,000.[26] Although emigration did continue among young people, this represented a significant change that brought to an end the 'second wave'.[27] As this work is primarily concerned with the period after the initial emigration experience, the end of the second wave, taken as 1971, is used as a starting point for the following demographic analysis.

London had contained Irish settlements for centuries but it was during the second wave that it acquired the novel position of being the premier city of the Irish abroad. The city increased its share of the Irish in Britain to higher levels than ever before as migrants largely shunned the industrial cities of the north of England and western Scotland for the booming south-east. By 1971 London was the adopted home of 32 per cent of the total Irish-born living in Britain, up from only 9 per cent at the beginning of the century.[28] After London, with its 240,000 ROI-born residents, the next largest group of Irish in Britain was the 44,000 in Birmingham.[29] Within the capital, the Irish made up the largest foreign-born group, with 3 per cent of the total population of the city and 17 per cent of all foreign-born residents. If one includes the Northern Irish population and children of Irish parents, who outnumbered the previous generation roughly 1.5:1, the Irish population in London in the decade could be estimated at 700,000, or nearly 9 per cent of the total population of the city.[30]

The Irish in London had a distinctive demographic profile. A higher proportion of ROI-born than Northern Ireland-born (hereafter NI-born) in Britain lived in London: 34 per cent of the ROI-born population (241,225 out of 709,235) but only 17 per cent of NI-born (42,175 out of 248,595).[31] Thus, in London the NI-born made up only 15 per cent of the total Irish population, whereas elsewhere in Britain they were a more significant 31 per cent, which reflects a much greater tendency to migrate to Scotland in particular. The Northern Irish in general were also less likely to emigrate. Thus, in 1971 people born in Northern Ireland made up only 28 per cent of the total Irish-born in Britain compared to 34 per cent of the island of Ireland's population.[32] Along with the Republic generally, rural areas and the west of Ireland were particularly well represented among emigrants to Britain. Rural counties were consistently the worst affected by emigration, and the Irish Commission on Emigration noted that for 1946–51, those from counties Cork, Galway, Kerry, Mayo, Donegal and Limerick made up 55 per cent of all emigrants from the Republic.[33] It has long been noted that a unique feature of Irish emigration is that women have usually outnumbered men. This was no different in London, where by 1971 females made up 54 per cent of the ROI-born population (compared to 52 per cent in the general British population).[34]

In 1971 the Irish across Britain were increasingly middle-aged and had settled down with families: 62 per cent of the ROI-born in Britain were aged 30–59, compared to only 47 per cent of the general population, and around 70 per cent of all the Irish were, or had, been married.[35] The age distribution of the Irish in Britain was due to the overwhelming majority of emigrants being young adults upon leaving Ireland. From 1943 to 1951, for instance, 84 per cent of women granted permits to travel to Britain from the twenty-six counties were below 30 years of age, as were 66 per cent of males.[36]

The Irish generally arrived in London with very little education; free post-primary education was not introduced in the Republic until 1967. It was estimated in the 1960s that only one-fifth of Irish people in Britain had any secondary education, and in 1950 only 0.23 per cent of the population in the Republic had attended university.[37] Even after being in Britain for a number of years, most did not acquire qualifications: in a 10 per cent sample of the British population in 1971, only 5.1 per cent of ROI-born men had qualifications above A-level and only 3.5 per cent had a bachelor's degree or higher. This compared to 8.7 per cent and 4.6 per cent respectively overall for men in Britain. Their female counterparts were in a more favourable situation, with 10.9 per cent having post-A Level qualifications, although four-fifths of these were nursing qualifications.[38] While secondary education was more common in Northern Ireland, by 1961 76 per cent of males and 73 per cent of females had no education past the age of 15.[39] This left the Irish in Britain worse off than their British counterparts and by 1981 ROI-born males were the least qualified of any ethnic group in London.[40] Thus, the majority of the Irish in Britain were clustered in lower status employment, with 74 per cent of males and 58 per cent of females in manual work in 1971, and unemployment was slightly higher than in the general population.[41] There was clustering within the building trade and nursing, with 38 per cent of ROI-born males working in the former in 1966 and 31,000 Irish-born nurses in Britain in 1971.[42] However, there was a small well-educated element within the post-war emigrant flood to Britain. There is some suggestion that the educated Irish were proportionally over-represented in the post-war migration.[43] The NHS in particular attracted Irish doctors, with the 4,000 Irish doctors in Britain outnumbering those in the Republic by 1971.[44] NI-born people consistently appeared between the British-born and ROI-born populations in occupation statistics, suggesting that coming from a similar education system and the opportunity of migrating within the same British company or public service held advantages.[45]

Within the capital the post-war Irish immigrants congregated in the north and west of the city. Brent had the highest numbers of ROI-born in 1971, with 21,761 people making up 8 per cent of the borough's total population. Ealing, Hammersmith, Westminster, Islington and Camden followed Brent in the absolute figures, all with over 12,000 ROI-born and all situated in the centre, west and north of the city. Significant numbers also lived in the south/south-west boroughs of Lambeth and Wandsworth. There was a certain element of clustering of Irish people in some areas. In 1971 3,731 ROI-born lived in the two Kilburn electoral wards, making up 17.4 per cent of the population; 1,492 lived in Cricklewood ward where they made up 15.4 per cent. Adding 15 per cent to the absolute figures for those from Northern Ireland and including the second generation as 1.5 times greater in number than their parents, it is reasonable to assume that around 40–50 per cent of these famously Hibernian areas were indeed Irish. Similar concentrations, if not quite as dramatic, existed throughout Brent and in other boroughs in places such as Queen's

Park and White City. In spite of these areas of high concentration, the Irish were by no means heavily ghettoized; over 65 per cent of ROI-born people in London in 1971 lived in electoral wards where less than 5 per cent of the population was also ROI-born.[46]

There were changes in the demographic picture of the Irish in London from 1971. This was most apparent in the changing Irish population of London and its distribution. Between the 1971 and 1981 censuses, ROI-born residents in London decreased by 15.6 per cent. This exceeded the 13.4 per cent fall in ROI-born residents across Britain. This disparity is possibly due to the growth of new towns in the south-east, which led to an 8.6 per cent fall in the London population overall, and a greater rate of return migration among the middle-aged London cohort than among the older Irish populations of Scotland and north-west England. The number of NI-born in London fell by roughly 9.1 per cent, close to the general population decline in London, perhaps due to a lack of desire to return to Northern Ireland during the Troubles and a trickle of people escaping the violence by moving to London.[47]

In spite of a general lack of social mobility in terms of occupation, residential patterns show that the Irish were moving up socially and out towards to the suburbs from 1971.[48] Inner-city boroughs lost enormous proportions of their ROI-born population. The largest proportional falls from 1971 to 1981 occurred in the inner-city boroughs of Kensington (-38 per cent), Hammersmith (-29 per cent) and Westminster (-26 per cent). At the same time, two boroughs on the outer north-west border of London experienced gains in their ROI-born figures: Enfield (+9 per cent) and Hillingdon (+3 per cent). Within Brent one sees the same pattern from 1971 to 1981, with wards closest to the centre of London, such as Kilburn and Queen's Park, losing a large proportion of their ROI-born population, and outer ones, such as Fryent, Kenton and Sudbury, experiencing modest rises.[49]

The pattern is even starker when one extends the analysis to 1991. While these figures were affected by the 'new wave' of emigration in the 1980s, it is still significant that the outer London boroughs saw dramatic rises in ROI-born populations, with Enfield experiencing a 46 per cent increase from 1971 to 1991 (4,600 to 6,600 people), Harrow 37 per cent (6,400 to 8,800) and Waltham Forest and Hillingdon both over 20 per cent. In the same two decades, Kensington, Westminster and Hammersmith lost 47 per cent (8,400 to 4,500), 39 per cent (12,800 to 7,800) and 36 per cent (13,500 to 8,600). By 1991 the ROI-born population of even the minor 'ghetto' of the Kilburn wards had fallen by 43 per cent, while the slightly less central Cricklewood lost only 11 per cent.[50] This ethnic drift to the suburbs is evidence of the Irish going through the process first recorded by the Chicago school of sociologists, of immigrant groups moving out from the centres of cities as they become better established.[51]

'Happier amongst your own': The Settled Irish Community

Of late I was transported, boys, from Erin's holy shore;
My case is sad, my crime is bad, for I was born poor.[1]

This chapter paints a picture of the Irish-born population of London who migrated to the English capital primarily in the two decades after the Second World War. It first considers the emigrants' narratives of leaving Ireland. Attention is then turned to the central question of whether the Irish-born in London built a coherent 'ethnic community'. The ultimate conclusion is that an Irish community did develop that impacted in real terms on the lives of Irish emigrants and became increasingly imagined as an ethnic community within London and Britain by the 1970s.

LEAVING

The quotation above is part of a song heard by John B. Keane on a ferry crossing to Britain in the 1950s. The song goes on to lament life in London: 'Oh Cricklewood! Oh Cricklewood! / You stole my youth away / For I was young and innocent / And you were old and grey.' This depressing picture of forced emigration has been the dominant portrayal of leaving home throughout the nineteenth and twentieth centuries. For instance, Kerby Miller's analysis of the letters of Irish emigrants in the nineteenth century has shown the language of exile to be prevalent.[2] Very often one comes across similar language in popular London-Irish 'community memory' – it is significant that both London Irish RFC and the London County GAA teams mirror that of the New York GAA in labelling themselves 'The Exiles'. Of the eleven second-generation interviewees for this work, only one expressed the opinion that their parent(s) leaving of Ireland was motivated by anything more than a 'sail or starve' choice.[3] Scully has characterized such a narrative of 1950s Irish emigration to Britain as part of the 'recognised story within which individuals can position their personal narratives'.[4] It is certainly noticeable throughout leaving narratives that interviewees relate their story to this overriding story of enforced emigration.

Other factors behind emigration, both 'push' and 'pull', have been identified by academics, notably the maintenance of social networks, the cultural pressures to leave and youthful adventure.[5] The aim here is not to provide the definitive set of reasons why people left Ireland but to give a picture of the myriad ways in which leaving is remembered by emigrants, to highlight that the Irish in London were not all simply economic migrants. One must bear in mind that the subsequent experiences of interviewees may well have played a part in their narratives – the emigrant who came looking for adventure but found only hardship may later only remember his or her leaving in terms of enforced exile; in light of the recent Troubles in Northern Ireland, the politically minded person may now place more emphasis on discrimination against Catholics in their emigration narrative than was the case at the time.

The most dominant theme in telling the story of leaving was indeed the economically motivated 'reluctant exile'.[6] Rose remembered the chronic emigration from her Wexford town: 'But [upon leaving school] you hadn't any jobs to go for, there wasn't anything to do. Because of that everyone had to go away ... There wasn't any work in the town apart from fishing.'[7] The prolific writer Donall MacAmhlaigh, who migrated to Northampton in 1951 and spent many years working as a labourer, opined: 'I don't believe the Irish were ever really afflicted with the wanderlust, going all over the globe for the fun of it. There may have been a few such but the bulk of my generation that came over here to Britain came for the good and sufficient reason that they had no prospects of work at home.'[8] On occasion an interviewee had a job in Ireland but it was too lowly in pay and status to stay in Ireland for. Oliver's dominant narrative was very much that of having been driven from home through lack of opportunity: 'There was nothing there! That [porter's job] was all I got offered! I had the potential of going to university and here I was, a hotel porter at the European hotel.'[9] One interviewee for Donnellan's film, *The Irishmen: An Impression of Exile* (1964), characterized himself and his countrymen as being 'forced to leave Ireland, there was nothing in it, it's poor, it's destitute. I'm sorry to say it's destitute, it's the best country in the world and they're the greatest people in the world.'[10]

However, in many cases the economic explanations of leaving were mixed with other motives and in some the alternative motives predominated. Very often moving to London was, as Liam Ryan points out, important in maintaining social ties rather than breaking them. Robert explained his emigration as due to work but there was also a strong element of maintaining the networks that he had grown up with:

> Like all the young lads in my time there was no work about so I hit the gravy train for London ... I was living in Willesden with my sister for a couple of weeks and then ... about twenty lads from my street at home all amalgamated and we got two houses and we were all living together. So I was with all me own lads, fellas I went to school with.[11]

Even those who remembered an extreme reluctance to leave home often mixed their economic explanations with joining up with relatives. When interviewed for a documentary on the Irish in London, one woman described her leaving in economic terms but also mentioned her family link:

> Interviewee: There was no employment over there and a number of my family were already in England and I decided there was nothing else for me but to leave. I didn't like it.
> Interviewer: You didn't want to leave?
> Interviewee: Who does?[12]

For some, the maintenance of social ties and the possibility of building new ones were the primary motivations for leaving. For instance, John Munally was too concerned about the dearth of young women left in his home parish to stay in Ireland: 'The girls we'd got to know went away to America and England, so you were lost, you had to go ... We wanted more excitement ... Most of my friends, including the young girls, came over here, and I wanted to get away.'[13] Indeed, the fact that in the Republic of Ireland in the 1950s one-third of men and one-quarter of women over 55 remained unmarried supports the idea that poor marriage prospects were motivation for leaving. The thoughts of the Irish Housewives Association that most young girls leaving were 'mostly attractive country girls who are striving to get away from the late marriage prospect in this country' is supported by the interviewees for this project, the great majority of whom met their spouses after emigrating.[14]

The picture of emigration as a necessity on the path to adulthood, including finding a spouse, was vividly portrayed by some. As Robert pointed out, it was on a person's horizon from a young age: 'When you became 9 or 10 emigration came on your mind.'[15] In *The Irishmen* one interviewee characterized the attitude in Ireland when growing up: 'there's a feeling there's something wrong with you if you haven't got out ... Somehow you're failing, you're not fully alive if you haven't got out.'[16] The seeming glamour of returning emigrants reinforced such a culture. Declan remembered that many emigrants going home would 'save up a bit of money, buy a suit, maybe hire a car in Dublin' and make a big impression on the young at home. Pat Sweeney remembered this being an important factor in him leaving: 'I came here because all my relations were coming here; my friends were coming back well dressed. They had the blue shirt, the white shirt, the brown shoes and they had money.'[17]

London offered opportunities for career development that Ireland did not, and a chance to take advantage of them was often a major reason for emigrating, particularly for the better educated. For instance, Evelyn initially moved to London in order to study for qualifications to become a professional piano performer and teacher; Diarmuid moved to embark on a PhD at a top university; Jack left home in Armagh with his band in search of a wider audience among the Irish abroad.[18] Others remembered leaving Ireland for pure adventure or to escape the constraints of a society that they perceived as suffocating. Brenda's motivations for leaving included the higher pay she stood to earn in London and the fun she had when visiting her sister, who was already in London: 'A lot of people came for work, but I had a job. I suppose I came because I thought that it would be better.'[19] In this vein, one interviewee for another project remembered that he initially 'only came over for a couple of years [to] have a bit of fun'.[20] Stephen said to his friend Paul during an interview: 'I was different, I had work. I just got pissed off.'[21] It is telling that Brenda and Stephen's comments also reflect the dominance of the view of the Irish as leaving solely through economic necessity by stressing their difference to the main narrative.

Stephen's getting 'pissed off' was a lesser version of the minority who left Ireland due to alienation from its social mores or due to traumatic experiences. While this applied to none of the interviewees for this book, it has been a theme found in other interviews and studies. This seems to have been particularly prevalent among women who wished to leave behind the constraints that their gender faced in Ireland. It also seems to have increased towards the end of our period, which reflects Ó Briain's survey, carried out among emigrants in the 1970s, that found four times as many women as men professing to be leaving for non-economic reasons.[22] For instance, one woman left Ireland to become a nurse in England in 1965 because she felt stifled by conservative morals that led to situations such as the ban on contraception and a 'pure fear of sex' as well as the 'class system and nepotism' she perceived in Irish society – 'I just knew I had to leave home to survive.'[23] The singer Sinéad O'Connor, who left Dublin for London in 1982 as a 16-year-old, put it this way: 'I was glad to leave Ireland (at 16), glad to get out … I hated the place. It was the most depressing place in the world for me because of my circumstances growing up ... Going to London meant *freedom*, it meant *escape*.' (emphasis added)[24]

Males also occasionally fled Irish morality, as with a homosexual couple who ended up at the London Irish Centre's hostel in the early 1970s.[25] The London Irish Survivors Outreach Service today works with those for whom London was an escape from the physical and mental abuse received in certain institutions.

Some had less of a choice in leaving. Ann Rossiter's work has described the 'abortion trail' of women travelling to England due to the illegal status of abortion in Ireland.[26] Before legal abortions in Britain, the trail of unmarried pregnant women was also a feature of Irish London. Sheila Dillon devoted her working life to help young women who left Ireland to protect the reputations of their families: 'I belonged to the Legion of Mary. We used to meet young Irish girls down at Euston Station ... We'd watch those girls getting off the train at Euston ... I used to know if they were pregnant just by looking at them ... Helping those young pregnant girls became my mission in life.'[27]

It was not just the conservative Republic that people fled from; Northern Irish society also drove alienated people out. In the 1972 annual report of the London Irish Centre it was noted that a number of 'Northern Ireland refugee families, driven out of their homes by intimidation or frustration, have arrived in London during the past year.'[28] Prior to the outbreak of the Troubles, people also left through frustration at the bigotry and heated political atmosphere that they found in the North, as Eoin, who emigrated for the first time in 1958, pointed out:

> My reason for being here is simply that in Northern Ireland, whenever I was looking for work, my involvement in nationalist organisations, well it wasn't well known, but it would have been easy enough to find out and it made things difficult. In those days they'd be blunt about it, they'd ask you what your religion was outright. And I came from Ardoyne [a Catholic area of north Belfast] which tells you about all you need to know.[29]

While it is clear that the economic position of Ireland in the post-war years was the underlying cause of most emigration, the narratives of leaving often bring out a web of reasons, sometimes several within the same interviewee. Memories and reasons for leaving are important for the study of the 'settled community' in London because they affected the operation of that community. For instance, the dominant motive of economic exile played a pivotal role in encouraging the persistence of a 'myth of return' to Ireland, and narratives that explain leaving Ireland in order to escape Irish society can account for the alienation of some from the core of the community in London.

Whatever the reason for leaving Ireland, arriving in London was an exciting, if slightly bewildering, experience for most emigrants, many of whom had never been to a city. Anna May Mangan was told that one of her father's first impressions was that 'Londoners [were] "miserable feckers" because no one ever greeted him in the street. When he first arrived the man was kept busy tipping his hat and offering a cheery "Howya?", "Good morning!" or "Good afternoon!" to everyone he met.'[30] David, who left for London in 1957, described a similarly strange but exciting world:

> You imagine a guy coming from a village in rural Ireland and landing in London, it being probably the first city he'd ever seen in his life, and to see the vastness of it, the width of the street, the houses, the amount of activity that was available to you, an absolute ball it was for the people who came in the '50s … You had a situation where people who came from Ireland at that time who had never been at anything other than a parish dance, where the priest would be looking around seeing what they're up to, and suddenly they're in London and you've got

all of these Irish establishments – the Round Tower, the Gresham, the Blarney – all of these big, big 'ballrooms of romance', and they used to flock there in their thousands ... You can imagine the difference ... it made to their lives.[31]

'THE IRISH COMMUNITY'?

The historians of the Irish in Britain have never managed a consensus on what characterized an 'Irish community' in a given place and time. Studies that have dismissed such a notion have pointed to a lack of sustained political organization, a perceived high speed of assimilation into British society and only low levels of residential clustering.[32] Hickman has rightly criticized much of this work for what she sees as the use of criteria that may be suitable in studying ethnic groups in America or elsewhere being used for the Irish in Britain.[33] A similar criticism of the use of generalized criteria for ethnic groups can be made of Hutchinson and O'Day's dismissal of an Irish 'ethnic community' in early-twentieth-century London that is based on Handelman's generic system of ranking ethnic groups that automatically relegates any without political organization and would thus immediately see the Irish in London as no more than an 'ethnic network'.[34] This work assesses the Irish population of London on its own merits rather than looking to place it within any uniform index, showing that there was a significant amount of social inter-action between Irish people in London, partly through residential and occupational distribution but primarily through a raft of generally non-political organizations, clubs and places that became consciously 'Irish spaces', which maintained and passed on an ethnic identity. It is the contention of this work that it is reasonable to say that the people involved in these environments were part of an 'Irish community', regardless of the facts of low levels of political organi-zation and only limited ghettoization. In addition to high levels of face-to-face interaction, a sense of belonging to an 'imagined' Irish community in London, and in Britain more widely, was common and its expression became stronger from the 1970s.[35]

The limited residential clustering of Irish people did lead to some areas having a distinctly 'Little Ireland' feel. Danny said that in the 1960s when 'walking about Camden or Kentish town [borough of Camden] you felt as though you were in an extension of Ireland'.[36] Likewise, Fr Terence said that when he was about to leave for his first parish in England in 1973 a recently returned Irish priest remarked: 'Oh, Kentish Town, there was an English person seen there once.'[37] An interviewee in Dunne's collection of interviews moved from Hampstead to Cricklewood in the mid-1960s partly because she wanted to live in a more Irish area: 'I felt more at home there than I had in Hampstead ... Kilburn and Cricklewood at that time were bursting at the seams with Irish.'[38] Common phrases among inter-viewees and the Irish in London generally such as 'County Kilburn' and 'the craic is good in Cricklewood' emphasize the particularly Irish atmospheres of these north-west London areas.

Such areas saw high levels of day-to-day interaction between Irish residents outside more obvious ethnic spaces such as Catholic churches or dance halls. Mentions of everyday contact between Irish people in London were frequent in interviews. Joe's memories are an example of how residential clustering could lead to interactions that, while perhaps relatively mundane, were important in building social ties among Irish people: 'Our next door neighbours were Irish and they came from Glenties up in Donegal. He was a fire engine driver so he would take my mother out to learn to drive ... and we'd take them to Ireland in the car. That was the deal.'[39]

This continued to be apparent among the post-war emigrants beyond the time frame of this book. For instance, during the interview for this project with Stephen in the relatively highly Irish populated Harrow, Paul (a Fermanagh man) came from over the road to let him know that Séamus Heaney had been on the radio.[40] Malone's 2001 study of the Irish population of Kensal Rise, in Brent, highlighted the regular interaction and culture of mutual help that existed. One elderly interviewee described her regular interaction with Irish people living nearby:

> Here I can go to the shops and have a chat with Jack across the road or Barbara and that keeps me going. If I need anything I can go next door to Sarah and Paul – they're very good neighbours ... I know it here. We all came here together, the Kellys and the Caseys – It would be bad to leave it now ...[41]

It is important to note that such ethnic networks also existed outside the main Irish areas, where a relatively small number of Irish people could still have a high level of interaction, as John Walsh remem-bered from his south London childhood:

> It was quite a gang this freemasonry of London Irish were

casually keeping each other, busy offering each other employment, implicitly refusing to trust the perfidious Brits to do any
job with honesty. The tribe may have been far from home, but
they brought their numbers together by way of network and
introduction, until everybody was sharing the same Cavan
osteopath, the same Wicklow plumber, the same Connemara
bookie.[42]

Some occupational clustering also enhanced this face-to-face
interaction. Irish men dominated some building companies and sites,
making them their own. Ciara showed this when saying that her
husband 'works for Murphy's [construction]' and thus 'has stayed in
the Irish working community'.[43] When asked if he had experienced
anti-Irish hostility, Timothy, who worked in construction, said that
he did not, and elaborated: 'The work didn't bring me in touch [with
English people] ... What could somebody do if they were in
construction and they didn't like you? They [the English] were in
the minority at that time.'[44] A similar but less common situation
existed in hospitals with large numbers of Irish nurses. One nurse
who began training in London in 1957 said that she felt homesick
for only a week and 'after that I felt as though I was in England all
my life because there were so many Irish girls there and they were
all in the same boat'.[45] Outside London and areas of concentrated
Irish settlement, MacAmhlaigh still found high levels of Irish interaction, due to having worked in both hospitals and construction: 'it's
mostly Irish that are here between nurses and others ... as in most of
these places that I've seen on building sites in this country, the Irish
stick together and don't have much social contact with the English'.[46]

As we have seen, the number of Irish living in areas of London
with large concentrations of their compatriots was not particularly
high and decreased over time due to return migration or movement
to the outer boroughs. Fr Terence noted this drift to outer London
when many of the people he met as parish priest in a nice area of
Ealing told him about starting 'in one room in Kilburn'.[47] But even by
1971 only 31 per cent of Republic of Ireland-born (ROI-born) people
in London lived in the five boroughs where over 5 per cent of the
population was also born in the twenty-six counties.[48] Even in the
most Irish borough of Brent, only just over half the Irish lived in
wards where over 10 per cent of the population was ROI-born.[49]
Likewise, while 30–40 per cent of working-age Irish males and 31,000
females were in construction or nursing, the majority were not in

these occupations and worked in jobs where most colleagues were not Irish.

As well as not being heavily ghettoized, the Irish did not engage in widespread political organization at any time up to and including the 1970s, something that is discussed further in Chapter Two. In spite of these points that may indicate a lack of a coherent community, the Irish in London showed high levels of organization in other areas, which brought them in to regular contact. The county associations in London, under the overarching Council of Irish County Associations, were important vehicles for ethnic interaction. The early preoccupations of the associations are illustrated in the 1957 minute book of the Fermanagh Association, where the initial pains of emigration were clearly expressed in the language of exile and inspiration was taken from another group of 'exiles':

> Our primary aim was the welfare of our people in London but we owed a great deal to Fermanagh and as emigrants we had a duty to do what we could for the county and in that way help ourselves by creating employment at home ... The Jews resembled the Irish in many ways, particularly in that five sixths of both peoples had to live outside their native land. The Jews had tackled their problems with much more energy than any Irish government or group had ever done.[50]

Help for recent emigrants remained a prominent feature of the associations, as can be seen from the records of the Kildare Association in the 1980s when adverts were placed in Kildare newspapers for emigrants to contact them and a cheque sent for the son of one Kildare woman who had been badly injured at work.[51] However, as time passed and emigration slowed, these associations became primarily social groups as well as touching points for emigrants and their children with 'home'. Dinner dances, with proceeds being for the benefit of a member or a good cause in their home county (or for the civil rights cause in the late 1960s and early 1970s) and often with the attendance of a bishop from Ireland, began to be the mainstay of these societies. The expanding priorities in the Fermanagh Association, which held its first annual dinner dance in the august surroundings of the Irish Club in Eaton Square in 1965, can be seen in its Annual Report of 1971, when it was reported that in addition to helping to raise money for hostels and the London Irish Centre it had held 'two successful dinner dances', several 'parties and outings' and helped to create the Ulster float in the St Patrick's Day parade.[52] Anne, a second-generation interviewee, was a regular attendee, along with her father, at the events of one of the few associations that focused on an area within a county, Bandon in Cork. She described the social aspect and the connection with Ireland the association promoted:

> We used to have meetings and they'd have big dinner dances … I was allowed to go, I remember we had long dresses, all dolled up. And then every July they had Bandon week so we went over to Bandon as a family and my dad had his relations there …. and there'd be loads of things going on … The whole Bandon Association went back there.[53]

The county associations were well remembered among interviewees. Indeed, Ciara, Robert and Peter were currently involved with their respective associations when interviewed. One other interviewee, Fr Tom McCabe, who worked at the London Irish Centre in Camden from 1969 until 1973, mentioned being formerly involved during the 1970s.[54]

Gaelic games also provided a focus for Irish people in London, there being several dozen clubs in the capital from the 1960s on. As well as helping new emigrants, particularly men, to settle in London quickly, Gaelic games became community events. David played a game of football within three days of arriving, found 'twenty-five or thirty friends just like that from being invited to play in a match' and became heavily involved in the GAA in Britain for the next twenty years.[55] Robert remembered fondly the atmosphere during his early years in the GAA from the mid 1960s: 'It was great because I'd just arrived and I'd met fifty people the first day … This was the mid-'60s and it [Gaelic games] was really for the families, a fun day out for everyone … and the radio would be blazing away with the matches at home and you'd meet so many people all day, it was brilliant actually.'[56] Peter found the communal aspect of his club so attractive that it appeared to have had a significant influence in his staying in London. In reply to the question 'Do you remember your emigration well?' he answered:

> 16 April 1956. I remember it very well. I was lucky enough; I got in with the football club. I had no intention of staying here – I came here to do a course and I intended to go back and start a business in Ireland and I got involved with the football and I

suppose the social scene as well and I enjoyed it. I really got involved with the football side of it from the very beginning; I would say I was an officer in the club after a year or two.[57]

On occasion the London Irish came out in force for displays of their native sports at Mitcham in the 1950s, and later at New Eltham and Ruislip. For a period, Gaelic games were held at Wembley Stadium for a day annually, a spectacle that attracted 18,000 spectators in 1974.[58]

The London Irish Centre in Camden had been providing welfare and temporary accommodation for newly arrived immigrants since it was founded by the Catholic Oblate order in the mid-1950s in order to provide a hostel for young men and advice 'to introduce the Irish working boy and girl to all that is best in the Irish, or Catholic, life in London'.[59] In 1969, 2,299 Irish people came to the London Irish Centre for help and advice with housing, jobs and welfare, and thousands continued to come through the 1970s.[60] It was also a lively social centre with bars and large halls for dances, *céilithe*, county association dinners and cultural events.[61] Ciara remembered in the 1970s the Irish Centre social scene as being 'excellent … it was packed, it was hard to get a seat'.[62] Organizations set up by and aimed at Irish people also existed outside explicitly cultural activities and religious institutions. Given impetus by coverage in *The Irish Post*, a newspaper founded in 1970s and aimed at the Irish in Britain, Irish social clubs and centres experienced somewhat of a golden age from the 1970s.[63] The Federation of Irish Societies, which was established on a Britain-wide scale in 1973, brought Irish organizations and centres together into one overarching structure.[64] There were a number of centres within London, such as the South London Irish Club, founded in the mid-1970s, and the Haringey Irish Centre in the 1980s.[65] However, while *Áras na nGael* (House of the Gael) in Kilburn was founded as a cultural haven, specifically Irish social centres never had a great presence in north-west London. Because there were enough establishments that catered for the Irish, it seems that a centre was not needed.

Irish dance halls, frequently referred to by interviewees as 'ballrooms of romance', were important in the creation and maintenance of an ethnic community. Pictures from nights at the halls and advertisements for Irish showbands, such as Big Tom and the Mainliners and The Indians, took up much space in *The Irish Post*. The Galtymore in Cricklewood, the National in Kilburn and the Gresham in Holloway were among the most frequently mentioned in interviews and it appears that many young Irish lives revolved around dancing.[66] Despite their 'golden age' probably ending with the reduction in new, young emigrants by the beginning of the 1970s, the five interviewees for this project who migrated to London in the late 1960s or early 1970s all mentioned frequenting such establishments.[67] Indeed, among the first-generation interviewees for this project who were based in London, only three – the well-educated Diarmuid who moved to London in 1977 and the middle-class Elizabeth and Evelyn – said that they did not frequent such dance halls with regularity.[68] When Donall MacAmhlaigh visited London in the late 1950s for a Gaelic football match, his diary entry was full of wonderment at the social life that such places provided: 'The Irish in London, I'd say, have a great life, plenty of their own people all around them, galore Irish dances and somewhere to go every night of the week.'[69] Interviewees for this and other projects certainly looked back on these dance halls with fondness, often due partly to meeting future spouses during a set dance or a jive. Kathleen Morrissey, who met her husband in the Galtymore and still frequented it when interviewed in the early 2000s, spoke of the real importance of the Cricklewood venue in the lives of the Irish in London: 'They weren't just places to dance. They played a very important part in the lives of young Irish people ... It was a great big network, really. For me, in so many ways, it [the Galtymore] was the most significant place in my life in London.'[70] A documentary released in 2002 to mark fifty years of the Galtymore highlighted this importance to the Irish in London in keeping in touch both with each other and with singers and bands from home: 'London was now another Irish parish. If you were anyone in Ireland you were a star in the Galtymore ... It was a meeting place for jobs, problems, fun, finding flats and rooms, whatever. You were sure to make friends at the Galtymore, it really was a mini-Ireland.'[71]

The plethora of Irish pubs (it has been estimated that up to half the pubs in London were Irish-run in the early 1970s) provided other foci for emigrants in London.[72] These often became exclusively Irish spaces and people clearly distinguished between 'Irish' and 'English' pubs. Danny, for instance, in the context of feeling more at ease talking about the political situation in Northern Ireland around Irish people, said that, 'you wouldn't have talked about them [the Troubles] at all in an *English* pub'.[73] One interviewee, George, who grew up in

Kilburn with an English father and a second-generation Irish mother, recalled the pubs in his area exercising a voluntary segregation:

> There was only one pub in Kilburn that had a predominantly English following and an English landlord, all the other pubs … were frequented by Irish … My dad tended to go in there. He was one of the few English builders and he was an employer… He never said to me that he went there to avoid the Irish pubs. But the people that were in there were very much that they wanted to be in an English environment … It had a different feel about it.[74]

Some called these Irish pubs and dance halls 'ghettos', including one Irish landlord, who said that for men coming in from the building sites, 'the pub became a ghetto system, perhaps, a community of sorts'.[75] Ryan has labelled Irish pubs 'stepping-stones to a larger society' in their role of providing an ethnic space in which emigrants were comfortable. Robert certainly felt that and put his smooth transition into London life down to pubs as well as Gaelic football: 'You got homesick from time to time, missed little things about home and that but from day one I was playing Gaelic football here, from day two all the pubs were Irish and I was singing, you had money and you could go out and you were working away.'[76] Moreover, pubs acted as banks to cash cheques and recruitment fairs for construction workers – 'Those days you could go into a pub and get a job', as John pointed out.[77]

The almost exclusively Irish nature of some Catholic parishes meant that going to Mass in London was seen as an opportunity to meet other emigrants socially. The church as 'a meeting place' was a strong theme in interviews and research. The Sacred Heart on Quex Road in Kilburn, in particular, was renowned for the huge numbers of Irish people who went there on Sunday, with a dozen or more services for roughly 12,000 people in the late 1960s.[78] One Irishman remembered it as 'A real Irish church, with great priests. You'd always meet someone you knew. A big plus was the number of Irish girls who would go there.'[79] Timothy spoke of how, if you were a newly arrived emigrant and 'you were living in the Kilburn area, you went to Quex Road on a Sunday … you went early, checked out who from your area [in Ireland] was there and had a chat with them and they tried to make you welcome'.[80]

Likewise, Brigid, who migrated to north London from Donegal in 1972 at 18 years of age, spoke of her parish church as a focus for the Irish: 'When I came here there were lots of young people my age from Ireland ... you'd go to church and you'd get to know them here, it was actually a lot of fun.'[81] The churches even became battle-grounds for the often hotly contested recruitment of promising Gaelic games players, as Packie Hughes found out in 1960 when he was recruited by St Brendan's after Mass in Hayes.[82]

The Catholic Church itself, perhaps unwittingly, did much to encourage the development of a sense of 'Irish parishes'. Priests from Ireland were either specifically placed as Irish chaplains or simply assigned as a priest to such parishes.[83] Fr Terence remembered this conscious policy of strategically placing Irish priests:

> What the diocese tried to do was, if there were a lot of Irish people there, they would try to have an Irish priest, at least one Irish priest in the parish ... so that he could be a link with Irish people but also cross the boundaries and help people to inte-grate ... That was the thing with the Irish chaplain. He was appointed to the parish with special care for the Irish people ... [They] loved to see an Irish priest, he was one of their own. They felt that he understood them.[84]

The mainly Irish parishioners of Fr Terence's first parish in Kentish Town were in luck, as all three priests at the time were from Ireland.[85] Indeed, long before the campaigns for recognition as an ethnic minority began in the 1980s and the multiplicity of Irish welfare organizations that sprang up, the Catholic Church recognized the particular needs of the Irish population of Britain by creating the Irish Emigrant Chaplaincy Scheme in 1957 and an Irish Welfare Bureau in Hammersmith in 1971.[86] Efforts such as this certainly aided the Irish, and priests such as Eamonn Casey are still held in high esteem by many today for help and advice on settling in Britain.[87]

As well as taking a leading role in the spiritual and welfare needs of the Irish in London, the Church set up parish clubs, partly, according to Fr Séamus Fullam, to provide a social scene outside of the pubs. In many cases they became family-friendly Irish clubs. Fr Fullam, who worked across London in predominantly Irish parishes for five decades from the early 1950s, spoke of how the Irish 'stay among themselves' and how he was irritated by people calling the clubs in his various parishes: ' "The Irish Catholic Club" – it's not. The Club was always intended to be for everyone. [But] of the people who came, 99.9 % were Irish.'[88] Mary Walker spoke of her local parish club in Edgware as 'a place in a big city where the Irish could feel at home ... The club used to have a big room, and that was their community, where they all used to meet.'[89] Two second-generation interviewees mentioned that their parents still socialize in such clubs today.[90]

Sending children to Catholic schools was very much the norm for the Irish in London, perhaps more so than in other parts of Britain that did not have as much choice in educational establishments. While this sample may be slightly biased due to the nature of a snowballing technique of finding interviewees, it is significant that of the fifteen interviewees for this project who had children in London or just outside, thirteen sent them all to Catholic schools.[91] Thus, the school run and school events became forums in which Irish-born people, particularly women, interacted with each other. Ciara and Brenda both mentioned knowing Irish people through their daughters' Catholic schools. The latter said: 'A lot of our friends are Irish. Not consciously, but with the kids at school, and at that time a lot of them at [name of RC primary school] were from Irish backgrounds, I suppose we had something in common with them [the other parents].'[92]

Brenda's children's school put on Irish dancing and music concerts on St Patrick's Day, further showing the way in which a Catholic institution became at least partly an Irish environment. Rose reflected how Catholic schools provided her with new Irish friends during her transition from living in a central borough to Enfield, and from her dance hall days to her school run days:

> Oh yes. We met up with a lot of Irish ... We went up to the Irish clubs up London. We used to go to Camden and we used to go to one in Tottenham Court Road, the Shamrock, the Round Tower, there was a lot of those around at the time ... Then when we moved out to Enfield there was quite a few Irish over there. Especially when we left the pub and the kids started school, in the Catholic school in Enfield, and naturally at that time they were all Irish that went to the Catholic school, or near enough. So, we all used to trot off to school in the mornings and then again in the evenings. That was how you break in to the Irish scene.[93]

Through some residential and occupational clustering, specifically Irish organizations – such as the county associations, the GAA, dance halls and pubs that catered for an Irish clientele and Catholic parishes and schools – Irish people created and were provided with structures through which regular face-to-face interaction was commonplace. Moreover, there was heavy overlap of interaction between these 'Irish spaces' among interviewees, meshing these spheres together into a coherent face-to-face community. Occasionally during interviews, almost all these Irish arenas found themselves expressed in a single person, such as Robert, who worked with Murphy's construction, lived in Brent, was heavily involved in the GAA and his county association, sent his child to a Catholic school, went to Mass and frequented Irish dance clubs and pubs.[94] This level of involvement was exceptional, yet, even among those interviewees professedly not involved in Irish activities, interaction with areas of the Irish community was in fact high. For instance, Brenda married an Englishman and was never involved in any organized Irish activity. Yet she has always gone to Mass, often in the London Irish Centre on a Saturday evening when she first arrived in London, where she would 'meet people from home', after which she would 'go to the dance and meet them again'. Later in life she sent her daughters, who briefly did Irish dancing when they were young, to Catholic schools where there were a great number of Irish parents who became friends, with whom she would still occasionally go to listen to traditional music in an Irish venue.[95]

The potency of the structures and Irish spaces was reflected in the social circles of many Irish people in London. Several interviewees talked of having an exclusively, or largely, Irish social network and sometimes expressed an unabashed preference for the company of Irish people. Timothy, for instance, worked in construction with mainly Irish people, and his friends were overwhelmingly Irish due to his involvement in the GAA: 'on the weekend on the sports side it was 100 per cent Irish'.[96] However, this was not limited to those who did not work with many English people or those involved in Irish cultural activities. While Danny and his wife Victoria were never involved in Irish cultural or sporting activity and both worked mainly with English people, their social circle was also '100 per cent' Irish, and Danny said: 'Most of the people I knew and mixed with were all Irish ... You were happier amongst your own.'[97] Similarly, Peter, who worked in a white-collar job, was asked about his social circle:

Peter: It would be mostly Irish. Now I worked with all English

> people. I did socialise quite a bit with them too ... but most of my association was with Irish people ... I felt more comfortable with them. I don't think I had any English person at my wedding. They were all right to work with.
>
> SS: Why did you feel more comfortable with Irish people?
>
> Peter: Well you were more at home with them because of your culture and everything else.[98]

The existence of entirely Irish social networks among emigrants has not been an isolated finding of this project. Catherine Dunne's collection of interviews with Irish people in London found a number who exhibited similar social behaviour. Kathleen Morrissey described her experience of the Irish social scene in north-west London: 'Long ago, people clung together almost as a matter of survival. They didn't integrate into the community in the way that young Irish people do now ... All my friends are Irish. I suppose I haven't really assimilated, but I have no regrets about that. I do mix with other nationalities at work, but my friends are Irish'.[99] A telling episode occurred in 1971 when the disc jockey Terry Wogan wrote a scathing article on the 'ghetto Irish' in an Dublin newspaper:

> For many being Irish in Britain is an excuse. An excuse for lack of self-improvement, an excuse for drunkenness and aggression, an excuse for poverty, an excuse for lack of involvement ... [Home] must be wherever you live. And that's [something] which many of the Irish in Britain have always refused to accept. Why else the Irish ghettos of Kilburn and Camden ...? Although many of these people have lived most of their lives in Britain ... they have never attempted to integrate ...[100]

Yet rather than deny such accusations, the general response was one of indignation that strong ethnic association should be questioned. In what was seemingly a contribution to the debate Wogan initiated, 'People who air such views' were dismissed at the 1971 Tipperary Association dinner as 'those who start out with ... educational and material advantages and who, sad to say, rarely lift a finger to help people with no such advantages'.[101] Donall MacAmhlaigh reflected the general tone of replies to Wogan in *The Irish Post* when he wrote:

> seemingly it would never occur to him that our people here are perfectly entitled to gather together, retaining what they can of

their Irishness ... I have a jar and the crack with my fellow Irishmen and all being equal, would prefer the company of an Irishman any day to that of other nationalities. If that is being 'ghetto Irish' then I am proud of it ...[102]

Other interviewees said their social circles were mixed or that they had separate groups of friends. Brigid remembered how she had two distinct social scenes. When asked if she felt part of an Irish community, she replied, 'Yes, yes, definitely. I had two lots of friends, I had my family and my Irish friends and I had my English friends and I always saw them separately.'[103] Sometimes a more mixed network came about after moving away from areas of high Irish settlement. David, for instance, although heavily involved in the Irish community since his emigration in 1957, became involved in other, non-Irish, activities when he moved just outside London in the 1960s and met English and other people through them.[104] Some Irish people in Britain purposely sought out mixed groups. While no interviewees for this project took such a course of avoidance of Irish social scenes, this was the case with Des Cusack, who lived outside of London in Sussex: 'I don't, and this is deliberate, I don't associate myself with clubs specifically for Irish people, because to me that is like colonisation ... but that doesn't restrict me from having many Irish friends, and as many English friends, and West Indian friends.'[105]

Those who mixed in the professional scene often had a wider group of friends, such as Evelyn who frequently referenced 'English friends', 'Irish friends' and friends who were 'a bit of everything' that she made in the 'very mixed area' in which she has lived with her family since the 1960s. While hard to fully substantiate, research would suggest a slight gender divide in which women had a more varied social network than men. The lower levels of congregation in one sector of work and the generally masculine nature of the GAA and pubs, through which many male interviewees met their friends and acquaintances, may have encouraged less of a 'ghetto Irish' outlook among women. This was certainly the case with the married Ciara and John; in interview, the former contrasted her husband's Irish oriented life within construction with her own, where she 'moved about a lot' in work and developed a mixed group of friends.[106]

It appears to have been rare in London, and certainly in the northwest of the city, for Irish people to unintentionally find themselves without some Irish friends and acquaintances, highlighting the particularly high frequency of Irish interaction in London. Nine of the seventeen first-generation interviewees from whom I got a good impression of their social circles had mainly or exclusively Irish friends throughout their lives.[107] This tallies with a survey in *The Irish Post* in 1992, which found 58 per cent of respondents saying they had only or mainly Irish friends (and 21 per cent of those surveyed were second-generation).[108] Diarmuid, involved in academia and living in south London away from the main Irish areas, was the only interviewee in this sample to profess to have had a very mixed group of friends among which Irish people were in a small minority.[109]

The high incidence, among the interviewees, of meeting an Irish spouse in London underscores the high level of emigrant interaction. Of twenty-one first-generation interviewees who were married and discussed their spouses, sixteen (including two married couples), were married to first-generation Irish people and at least eleven of these met in London. Two more were married to second-generation Irish people. Across Britain as a whole, the 10 per cent census sample in 1971 found that only 31 per cent of married ROI-born people had an ROI-born spouse, and only 28 per cent of second-generation Irish people had both parents born in the Republic.[110] Higher figures were recorded for London in the same year, where the 1 per cent longitudinal survey found that 46 per cent of married ROI-born women had spouses also born in the twenty-six counties.[111] These figures are misleadingly low as Northern Irish, second- or subsequent-generation Irish and Irish people who happened to be born elsewhere are excluded from such figures.[112] Just within the small sample for this project, six marriages included one ROI-born and one NI-born or second-generation person. The marriage of the Northern Irish couple, Danny and Victoria, would not even feature in the endogamous marriages figure for 1971. Given the overwhelming predominance of the Irish and Irish-descent among urban Catholics in England and Wales, one would suggest that a more telling figure lies somewhere between the 31 per cent of endogamous ROI-born marriages and the 71 per cent of marriages of Irish-born Catholics that were to other Catholics as reported by Hornsby-Smith and Lee in 1979.[113] In spite of problems with the statistics, the significantly lower figure recorded for endogamous ROI-born marriages across the whole of Britain does suggest a peculiarity in the strength and the impact of ethnic spheres on Irish lives in London. One also notes that the 1950s generation seemingly married among themselves more than earlier or later emigrants. As Caulfield and Bhat noted, in 1971 only 19 per cent of ROI-born over the age of 60 in Britain were married to a similarly born spouse, whereas 34 per cent of those aged 25 to 44 were. In addition to this, they found that the percentage of births to an ROI-born parent where both parents were ROI-born fell from the start to the end of the 1970s.[114]

A DIVIDED COMMUNITY

The evidence points towards a very high level of interaction and organization that supported and maintained an Irish community within London. This community was largely poorly educated, of rural or working-class urban backgrounds and was Catholic and conservative in its social behaviour. However, while this may have applied to the majority of Irish in London, there were those who were only on the fringes of this 'core community' or were not part of it at all. Perhaps the most notable division among the Irish in London was that of class; those who emigrated as professionals to improve career development generally involved themselves to only a small extent in some of the same Irish structures as the core community. There was certainly some overlap between the professional classes and their working-class compatriots but largely only in philanthropic or business matters. For instance, there was some involvement in the running of the Irish Centre, as remembered by Fr McCabe. Likewise, *The Irish Post*, read by interviewees of all social hues, was founded by the chartered accountant Tony Beatty, who claimed to have formulated the idea on 'hectic business trips'.[115] Perhaps not unusually, socially the barriers between classes were high. This reality was shown by Fr McCabe when he tried to illustrate that differences were breaking down but in fact described the involvement only in philanthropic roles:

Fr McCabe: As you probably know there were many splits in the Irish community. There was a feeling that the Irish Club in Eaton Square was a different class, that's where the professionals went. But in fact those social barriers were breaking down and people from Eaton Square ... got very involved in the Irish Centre.

SS: Did you find that they got involved in other societies like the county associations?

Fr McCabe: No, not the county associations ... There was more meaning in the Irish Centre for those who were thinking of doing something more meaningful for those coming over.[116]

Although John Walsh pointed to the 'freemasonry of London Irish' which his parents were a part of, and that included those in working-class jobs, it was the 'London-Irish professional mates' who visited in the evenings. While the Irish 'charladies and gardeners' that his parents hired were on friendly terms, they would 'not get invited to supper'.[117]

Those in the Irish professional class interviewed for the project lived in different areas, sent their children to high-end grammar or independent schools and attended different churches and thus had little day-to-day contact with their less well-off compatriots. They had their own institutions for social interaction: the Irish Club in Eaton Square, the National University of Ireland Dining Club and the Irish Embassy were the haunts of Irish high society, while London Irish Rugby Football Club was its GAA. It was in such places that one found, as Evelyn put it, 'middle-class people doing things that middle-class people like to do'.[118] The February 1971 issue of the *Irish Club Bulletin* gives a flavour of what this was. Noteworthy news pieces included: the St Patrick's Day Banquet and Ball, to which invites were extended to MPs, TDs, Catholic Cardinals and Val Doonican; a Gaelic League choral music concert; a wine and cheese reception; an article on Irish theatre; and an upcoming debating society clash between the NUI Club and the Irish Club, where the former's motion was, rather controversially, 'This house believes that women do not know their place in society.'[119]

Several interviewees described the reality of the social divide. While the Irish dance halls held fond memories for most of the interviewees, Evelyn quickly found that 'the Galtymore wasn't for us – we were much more at home in the Irish Club'.[120] Likewise, Elizabeth 'was in the Gresham once, but ... didn't frequent it'.[121] Some working-class interviewees were simply unaware of the existence of an Irish professional scene in Britain. When asked if he had met any middle-class Irish people in his time in London, Danny replied: 'If they were over there we certainly didn't meet them.' He then remembered that he once had a dentist from Belfast, 'but if you'd met him outside he'd have walked past you'.[122] Others knew of their existence but remained similarly aloof from them. For example, Ciara and John found that they 'tended not to mix in the same circles ... [The Irish Club] was upper class so we didn't think that we'd fit in there. We'd have gone to the more working-class clubs.'[123] From those more involved in Irish community activities, hostility or irritation was sometimes expressed at the division which existed. Oneinterviewee displayed outright disdain for those who attended the Irish Club, calling them 'phonies' and 'upstarts who forgot themselves in the euphoria of their new status in life and aped the culture of the "Big House" '.[124] Likewise, Timothy, a prominent member of the GAA in London, was scathing in his assessment of London Irish Rugby as the sporting focus of the professional class:

> You'd have people in certain jobs or have a certain amount of money, it'd be important for them to bring their kids to Sunbury [where London Irish is based] on a Saturday morning. It wasn't because they wanted to bring their kids to Sunbury, it was a pain in the arse to bring their kids to Sunbury ... [but] they felt that they would be hobnobbing with people.[125]

Timothy was not alone in his frustration at the lack of involvement of the middle class in wider community activities; David was also bemused at the difficulties he had in persuading them to sit on committees within Irish organizations.[126] The memoirs of the second-generation Irish are also indicative of this social reality. Brian Dooley, in his work on second-generation Irish people in Britain, was struck by the contrast between John Walsh's upbringing, as the son of an Irish doctor in south London, and his own, in spite of them living only a mile apart as children: 'His parents went to posh dinner and dances at the Irish club in Eaton Square, and existed in a different Irish London to mine. Walsh's father was our family doctor when I was a boy ... but socially our families' paths would never have intersected. His London Irish upbringing was an oddly solitary one.'[127] As with Walsh, Mary Clancy, the daughter of a highly successful family involved in engineering, remarked that upon involving herself in an Irish charity later in life, it 'opened up a whole new world for me, a dimension which I really didn't know existed – the whole Irish community ... Living outside London and working in civil engineering, we were never part of the Irish community as such.'[128]

The social circles of the professional Irish, as noted above, tended to be less exclusively composed of their fellow emigrants. Eoin, who dabbled in the lives of the working and professional classes of Irish people without ever truly being a paid-up member of either, characterized the latter as being far more adept at being social chameleons with less of an immediate need to be among their fellow Irish:

> The Irish in Cricklewood, they felt the need, because of the work they were doing, the level of education and so forth, they felt the need to congregate, join their fellows in pubs and clubs, whereas the professional people didn't feel that need. They were free agents, they could come and go, they had choices. The labouring class didn't have choices, even over where they lived ... The middle classes, they're dispersed – Hampstead, Weybridge and so forth.[129]

Certainly there were no middle-class Irish ghettos, no County Kilburn reserved for doctors, and this led to lower levels of everyday interaction. With attendance at different churches, children at different schools and a smaller sporting scene, social interaction was limited to personal friendships often made through the small number of organized societies and clubs.

It is suggested that the Irish middle class made up an ethnic network within a wide Irish community. It overlapped with and provided limited leadership for the rest of the community in organizations, and to some extent its members were within Irish networks of mutual help. This social divide was also not set in stone; some of the interviewees for this project were either well qualified upon emigration or became so in London and involved themselves heavily in the institutions of the core community, such as Stephen with the GAA.[130] Nevertheless, a prominent social divide existed and the London Irish professional class from the 1950s onwards never played the central role in ethnic leadership that their predecessors elsewhere within the historic diaspora had done, such as in nineteenth-century America and Liverpool.[131]

Within the less affluent Irish community there were more subtle social divides. Harrison noted in 1973 that in Birmingham at the weekend, the 'building workers and shopgirls go more often to the Shamrock [dance hall], and the teachers, nurses and social workers go off to the Mayfair'.[132] This appears to have also been the case in London to a small extent. Ryan's study of Irish nurses in north London found some level of class consciousness, as with one nurse who told Ryan that her Irish senior sister would say: 'you don't want to be going down to that Garryowen [dance hall in Hammersmith] place, you know, they are all working on the roads and the buildings'. Instead, they were sent to sing carols in the London Irish Rugby Club.[133] Similarly, Victoria saw the Buffalo in Camden Town, popular with labourers, as too rough to go to.[134] Phyllis Izzard, who improved her lot in London when she entered accountancy, recounted a story of once going out with a labourer from Connemara and being far from impressed: 'I think the West of Ireland men had the reputation among us girls of being a bit "culchie", a bit uncouth, like ... we were looking for something a little bit more refined!'[135]

These quotations point to a number of themes and divisions within the Irish in London. They suggest that the oft-observed minor snobbery that existed in rural Ireland, the 'tuppence ha'penny looking down on tuppence' as one interviewee put it, to some extent survived the journey to London – migration for economic reasons was not necessarily a leveller.[136] It is significant that all such comments noted were from female interviewees. As noted above, women were less clustered in manual labour. Indeed, the employment in which there was the greatest level of concentration, nursing, was a route to qualifications and a respected profession. This in many cases elevated female emigrants above their male counterparts socially and thus they were encouraged to aspire to the Rugby Club world over the Garryowen dance hall. Phyllis's comment also highlights the minor level of regional favouritism and division that remained among the Irish in London, something also noted by Brendan McGowan in his study of the Irish in Leeds, where Mayo people were accused of being 'clannish' by some.[137] Diarmuid, from Belfast, well educated and outside the core of the Irish community in London, dismissed the dance halls as for the 'country Irish'. Victoria, Jack and Evelyn felt that they were stereotyped on occasion by those from the Republic because they came from the 'black North'.[138] Donall MacAmhlaigh's *Diary* portrays the Connemara men and Dublin men as having a particular taste for fighting one another.[139]

As well as being a possible marker of social aspirations and potential, gender was an important division within the spheres of social interaction within the Irish community. Without intending any crass generalizations, it might not have been uncommon for an Irish emigrant male to have worked on a building site exclusively with men, spent most evenings in an Irish pub, where men predominated, and played Gaelic football at the weekend, again among his male counterparts. The masculine nature of the Irish pub has been regularly noted. For instance, Popoviciu, Haywood and Mac an Ghaill explored the 'highly gendered' world of Irish men in London in which the pub was seen as a key Irish and male space.[140] Some interviewees for this project and others mentioned a gender divide that expressed itself through pubs, such as Fr Bobby Gilmore who characterized Irish men as having more contacts to work within the Irish community because 'they had the pubs; women didn't have the networks'.[141] Some women spoke of the pubs as male domains, as with Anne O'Neill, who had great sympathy for the Irish builders who 'used to come from work, go into the pub and get drunk ... Those fellows did not have a drink problem when they arrived here – they developed it because they were here, living in conditions like that.'[142] Such statements point to the well-noted phenomenon of the Irish male's problem with alcohol when in Britain, which contributed to the rates of admission to psychiatric wards in the 1970s for Irish men being eight times higher than for their English counterparts and the oft-quoted fact that the Irish male in the 1970s/1980s was the only immigrant to experience a fall in his life expectancy upon arriving in Britain.[143] In spite of the general picture, however, the masculinity of the Irish pub was not monolithic and has perhaps been slightly exaggerated elsewhere. The Galway man John Lydon Senior mentions in his infamous son's autobiography that he met his Irish wife in a pub in London and there were a number of references in interviews to women being in pubs, such as Ciara who spoke of frequenting Irish pubs that her visiting friends from Ireland found 'more Irish here than at home'.[144] Hornsby-Smith and Dale's observation that children of an Irish mother and an English father were more socially mobile than those where the nationalities of the parents were reversed could perhaps be seen as partly due to the highly masculine nature of the worlds of many Irish male emigrants, worlds in which education was not valued.[145] This was certainly the case with one second-generation interviewee, the son of a labourer, who said: 'My mum would have been very aspirational, particularly regarding the kids and education. You know, in another life, she would have studied and had a professional career ... She was very keen to see her kids get on ... Whereas my dad ... always distrusted education ... he would have thought it was work avoidance.'[146]

While Irish female spheres may not have been as numerous or as

highly gendered as those for men, one would not have been too sur-
prised to have found an Irish female nurse working largely among
women and to have found her later in life primarily interacting with
Irish women through Catholic schools and cultural activities for the
second-generation – with women often taking a leading role in
ferrying children to Irish dancing and music classes.[147] The interviewees for this project who mentioned friends through school
networks were all female, except for one male teacher. Interestingly,
considering the high male attendance at Mass among interviewees,
females also seemingly found the parish church to be a place of Irish
interaction more than males did. It featured more often in the
narratives of females. Kathleen Morrissey characterized the Irish in
London as follows: 'Women tended to join the Church; men went
to the pub.'[148]

The community structures were often masculine in their imagery
and leadership. Both male and female emigrants might have stood
for the military (and thus masculine) themed 'Amhrán na bhFiann'
at the end of Saturday evening's entertainment in an Irish dance hall
and been ministered to by a member of the exclusively male Catholic
hierarchy on a Sunday morning.[149] They might have read *The Irish
Post*, which a number of women complained about being too male
oriented in 1971, attended functions of the county associations (most
of which began life as the 'Tipperary/Galway/Clare*mens*' Association') at the clerically administered London Irish Centre and heard
speeches from visiting bishops or (most likely male) politicians.[150]
Indeed, the domination by men of the leadership of many Irish
organizations up until the 1980s was noticed by this researcher when
the search for interviewees often resulted only in male candidates.

This masculinity was seemingly one of the reasons why there was
a minority of Irish people who consciously distanced themselves
from the core Irish community. Such feelings of alienation were
prominently expressed by some women in the mid-1980s when
conferences held by the London Irish Women's Centre (LIWC) noted
the gendered nature of the Irish community: 'The existing Irish
community and cultural organisations are dominated by men. Not
only are Irish women's needs inadequately met by those organisations, many needs are not met at all.'[151] Such women often did not
interact at all with the Irish community and in the 1980s formed
what Rossiter terms 'the *alternative* Irish community in London'.[152]
(original emphasis) Very often it was those whose leaving Ireland

was motivated by a need to 'escape' who found the London Irish scene too similar in its masculinity and its morals to that which they left behind. Thus it is those who emigrated during the 1970s, when the Irish economy was attracting return migrants in large numbers, as well as some of the 'new wave' of emigration in the 1980s, who feature most prominently when one investigates people who rejected the 'traditional' community. Rossiter brings out a number of examples in her portrayal of 'the alternative Irish community'. For instance, Joan Neary, who migrated to London in 1973 and was involved in feminist groups, had never participated in the activities or attended the venues of the core Irish community apart from the occasional 'feminist *céilí*' held at an Irish Centre: 'I wouldn't be at home in those kind of places because it's not who I am ... I would hate some of the values, the ones I ran away from, probably. My not making forays into those areas is about my own past.'[153] Likewise, Tricia Darragh's account of when she moved to London in the mid-1970s after rejecting Catholicism, having a secret baby and becoming interested in communism contained a sense of alienation from the values of the majority in the Irish community: 'I found that time quite difficult, because I was very much in an Irish community, you know, round Kilburn, Willesden and I just didn't want to have anything to do with it. It was like I was rejecting everything about it.'[154]

Some men and women escaped the homophobia of Ireland. Frank Byrne, a gay man who left for London in the early 1960s, said that he needed the 'anonymity' London could provide and has only ever had very limited contact with the Irish community.[155] By the 1980s the LIWC was fighting the 'discrimination against Lesbians both within the Irish community and the wider London community' that had left Irish lesbians without support networks before that decade.[156]

Joan's and Tricia's accounts of alienation highlight not only a gender divide but a generational divide that was also beginning to emerge. While this was not fully realized until the influx of 1980s migrants to London created new organizations and networks, some of those who came in the 1970s were already experiencing this. Older organizations, such as the county associations and the structures of Irish Catholicism, often did not appeal to better-educated, frequently urban-origin, Irish men and women. For instance, neither Diarmuid nor Noelle, university educated and in their twenties when they moved to London in the 1970s, gave a narrative of escape from

Ireland, yet they both expressed a social distance from the older Irish community – what the latter labelled the 'Aran sweater and shamrock brigade'.[157] Again, while not entirely apparent until the later 1970s and 1980s, there was a generational divide between Irish immigrants and their children, who, like their incoming Irish contemporaries, often saw the older community structures as irrelevant.[158] There were other Irish people in London who simply did not move in Irish social circles, more by chance than design, something which one would suggest was particularly evident among those who married non-Irish spouses or lived away from the main area of Irish settlement in north-west London, or were professionals.[159]

It would be wrong to portray the Irish who arrived at Euston in their entirety entering a coherent ethnic community in which everybody lived happily together and interacted in the same ways. There were divisions within the Irish community, most notably with regard to class but also with regard to gender and, to a lesser extent, regional cliques. There were also those who could barely be described as a part of the Irish community, so fitfully did they interact with it, namely Rossiter's 'alternative' community of a feminist persuasion and some who came to London and simply found themselves not in Irish social circles, something particularly evident among a younger, better-educated generation who emerged from the 1970s. Nevertheless, a series of overlapping institutions and spheres of Irish interaction undoubtedly sustained an ethnic community for the majority of the Irish in London, particularly in the north-west, which affected in their everyday interactions in concrete ways.

IDENTITIES IN EXILE

The expression of Irishness in London was in many ways similar to the mid-century Ireland that emigrants had left behind. The terminology of personal identity was usually very one-dimensional among interviewees and involved the setting up of a mutually exclusive dichotomy between Irishness and Britishness. Among the interviewees the almost unanimous answer to a question about identity was a straightforward 'Irish'. For instance, Brenda answered: 'For me I'm still Irish, I'm still the same.' Likewise, Peter replied: 'I never changed a bit, never one bit in the world.'[160] Evelyn fiercely rejected any compromise when asked if her identity had ever changed: 'Absolutely not. When there was talk that we'd all have to have

British passports I thought, "over my dead body", there's no way I'd ever have a British passport.'[161] The only two first-generation inter- viewees to acknowledge a non-Irish portion of their identity were Victoria, who moved to London at 8 years of age and said that in some ways she sees herself as 'half English', and Oliver, whose study of, and subsequent alienation from, Irish nationalism has led him to question his identity.[162] Deep emotional attachment to counties, cities, parishes and townlands survived the crossing to Holyhead. This expressed itself in the county associations, GAA clubs originally devoted to people from certain counties (the Kingdom for Kerry men, Tir Chonnail Gaels for Donegal men) and loyal support of one's home county football or hurling teams.

The Irish in London brought an instinctive nationalism across the Irish Sea with them. While for some this nationalism was expressed through political activity in London, for the vast majority who were not politically active it was a vague and latent feeling. There were frequent references to this: for instance, Diarmuid said of his co-workers on building sites in the 1960s that 'they weren't politically motivated but they'd have Irish nationalism like almost every Irish person had'.[163] Maurice O'Neill confidently proclaimed that 'Every Irish person believes in the objectives of Sinn Féin, the objectives of the IRA.'[164] There were some brief periods of nationalism breaking out into action, as when thousands gathered in Trafalgar Square in 1966 to celebrate the 1916 Rising's fiftieth anniversary, during the outrage over internment in Northern Ireland that led to the short- lived success of the Anti-Internment League, and at the funeral of the IRA hunger striker Michael Gaughan, which attracted a few thousand marchers in Kilburn in 1974.[165] However, these were exceptions to the rule and nationalism more often expressed itself in the 'pub patriotism' of rebel songs or loosely held convictions. Danny and Robert were among those who reminisced about singing rebel songs, while adding caveats that dissociated the nationalist lyrics from violent republicanism, betraying an anxiety over such matters that is discussed in Chapter Two: 'I used to sing "Bold Fenian Men". But I'd only sing it around Irish people ... It's just a song. I did feel proud to be Irish'; 'I liked singing rebel songs because I loved the songs, not because I wanted to shoot or kill anybody.'[166] While such statements and tales were less common among female interviewees, there was certainly a nationalism that was present, as when Ciara said that she would vote 'for a united Ireland in the morning'.[167]

Fr McCabe neatly summed up the ambivalent nationalism of Irish London: 'Yes, nationalist, without being that sympathetic for the cause itself.'[168]

As when they were at home, the Irish in London were generally practising Catholics. A significant majority, twenty-one out of twenty-nine first-generation interviewees, still attended Mass regularly when interviewed.[169] For many, Catholicism was integral to their lives and their identities in London. Evelyn, for instance, said: 'Put it this way, I think the most important thing in my life is my Catholicism.'[170] Likewise, Abigail said: 'The Catholic Church has been very central to my life.'[171] The importance of Catholicism in an actual religious sense was most evident among female interviewees, who appear to have generally found more comfort in religion than their male counterparts – all eight of those who had lapsed in practice were men and at least two of these had wives who still practised. The interviews consistently showed how fundamental the link between Catholicism and Irishness was in the eyes of many who came from Ireland in the post-war years. Evelyn said that she has always 'hated being called a *"Roman* Catholic", I feel I'm an *"Irish* Catholic" '.[172] Stephen followed a common theme in portraying the Irish in London as demonstrating a 'purer' form of Irishness and immediately linked it with Catholicism: 'The parishioners down there at [our local church] are more Irish than they are back in Ireland, certainly more *Catholic* than they are back in Ireland.'[173] Even among those whose practice had lapsed, this sense of Catholicism as an essential badge of Irishness remained. Eoin admitted that Catholicism still played a major part in his identity, particularly as an Ulsterman, and he labelled himself a 'cultural Catholic'. Similarly, Con continued to acknowledge that 'Catholicism is still part of my culture' and he continues to attend a choir that sings Mass in the Irish language.[174] Declan showed how significant nationalism and Catholicism remained to his identity in London at first, even if their importance waned later under the weight of left-wing political ideas: '[In England] you had to defend the politics and religion that you thought was central to your identity. At the time, nationalism and Catholicism were central to my identity … I was very much taken by the IRA, I thought the IRA was a great idea.'[175]

The Irish Post had a priest as a regular columnist in its early years and still today includes a section on Church matters, highlighting the continued importance of Catholicism to its audience.[176] This is not to say that Catholicism was central in the lives of all Irish people. Certainly, some felt 'lucky to have escaped the Catholic religion' and the 1980s 'alternative community' were resolutely Irish but (mostly) not Catholic.[177] As Ireland itself began to modernize, Catholicism became less central to national identity, and among some of the interviewees who had lapsed there appeared little difficulty in articulating an Irishness without religion.[178] Nevertheless, Catholicism was undoubtedly a characterizing feature of the community as a whole and an important feature of identity for most within it.

While the expression in words of Irishness in many ways remained a one-dimensional assertion of nationality infused with Catholicism, the Irish in London could not truly maintain an identity that was at one with those at home, developing in the same direction. The image of being exiled that was strong during narratives of leaving, and has been noted in the early formation of the county associations, lingered among the Irish in London and became part of how the community and individuals positioned their sense of self in relation to Ireland. On occasion this sense of exile has lasted a lifetime. This is particularly the case when the economic emigrant is disillusioned with the modern Ireland and feels exiled in both time and space. Patrick Kenny, who was interviewed nearly half a century after his family left their Tipperary farm said: 'I would have been much happier had I stayed in Ireland … because the one thing that troubles me most is my sense of exile … It's weird when you have those strong memories of a place and when you return to the place, you find that your memory is the only thing that you're attached to.'[179]

John Walsh's and Brian Kearney's autobiographies describe the strong sense of exile that their parents felt. For instance, Kearney reminisces: 'My mum and dad lived in England for thirty years. They changed a lot in that time; but one thing about them that didn't change was their Irishness. As far as they were concerned they weren't living in England at all, just visiting.'[180] A deep longing for Ireland was sometimes mirrored by a sense of alienation from British society. Interviewees generally did not express any strong sense of alienation but articles and letters in *The Irish Post* hint that it may have been stronger for some in the past. For instance, after Bloody Sunday in 1972, an article by John Kavanagh appeared in the paper opining 'that the Irish in Britain should go home … We are a different people. We should not be here … We have less in common with the British than with most other Western races.'[181] In February 1974 the weekly opinion column 'Frank Dolan' – in fact written by the editor Breandán MacLua – opened a discussion on the upcoming general election with the comment: 'The Irish should never have come to Britain. It was already a rigid society with its fixed customs, class structure, traditions and centuries of pathological anti-Irishness.' The article went on to deride the Conservative Party, saying: 'You will never be at home among them. All that they stand for is alien to all that you come from.'[182] Both these articles stated that the Irish in Britain would have got on far better in the other English-speaking countries to which other Irish people had emigrated. Such sentiments also appeared in the lively letters page: for instance, in January 1981 one letter about returning to Ireland, 'where we belong', spoke of Britain having a 'culture and way of life totally alien to us'.[183]

It is significant that both Walsh's and Kearney's parents eventually moved back to Ireland because a desire to return was the strongest expression of the sense of exile. This was almost universal among economic migrants. It is an irony that being closer to Ireland than their cousins in America or Australia were could make the exile mindset more powerful, due to the seeming attainability of return to Ireland. Fr Terence noticed this failure to make a clean break between past and future upon emigration: 'At that time nearly everybody who came to England was only staying for a few years. Some had said that forty years before. But they were going back, that was the theory, they were going back sometime when things were better.'[184] The 'theory' of coming over for a short period was widespread in leaving narratives. Mary Allen, when interviewed in the 1980s around twenty-five years after emigrating, said she had initially envisaged a stay of mere months: 'I was so homesick ... But the thought was, that was May and the idea was we were going back at the end of July, and I thought, "well I can stand it for that long".'[185]

Con had a similar idea upon migration to London: 'My idea was that I was going to make my fortune and then go home again.'[186] Several interviewees said that they had seriously attempted to return to Ireland permanently at some point since their initial emigration. David found a job advertised on one of his annual trips back to Ireland, applied and was offered the job before deciding against return.[187] Danny, whose initial plan of a 'few months' in London became a stay of over four decades, eventually permanently returned to Northern Ireland in the 1990s, where he had 'always felt that one day' he would return.[188]

The Irish Post often had features about return migration, reflecting the high numbers who were going back to Ireland in the 1970s. In its very first issue there were two features on this topic. One was a consideration of qualifications needed to get work in Ireland and the second asked Irish people around Britain if they would return to Ireland if they found a job with similar pay and conditions, a question to which five out of eight said yes and a sixth said he would work in England but retire to Ireland.[189] In 1994 MacLua summed up what he had seen during his decades at the forefront of the Irish community: 'The man from the Punjab dreamed of the good life represented by owning a house in Slough or Southall; the man from Co. Mayo dreamed of returning to his own green fields and he was bitter about being away from them in a strange land.'[190] As the Irish economy modernized, the dream was realized for many and there was a high level of return migration in the 1960s and particularly the 1970s. While no exact figures exist for return emigration from London, a number of statistics have been highlighted by academics that point to this significant phenomenon. Garvey found that in spite of a continuing net outflow of people from the Republic between the 1961 and 1971 censuses, there was a gain of roughly 32,000 children under 15 who had been born in Britain, suggesting return migration of families partly offsetting continued migration of younger people. Likewise, from 1971 to 1981 the number of people in the Republic born in Britain rose by 62,370, or 74 per cent.[191] In the same decade, while there was continuing net emigration in the age group 15–34, there was an overall net inflow of people to the Republic of 104,000 and positive migration figures for twenty-one of twenty-six counties. Meanwhile, the Irish-born population of Britain fell 11 per cent to 850,000.[192]

The myth of return was something held more deeply by those who felt that they had to leave Ireland out of economic necessity, or a necessity to further their chosen career due to lack of opportunity in Ireland; those who left Ireland for adventure or who abandoned a society that they disliked were less likely to express any great sense of desire to return, although the latter may have felt exiled in the sense of not belonging in their own society or that of the country that they moved to. The trend among interviewees and in memoirs was for men to have held on to this more commonly than women, which mirrors the earlier observation that the domination of leaving narratives of economic forces was more clear in males than females.

With the return migrants Danny and Victoria, it was the former who was clearly the driving force behind the move back to Ireland. Con said that he would have returned were it not for his wife's refusal.[193] The 'travel brochure image of Ireland', to quote Fr Gilmore, was in the hearts of many who longed to return. Danny freely admitted to being a 'sentimental eejit' and Stephen, who had never made an attempt to return, told of having the occasional 'very romantic mood' where it crossed his mind.[194] Female interviewees less frequently expressed any great desire to return to Ireland; apart from Victoria, only two out of seven with whom return was discussed said that they had attempted to or wished to move back permanently, although three more had houses in Ireland so that they could visit frequently.

In second-generation interviews this gender divide was also a noticeable trend. Rory summed up his parent's feelings:

> Dad always spoke about going back ... There was never a time that I remember him not talking about it ... When his brother went back in the 70s ... there was talk about it then. And then in the 80s there was talk and when we went over there we'd look around ... Whereas Mum has no intention of going back, absolutely none.[195]

Likewise, John Walsh's parents' return was due entirely to his father's persistence and it took several years of buying properties across Ireland to persuade his wife to go.[196] Fr Liam also noted this among his own parents and those of his peers: 'My dad had a hankering to go back to Ireland, but my mum didn't. And I think it was quite typical, I knew other similar families – the dads had this kind of romantic notion of going to retire or live back in Ireland.'[197] Such qualitative accounts are given weight by the quantitative evidence from census figures that show consistently higher male return migration. From 1971 to 1981, net male immigration to the Republic for males between the ages of 35 and 64 (pre-retirement and thus most likely involving the need to keep working in Ireland) was 30,700, 64 per cent higher than the 18,700 net female immigration.[198]

Among health academics, Walsh and McGrath have attempted the tricky task of linking a failure to form a positive identity in exile to mental and physical health problems among the Irish in Britain. They found that those in their sample with a positive identity and view of Irishness were healthier than those without.[199] While such a theory is hard for an historian to prove, it is suggested here that for some, particularly men, an obsession with exile and a failure to ever finish their emigration 'journey' mentally caused anger, bitterness and bad health. Angry, and all too often inebriated, Irish men feature alarmingly frequently in memoirs, such Maura Murphy's husband in her account of her life in Birmingham, Anna May Mangan's multiplicity of beer-swilling violent uncles and MacAmhlaigh's fellow labourers, among whom pub brawls were commonplace.[200] Brendan O'Hara's explanation of his becoming an alcoholic suggests strongly that a failure to process being Ireland in England and a feeling of not being the Englishman's equal was instrumental in his failed emigration: 'I had that inferiority complex; I used to hide me accent, I didn't want people to know where I come from, being called Pat, that was irritating. I went along with it kind of, it was to be a man, take it on the chin like, so I did with copious amounts of alcohol.'[201]

For Declan, the anger at the emasculation of emigration and the failure to deal with it emotionally was a strong theme in his experience of Irish emigrants:

> There was enormous pent up anger ... huge amounts of suppressed desire, humiliation. The very act of coming to England was humiliation, having been brought up in this wonderful culture of Catholicism and nationalism where everybody knew each other and now you find yourself in this big anonymous world where nobody knew you, nobody ... Fights broke out in pubs to an enormous extent.[202]

One might think that some of this anger would be directed towards Ireland, among those who felt that they were forced to leave for economic reasons, but this was surprisingly rare. Such feelings very occasionally were evident in letters to *The Irish Post*, such as when one contributor wrote: 'The Irish have no reason to love their country. Has their country loved them?'[203] Yet only one interviewee, Oliver, was palpably bitter towards Ireland for forcing him to emigrate to what he saw as a hostile country: 'I am passionately concerned to get across how much we suffered ... and how much that lot back there [in Ireland] didn't give a damn.'[204] He found himself bemused by his fellow emigrants' lack of similar feelings, quoting the historian J.J. Lee's comment about the architects of the Irish revolution who oversaw the departure of the post-war emigrants: 'In one respect only did they display true talent. So effectively did they master the techniques of indoctrination that many of their victims would continue to cherish the values responsible for their own plight.'[205]

The myth of return hindered the expression of an ethnic community identity beyond a shared sense of being Irish, Catholic and exiled. The death, or at least moderation, of the myth of return from around the early 1970s was of key importance in the development of an ethnic community identity within London and Britain. For the first time in the 1970s we see the beginnings of a widespread acceptance of permanence in Britain rather than an existence in transit. As well as the impracticalities for many of moving back to Ireland, after perhaps two decades away, the majority had begun to settle in Britain. With a growing second-generation by the start of our period, Irish Londoners realized that going 'home' was no longer an option in the short term. Several interviewees said that they would not go back to Ireland due to their families being in London, a trait particularly strong with females, which was reflected in their lower rates of return migration.[206] Phyllis Izzard showed that children began to make leaving London a less desirable option: 'I think, too, that the longer you stay here the more difficult it is to make the break and go back to Ireland ... The problems begin once you've had your children and the children go to school ... you'd be loath to do anything that would change their lives.'[207] Eoin also reflected this feeling: 'Sometimes I get a bit nostalgic for the place. But it's [just] a place ... Our friends are here, our family are growing up here.'[208] Ciara's reluctance to go back to Ireland was motivated by both family and a feeling of being at home in London: 'I feel that I would find it hard to leave my children and my grandchildren. Plus I really like London.'[209]

The passage of time made the London Irish see their counterparts in Ireland differently and realize that they were no longer fully at home in their old communities. By the time of the interviews, some criticized the Irish at home for various traits. Ultan, for instance, derided the nepotism and parochialism rife in Ireland.[210] Brenda expressed this most strongly:

> I definitely wouldn't want to go back to where I come from. I don't mean to be anonymous but I don't like this everybody knowing everything and analysing everything you say. I don't think it's like that in all of Ireland. Even when I go back now I think that they're so petty over silly little things and I don't

think I could take it. I love going back to Ireland and I love everything Irish but I don't think I could live there. But I also think that they've changed and I've probably changed … And I'm not sure if you'd be that welcome either … Unless you go back when you're young.[211]

A theme among interviewees was that they felt that they had moved on from their often rural or small-town youth and were now 'city people'. While Evelyn said that she would go back to Ireland, she couldn't go to where she grew up: 'I'd go to a city, I couldn't go to live in the country. I'm a city person now.'[212] Stephen said he could not go back because he'd miss 'that buzz' of London.[213] One very telling comment was from Tony Maher, of Harlow and formerly Kildare. It shows that England had changed him to the extent that he felt more comfortable with fellow emigrants than those who had never left and also provides a criticism of the petty suspicion of those at home:

I find now if I want to know anything about what's going on in my own village, the first thing I have to do is find somebody who's been over in this country, lived here, worked here and gone back home to Ireland. I can sit down with them and they'll tell me … all about the people, the work situation … Try to talk to somebody who has never left Ireland about the work opportunities or the wages and … they think that you want to steal their job, their house, their wife![214]

Such sentiments were presumably behind return migrants in County Carlow establishing the Carlow Emigrants Association in 1979 where ex-emigrants (and those home from London) met in a county association-style dinner dance.[215]

While the comments from interviewees were collected many years after the 1970s, it is reasonable to assume that by then, when many of the 1950s emigrants were well into their second decade in London, similar feelings had begun to emerge. Certainly, the experiences of 1970s return emigrants began to help the Irish in London realize that they and the people in Ireland had changed. Gmelch's study of return migrants in the West of Ireland in 1977–78 found that over half of the 606 people whom he surveyed were unhappy with their return migration experience in the first year. This disillusionment with the dream of return filtered back to London, especially from those who returned to Britain again, as was the case with the 5–10 per cent of Gmelch's sample.[216] One interviewee for this work, Abigail, returned briefly to Donegal in 1971 only to find it too hard to settle in, particularly when her children were shunned in the local school as 'English'.[217] Among the reasons for deciding on a permanent home in England for David were his children's well-being and a feeling of being settled, but also what he had heard from others about the difficulties in fitting in as a return migrant:

> I decided that all I'd be doing was putting the emigration thing into reverse, the kids might not get on in the schools over there and everything else ... it might not have been the right thing for them ... I said I'm not going to risk it ... I know five couples who returned [to Ireland] and three of them came back again. They couldn't cut it. People make huge mistakes.[218]

For many emigrants, in spite of the universal continued use of the word 'home' when referring to Ireland, London became a home for them with families and friends around them, a process that gathered pace as the second-generation grew. By the time of the interviews, only Peter and Evelyn said that they might still return, although neither appeared to be seriously considering it. A dual sense of 'home' developed for the London Irish and was a common theme among interviewees.[219] After Brigid was asked why she would never move back to Ireland she replied: 'Because this [London] is home.' When asked if this use of 'home' was usual, she said: 'Yes. But I still call it home when I'm going back home, that's where I come from.'[220] Similarly, Eoin answered the question 'Where is home?' with 'Home? Belfast! Yep, I still think of it as my home. Although this is my home, this is where I live.'[221] Norrie Fox's comments also show the duality that made defining 'home' such a difficult job for many emigrants:

> I've seen lots of changes, but I like London, I love London. But when, if I was asked, not so much now I suppose, but in years gone by when I was asked, at this time of the year particularly, they'd say, 'Norrie are you going on holiday', I'd say 'yes ... home' ... And then I'd stop and think, yes this [London] is my home but at that stage no, because whatever it is as soon as I hit Ireland I feel I belong. Same culture, same everything. I don't know, I don't feel foreign here.[222]

Like Norrie, for many Irish people an acceptance of London as one of two homes was partly due to a genuine attachment to their

adopted city and country. Robert said that in spite of only initially intending to emigrate for a few years, and still loving everything about
Ireland, 'after a little while I loved London ... We had a big conversation about this recently, about twenty of us, all GAA men, all people here who had their own houses and families. And we all came to
the one conclusion, it's the best town in the world we've ever been
in and we'd have been totally lost without it.'[223]

The realization that life in London was not temporary forced
the Irish to develop their own sense of identity as an Irish person
permanently abroad, 'imagine' an identity for their community and
establish organs to maintain it, something that they had been reluctant to do beforehand. The foundation of *The Irish Post* can perhaps
be seen as the symbolic beginning of this process, although it may
have been expressed earlier. In June 1970, Tony Beatty, founder
of the newspaper, spoke at the newly opened Leeds Irish Centre,
saying: 'The Irish Centre in Leeds and *The Irish Post* are about the
same thing ... They mean that we, the Irish community in Britain,
recognise some degree of permanency in our stay and are taking
steps to ensure that, while we are here, we will not abandon our own
Irish individuality and traditions.'[224] The raison d'être of the paper,
whose banner was 'the voice of the Irish in Britain', was the
existence of a group of people who defined themselves as an Irish
community, coherent and different from British society en masse,
and its success, which included a readership in the low hundreds of
thousands, is testament to the appeal of this idea.[225] Breandán
MacLua, reminiscing about the impact of the newspaper, said: 'One
achievement overrides all others. The newspaper played a very large
part in creating a sense of community which involved all the Irish
in Britain.'[226] Perusing editions of the *Post* from the 1970s and 1980s
certainly shows that this theme was to the fore. For those outside
London especially, *The Irish Post* provided contact with other Irish
people that had not been possible before, as one letter writer from
Kent in 1975 said: 'I knew next to nothing about the Irish community
until I began to read *The Irish Post* ... Without our own newspaper
we could have never been a real community.'[227] As well as news from
Ireland and regular political comment, it covered Irish social and
cultural activities in Britain in detail, printing pictures every week
from Irish clubs around Britain, often with a section describing the
local Irish community that the clubs represented, Irish music and
dance in Britain and the results of GAA matches in Britain. It provided

a large and lively letters section entitled 'You say – the forum of the Irish in Britain'.[228] During the 1970s it encouraged the development of Irish centres and the Federation of Irish Societies, with features on how to set up 'your own Irish Club', and celebrated the success of Irish people in Britain through annual awards.[229] The paper even initially tried to encourage the idea of ethnic bloc-voting.[230] The foundation of more Irish clubs around the country, including the South London Irish Club in Wimbledon in 1975, was, as Beatty pointed out, a sign that the Irish found themselves in need of more permanent facilities in which to carry on their way of life now that there was recognition of permanence in Britain. There may also have been an element of these new clubs replacing contact that was previously more regular before people moved to the suburbs.

By the 1970s the activities of the Irish community clearly showed a desire to assert their Irishness in a context of some permanency in London and ensure that their British-born children would remember their roots. At the Tipperary Association in 1971 the Bishop of Killaloe's speech included the advice to allow thoughts 'To turn to the next generation, namely the British born children of Irish parents here. These will number several million in our time. We do not want to prevent them from being fully integrated citizens of the country of their birth but we would like to think that their Irishness can enrich them and their country.'[231]

By 1977 the annual concert arranged by the Council of Irish County Associations had been replaced by the London Irish Festival at Roundwood Park, a day aimed at families that was seen as 'a golden opportunity ... for youth involvement' and for 'giving second-generation Irish a sense of identity'.[232] Indeed, the growth of the second-generation was of paramount importance for the Irish in London as they began to define and assert their identity more strongly in an organized fashion, in order to pass on their sense of identity, a trait that sometimes led to them seeing themselves as 'more Irish' than the Irish in Ireland.[233] Interviewees with children almost unanimously told of the importance they attached to passing on their Irishness. Peter said: 'I think it's very important, very important. Because I think you have better people [if you pass on Irishness] ... it's very important for them to have their roots.'[234] Rose took her children Irish dancing and made an effort to pass on a sense of Irishness:

> SS: Was it important to you to pass on your Irishness to your children?

Rose: Yeah, yeah, very much so.
SS: Do they feel Irish?
Rose: I like to think so, they visit Ireland like yourself I suppose,
       and I hope they keep it up.[235]

Likewise, it was of great importance to Paul that his family should share his identity and he was encouraged that they did: 'It's good to see the kids dancing on Patrick's day.'[236] The growth of Irish dancing and music, evidenced both in interviews and *The Irish Post*, was due primarily to the enthusiasm of Irish parents for their children to get a taste of their culture.[237] There was often a sense of disappointment when some emigrants realized that many of their children would have a different sense of Irishness to their own. David, for instance, in spite of his daughters holding Irish passports and having an interest in things Irish, expressed disappointment that they did not feel the need to join Irish organizations: 'I was always very sorry about that because I felt I was being as Irish as I possibly could but it never rubbed off on them.'[238] As well as an expansion in cultural activities, the late 1970s saw the foundation of Brent Irish Advisory Service, the first Irish welfare service in London not set up and run by the Church, the beginning of a trend for Irish community groups that would expand greatly in the 1980s.[239]

Hickman argues that focusing on residential dispersal or political organization in the assessment of the strength of ethnic groups leaves no room for what she terms 'creative consciousness' or a 'sense of belonging'.[240] It is certainly clear that the Irish in London had a sense of belonging to an Irish nation and to their home town-lands and counties. Evidence from interviews and *The Irish Post* suggest that the 1970s was a pivotal decade in the workings of the London Irish 'creative consciousness' that created a 'sense of belonging' to a community outside of the imagined Irish nation. By the time of this research, interviewees were also very much aware of their place within an ethnic community in London. They were aware of the phrase 'Irish community' and used it frequently without prompting to reference the Irish in London, parts of London and, occasionally, all of Britain. The term was often used when interviewees expressed the strength of the community spirit which they felt. For instance, Fr Terence, who first went to a church in Kentish Town in the borough of Camden in 1973, in the context of not sensing any backlash to IRA bombings in London, said 'but you see I was in a very strong Irish community'.[241] Peter also suggested that he did not come across anti-Irish feeling because of 'the very strong Irish community' in London.[242] Even those, such as Fr Bobby Gilmore, who stressed differences among the Irish, spoke of a unitary, if varied, entity: 'The Irish community had forty shades of green.'[243] Those who rejected the Irishness they found in London also acknowledged an 'Irish community', as with Tricia Darragh above.

Admittedly, this terminology and an imagining of the Irish community as a definable body of people was a more prominent feature of interviews with those involved in Irish activities and organizations. Certainly the 'Irish community in Britain' was an almost entirely imagined community that only had real impact on people's lives in such organizations such as the GAA and the Federation of Irish Societies and thus was rarely referred to except by those involved in these organizations on a national basis.[244] Yet a sense of belonging in a less abstract sense was present almost unanimously across first-generation interviewees. If they had not given any clear indication of a sense of belonging to a wider 'Irish community', interviewees were asked directly, to which the reply was usually along the lines of Rose's 'Oh yeah, and I still do', or Danny's 'Oh you would do yeah ... Most of the people that I did know were Irish', often in a tone that suggested that the answer was a bit too obvious for the researcher to be asking the question.[245]

One usually absent feature of the identities of the interviewees was that of class. Fielding and Hickman have both argued that assimilation into the English working class is something that has been too readily assumed in the case of the Irish.[246] The evidence from the research for this project certainly supports such arguments. In spite of the core community being overwhelmingly working class in social status, class played a minor or non-existent role in the narratives of the interviewees from rural areas, from which the great majority of post-war emigrants originated. Those from urban backgrounds used the language of class with more frequency than those from rural areas. For instance, Danny from the Falls Road in Belfast said that he could never have voted for the Conservative Party, because he and his wife were 'working-class people'. Similar language was used by the left-wing politically active interviewees, of whom two were from Belfast, one from Dublin, and the only rural-origin one from Connemara.[247] Second-generation interviewees were asked if class was ever mentioned when they were growing up. Rory said: 'I don't ever recall that phrase [working class] being used really.

I mean obviously they were working class, but I don't think they ever associated themselves with a working class. I suppose the nearest we ever got to it was politics ... God forbid if I ever vote Tory.'[248] Likewise, Gerry recalled his family voting Labour, 'but it certainly wasn't built on class solidarity, it was a pragmatic thing'.[249]

The Irish in London in our period began to look upon themselves personally and as a group in a new way. For the first-generation Irish in London the expression of an identity in exile never led to the use of a hyphenated identity such as that of the 'Irish-American', but many of the Irish in Britain began to recognize themselves as distinct from the Irish at home and as a group within wider British society. The 1970s was a key decade in the transformation of the community of post-war emigrants from a connected set of impermanent exiles to a self-expressed community within London and Britain.

CHAPTER TWO

'A besieged community'? The Troubles and Irish London

This chapter first briefly outlines the political activity of Irish emigrants in London and of the groups who were demonstrating about the Northern Ireland issue, both in the run up to the Troubles and throughout its first decade up until the 1981 republican hunger strikes. This is not meant to be a comprehensive history: rather, it highlights in a broad way that there was a plethora of groups and demonstrations but they never inspired the great majority of the Irish in London to become involved, either in the 1960s or after the Troubles in Northern Ireland had begun in earnest. The chapter then analyses the experiences of the interviewees with regards to the assertions from many commentators that the 1970s represented a time of widespread anti-Irishness, from within the British Establishment and among ordinary British people, relating to the IRA attacks. The ultimate conclusion is that while the Irish suffered a certain level of police harassment and media attention, and were the butt of anti-Irish jokes, claims that these phenomena gagged the Irish community politically ignore far more fundamental underlying reasons why the Irish largely failed to involve themselves in politics in the 1970s. Moreover, these things did not play major roles in the lives and identities of most Irish people in London.

THE IRISH AND POLITICS UP TO THE CIVIL RIGHTS MOVEMENT

The political quiescence of the Irish in Britain has historically contrasted with the successes of the Irish in parts of the United States. The Irish in Britain largely involved themselves with Catholic matters such as schooling and many got involved with trade unions, but there was never anything approaching a British Tammany Hall. On the one hand, Ó Tuathaigh and others have stressed the debilitating effect of the national question in Ireland on any efforts for the

Irish to find a normative political voice in Britain.[1] On the other, the Irish in Britain never even managed to focus enough energy on that to build a significant and sustained nationalist movement, with only small instances of longevity such as the nationalist T.P. O'Connor's parliamentary seat in Liverpool or brief instances of widespread involvement such as the Irish Self-Determination League's (ISDL) success as a mass movement during the War of Independence.[2] Regarding Irish politics in London, Lees charted political involvement across the nineteenth century among the 'first wave' of Irish emigrants. She painted a picture of limited participation in nationalist causes; only briefly around the time of the Young Irelanders' rebellion in 1848 was this on a large scale, with several groups apparently with thousands of members. As was the case elsewhere in Britain, Victorian Irish Londoners were generally more concerned with matters of Catholicism's liberty in Britain and involvement in trade unions; they had a 'very limited' role in leadership positions of conventional electoral politics. By 1900 the Irish, while still in many ways culturally distinctive, had been absorbed into the structures of English political life.[3] The 'second wave' emigrants after the Second World War largely followed the patterns of their predecessors: with interest in but limited leadership of local or parliamentary politics and no widespread active support for the groups campaigning about Northern Ireland.

For most of the twentieth century the Irish vote was wedded to the Labour Party.[4] By the 1960s the post-war generation of emigrants was continuing this trend. In 1966 a poll of the Irish-born across Britain found 66 per cent intending to vote Labour and 25 per cent Conservative. An *Irish Post* poll in 1970 found that 80 per cent said they had voted Labour in the recent election.[5] It is clear that the Irish, who were largely in working-class employment, quickly identified their needs as being met by the Labour Party. The majority of interviewees were inclined towards the party and said that they had always been so. Danny went so far as to estimate that '99.9 per cent' of his Irish peers would have voted Labour.[6] Active political involvement of the Irish-born appears to have been increasing through the 1960s as the post-war emigrants became settled. Ultan, heavily involved in Labour since he migrated to London in 1957, claimed that 'lots and lots of Irish people became members of the Labour Party at that time [the 1960s]'.[7] Looking back in 1979, Breandán MacLua said that 1963–69 was a high point of Irish involvement.[8] The Irish did begin to make themselves felt in the boroughs where they had settled in large numbers. For instance, the Labour councillor Paddy O'Connor became Camden's first Irish-born mayor (1966–67) and in 1969 Michael O'Halloran, a working-class Irishman originally from County Clare who was part of the post-war exodus from Ireland, was elected as Labour MP for Islington North.

This rise in Irish involvement should not be exaggerated. As with voters of whatever background, most of this Irish support was vague and involvement limited to the ballot, although sometimes not even that, as Rory pointed out about his father: 'He used to say he supported the Labour Party but I don't think he voted until about 1987 or something.'[9] Delaney has pointed out the low voting figures for the Irish, with only half of those in Sparkbrook (Birmingham's equivalent of Kilburn) who were eligible to vote in the mid-1960s actually on the electoral roll.[10] Those active in politics were in the tiny minority and while some Irish councillors were involved with the London Irish Centre, at no point before the 1980s was there cooperation between them to work together on issues regarding either the Irish in London or Ireland itself. An illustration of this was that Ultan said he knew only three Irish councillors in London from his time as a west London councillor from the late 1960s through the 1970s, in spite of there being double that elected in Islington in 1971.[11] One of the councillors Ultan mentioned was in fact a Conservative, showing that there was some, if smaller, involvement in the Conservative Party.[12] There was also some involvement in trade union activity, but again not on any ethnic basis. Indeed, such involvement seemed more likely to simply align Irish immigrants with the general British working class; in 1983 a Dublin-born trade unionist, Bill Taylor, said that he was 'proud' at how the Irish had 'repaid ... the British working class' through their involvement.[13]

As noted in Chapter One, it seems safe to say that whatever shade of green they were, the Irish in London were generally instinctively nationalist. While most were never motivated to take their patriotism beyond the singing of rebel songs, memories of nationalism ingrained through school and republican families came up frequently in the interviews of those who were politically active in London from the 1960s. Peter, who was to join pre-split Sinn Féin in London after emigrating, said that he got his strong views from his schoolteacher, and Timothy's upbringing in a family steeped in stories of the Old IRA and anti-Treaty forces was followed by his own involvement in

Clann na hÉireann, the British wing of Official Sinn Féin.[14] Ultan was brought up by a fiercely republican father and became heavily involved in the Campaign for Democracy in Ulster's (CDU) campaign for civil rights in Northern Ireland.[15]

The two most active political groups focusing on Northern Ireland in the 1960s were the Connolly Association and the CDU. Christopher, a member of the Connolly Association for over half a century, looked back on the 1960s as a time of growing membership.[16] Indeed, the group, whose aim is to act as the vehicle of the Irish in Britain in pursuit of a thirty-two-county socialist republic, saw its greatest period of influence in the 1960s. Its English leader, C. Desmond Greaves, has recently been identified by an historian of Northern Irish politics in the 1960s as 'the intellectual progenitor of the civil rights movement'.[17] Working as a lobby group, the association had success in gaining support from twenty-four MPs in 1962 and was a key player in convincing figures such as Paul Rose to pressure the government over the Northern Ireland issue.[18] Partly arising from the efforts of the Connolly Association, the CDU was founded in 1965. The founding members and leaders were largely Irish immigrants and members of the British Labour Party. Despite its stated aims of pushing solely for civil rights in Northern Ireland, the key founding members certainly had a nationalist streak: Paddy Byrne, the founding vice-president, had been active in the Republican Congress in 1934 and Ultan told this author that CDU's stated aims were 'the thin end of the wedge' that would lead to a united Ireland.[19] The CDU had success in recruiting MPs to its cause, with Paul Rose and Gerry Fitt being among its members, and overall having 100 supporters in Parliament.[20] Demonstrations, as well as political groups, in London grew along with the civil rights movement in Northern Ireland in the late 1960s. Information on political protests prior to the launch of *The Irish Post* in February 1970 is scarce because the British media tended to report in detail only those in London if they caused violence or if they were particularly large. Yet the three interviewees who were active in organizations that were protesting for civil rights in London – Christopher with the Connolly Association, Ultan with CDU and Timothy with *Clann na hÉireann* – looked back on the late 1960s as a time of great political activity: 'whether it was in the city or at the embassies, Hyde Park, Trafalgar Square, there were demonstrations every weekend ... you protested all the time'.[21]

In spite of the limited success of the Connolly Association and the

CDU and the existence of several other groups campaigning about Northern Ireland, there was minimal involvement among the Irish in London. The Irish Unity and Civil Rights Association was set up in the late 1960s and gained the nominal support of the GAA, county associations, the Irish Club, the NUI Club and the London Irish Centre.[22] However, it appears to have actually done very little and the Irish community generally was limited to passive support that at most extended to the purchasing of radical newspapers in pubs, benefit dances for civil rights associations and sending delegates from the county associations to meetings of moderate groups.[23] Christopher estimated that only 400 to 450 people were in the Connolly Association across Britain, with perhaps 10 per cent of these being English radicals, and he looked upon the average attendance at meetings of eight to sixteen people in the 1960s as an historical high.[24] Jackson's unsupported claim that the Connolly Association's organ, the monthly *Irish Democrat*, had a circulation of over 6,000 in the early 1960s seems far-fetched. Yet even if this estimate was accurate, this would simply underline the sentimental nationalism which would perhaps motivate the Irish to buy a political paper in a pub but not much else.[25] The CDU failed miserably in its attempts to gain a mass following among the Irish in Britain – it printed 2,000 copies of its first and only edition of its newspaper, *Spotlight Ulster*, and only managed to distribute 700 – and by 1968 had largely disintegrated as a force.[26] The lack of support among the Irish in London for political groups such as these in the late 1960s is highlighted best by the comparison made by Purdie between the 7,000 Irish people who attended Mass at Quex Road in Kilburn on Sundays in 1968 and the twenty who attended the CDU meeting in Kilburn in April of that year, in spite of heavy advertisement.[27]

While marches and demonstrations in support of the civil rights movement in Northern Ireland did take place regularly, as the interviewees remember, they appear to have usually been small. The highest estimate of numbers for a London demonstration in either *The Times* or the *Irish Times* (admittedly conservative papers that may have underestimated attendance or not reported demonstrations) in the late 1960s was 1,500 for one in Trafalgar Square on 20 October 1968 at which Gerry Fitt was speaking. The crowd at this event included myriad organizations from across the political spectrum, from the Irish immigrant-led CDU and the mainstream United Ireland Association (chaired by the one-time mayor of Camden Paddy

O'Connor) to the British working-class-based Sheet Metalworkers Union and far-left groups such as the West Ham Anarchists and Other Young Communists.[28] More typical demonstrations numbered 100 to 200, with one particular low point being a Connolly Association march in January 1969 that attracted twelve people.[29] To put these demonstrations in context, an anti-Vietnam demonstration in London on 27 October 1968 attracted several tens of thousands.[30] While Sinn Féin did exist in London in the early-to-mid 1960s, judging from the lack of documentary trace, and the testimony of interviewees Peter, Timothy and Con, it was essentially a talking shop, with members who attended civil rights and left-wing marches and sold their organ *The United Irishman*.[31] Likewise, a variety of ultra-left organizations involved Irish people in prominent positions without ever gaining any mainstream support among their compatriots, such as Gerry Lawless's Trotskyite Irish Workers Group and Brendan Clifford's British and Irish Communist Organization.[32]

The picture on the eve of the Troubles, therefore, was one in which there was widespread sympathy for Labour along with some modest electoral successes for Irish immigrants, but only low-levels of involvement. Similarly, there were some successes for the Connolly Association and the CDU but only a general and vague attachment to the sentiments of Irish nationalism in the wider Irish population. It is notable that most Irish organizations simply did not involve themselves in political matters, or in some cases studiously avoided them. When the county associations were set up in the 1950s, with the exception of some northern counties, they followed the traditional line of many Irish organizations such as the GAA in being explicitly 'non-political and non-sectarian'.[33] The Irish Club in Eaton Square reportedly took pride in no politics being discussed on its premises.[34] This is an important context to bear in mind when analysing reasons for the lack of political involvement in the 1970s.

THE TROUBLES

From mid-1971 to spring 1972 the worsening situation in Northern Ireland prompted thousands of Irish people and socialist activists to go out onto the streets in protest. The first demonstrations of note took place on 11 July 1971 when 5,000 gathered in Trafalgar Square, along with 3,000 in the next largest centre of concentration of Irish-born in

Britain, Birmingham. Bernadette Devlin and Bowes Egan of People's Democracy spoke in London and three MPs did so in Birmingham.[35] On the introduction of internment without trial in Northern Ireland in August 1971, the Anti-Internment League (AIL) was set up, campaigning for the unconditional release of the internees and the withdrawal of British troops from Ireland, adding 'self-determination of the Irish people' to their aims in May 1972.[36] It had its roots among the Irish in London, being set up at a meeting at the London Irish Centre.[37] The AIL campaigned in many different ways, sending delegates to Northern Ireland as well as to European left-wing groups, staging small-scale protests and holding conferences. However, its greatest successes came in the form of two mass protests. The first, against internment, was estimated in various sources as being from 10,000 to 25,000 strong.[38] The level of Irish participation within this number is open to speculation, but the fact that the overall demonstration was made up of three converging marches all coming from areas with large Irish populations (Cricklewood, Hammersmith and Archway –*The Irish Post* reported that the largest contingent came from the most Irish of these areas, Cricklewood) does suggest that this demonstration was at least aimed at the Irish communities in these places.[39] The second march, on 5 February 1972, was to protest at Bloody Sunday. Beginning outside the Crown pub in Cricklewood, renowned as where Irish labourers waited in the mornings for a day's work, the march of several thousand people (the organizers said 20,000; *The Times* reported that 4,000 ended up at Downing Street) proceeded to Trafalgar Square replete with tricolours, coffins and republican-styled berets for three minutes of silence.[40] Reinforcing the Irish emphasis of the AIL, Maguire's research shows that two of the three most profitable branches for funding were Kilburn, where Derek Highstead of the PIRA (Provisional IRA) organized large collections, and Slough, where a sympathetic Irish subcontractor collected among his labourers.[41]

All of those interviewed for this book who were usually politically active remembered being at the Bloody Sunday march.[42] The important point, however, is that many usually non-political Irish people also attended. Stephen and Paul said that this was the only march they ever went on, with the latter saying that 'everyone from the building trade' was there.[43] Fr McCabe, very much the moderate, remembered that 'I was on marches down to Downing Street myself, and I wouldn't be a natural marching person. After Bloody Sunday I went on at least two or three ... Bloody Sunday was the big one. It galvanised people into a sense that we must register that something awful has happened here ... They were carrying coffins.'[44] Trouble flared as attempts to place thirteen coffins in Downing Street were thwarted by the police and 122 people were arrested.[45] A few days later, three of the AIL's leaders (two London-based Irishmen and one People's Democracy member from Belfast) were arrested and charged with conspiracy to break the Public Order Act. Protests regarding Northern Ireland were soon officially banned from being staged in Trafalgar Square by the Conservative government, a ban not lifted until the 1990s.[46] Outside supporting marches, Irish community groups displayed some initiative over the Northern Ireland situation in the early 1970s. Fr Paddy Mee at the Irish Centre set up a fund for families of internees in December 1971.[47] The GAA held dances and collections for similar funds. Ironically, one was organized at the Gresham dance hall for 30 January 1972, Bloody Sunday.[48] Clann Connacht, an over- arching body for the five Connacht county associations, reacted to Bloody Sunday by pulling out of the 1972 St Patrick's parade in London in order to donate the funds set aside for it to the Northern Ireland Distress Fund.[49]

Following the protests surrounding Bloody Sunday, however, the scale of demonstrations collapsed dramatically. The AIL's next march on 26 February attracted only 5,000, when it had aimed for 'at least 50,000', and it had entirely faded out by 1973.[50] By April 1973 *The Irish Post* was bemoaning the fact that only a core element of 100 people turned up to Irish protests in London.[51] Probably the most influential group concerned with Northern Ireland for the rest of the 1970s, the Troops Out Movement, was formed in West London in 1973.[52] It was successful in gaining the support of some left-wing elements in the Labour Party who in 1980 set up the Labour Committee on Ireland.[53] Even at fewer than 1,000 members throughout Britain, the Troops Out Movement was the most significant organization campaigning about Ireland; while there were several other left-wing groups, they were tiny in numbers and they did not consistently focus on Ireland, something that a Troops Out Movement member complained about in 1977.[54] Yet in spite of its Irish focus, the Troops Out Movement had very little Irish involvement or leadership. One interviewee, Diarmuid, who came to London from Belfast in 1977, joined the group soon after arriving in London but could not remember any significant Irish, or even a second-generation Irish, presence.[55] There were also other small groups, with Provisional Sinn Féin having wings in England, one of which Con set up in 1973 before his imprisonment for violent republican activity in England.[56]

The only noteworthy incident for the remainder of the 1970s that involved the Irish community in a large way was a funeral cortège through Kilburn for the Requiem Mass of the IRA hunger striker Michael Gaughan, who died in Parkhurst prison in June 1974. *The Irish Times* reported that 5,000 people attended, a significant figure for a man convicted of IRA activity. Eight men dressed in quasi-paramilitary garb led a coffin draped in a tricolour to the Sacred Heart Church, Quex Road, Kilburn. Along the way the controversial and overtly republican priest Fr Michael Connolly praised Gaughan as 'a great man' and said that 'the price of freedom is very high and Irishmen have always been willing to pay it in full'.[57] This march was well remembered among interviewees. The politically active Timothy said that 'there were thousands in Kilburn ... people came out, everybody supported that'.[58] The march also attracted many who were usually politically passive, such as Robert, who said that he attended out of a sense of it being 'a historic thing'.[59] One of the more politically minded chaplains at the London Irish Centre, Fr Paddy Mee, was also apparently present.[60]

Generally, however, there developed among Irish organizations a determined policy of keeping out of politics – what has often been described as a 'heads down' attitude.[61] This was to an extent a continuation of the previous apolitical practices of Irish organizations, although the extreme reluctance even to discuss anything remotely political was at times extraordinary, considering that the 'non-political, non-sectarian' tag had not prevented organizations such as the GAA in Ireland historically being overtly nationalist.[62] Fr Bobby Gilmore, who came to London to work with the Irish Chaplaincy in 1979, was amazed by the almost total lack of attention that had been paid to matters such as the operation of the Prevention of Terrorism Act (PTA) and anti-Irish incidents, which hardly appear in the reports of the London Irish Centre.[63] Robert, who was heavily involved in the London GAA at the time, remembers only one episode when the organization spoke to politicians, and that was regarding the British Army's taking over of GAA grounds in Crossmaglen, County Armagh: 'If the GAA were ever to go into politics they'd just be split down the middle ... At times you felt like getting involved with this or that but they backed off it.'[64] The county associations from the

Republic of Ireland began to steer clear of any involvement in nationalist causes, although the support of northern associations for the
republican cause did surface occasionally.[65]

The Federation of Irish Societies also remained almost entirely
apolitical, which at times caused some controversy among its members.
In 1974 a debate was set off by an apparently innocuous action of the
chairman when he sent letters to political parties asking for clarification
of their policies on Northern Ireland.[66] Political tensions within
the Irish community as the Troubles escalated were mentioned
occasionally in interviews. Robert remembered telling collectors for
the PIRA that he 'didn't care' about their cause, and Timothy, who
collected money and sold papers for *Clann na hÉireann*, found some
hostility in Irish clubs and pubs, 'depending what was in the news'.[67]
The difficulty in mobilizing the Irish community to act politically on
the Northern Ireland issue is perhaps best shown by the Irish Civil
Rights Association's running of seven candidates for parliament in
Irish-populated constituencies for the October 1974 election. This
failed spectacularly, with the most successful of their seven candidates
polling only 633 in Hammersmith North.[68]

In mainstream British politics, reports in *The Irish Post* suggest that
Irish vote for Labour held in the February 1974 general election,
although the 80 per cent which the paper's post-election poll found
had voted Labour in 1970 had dropped to 66 per cent.[69] The
Conservatives had polled 14 per cent and 10 per cent in the respective
elections. However, in 1979 the paper's pre-election poll suggested
that Labour had lost the Irish vote. Of the 400 Irish-born and 200
second-generation Irish in Britain who were polled, only 22 per cent
intended to vote Labour, with 20 per cent in support of the Conservatives.[70] The poll found 32 per cent intending not to vote and 12 per
cent undecided, with the vast majority of these apparently being
traditional Labour supporters. Unfortunately, the reports in this
paper are the closest that we come to statistical evidence of the Irish
vote. Nevertheless, if we allow for a wide margin of error on these
figures and only tentatively suggest conclusions, the polls can be
illustrative. The Conservative Party appears still not to have made the
inroads among the Irish population that it had generally across the
country by 1979, where it polled 44 per cent of the vote. On the other
hand, the 1979 poll puts the Irish Labour vote far below the party's
eventual poll of 37 per cent.[71] The most striking thing, therefore, is
the disenchantment of the Irish with the two main parties by 1979.

Nevertheless, some interviewees do remember an interest in mainstream politics. Fr McCabe describes the period in London in the 1970s:

Fr McCabe: There was a lot of interest, particularly in Labour. I was amazed that there was so much interest in British politics. I remember politicians used to turn up for events, including the conservative member for our area. The parties were aware of the Irish vote.

SS: Who did you find that most people supported?

Fr McCabe: Oh the vast majority were Labour.[72]

Likewise, Eoin, a Labour councillor and candidate for a parliamentary election in the 1970s, found that 'Every Labour Party [branch] I've ever attended has had Irish people … Chelmsford, Stretham, Croydon, Greenwich, Twickenham, Crewe, Rochdale, Wolverhampton'.[73]

In terms of the electoral success of Irish people in the 1970s, there were some small successes among Labour Party politicians: in 1971 six Irish councillors were elected in Islington; Brian Duggan became Camden's second Irish-born mayor in 1972–73; and in 1974, Alfred O'Reilly became mayor of Waltham Forest, a borough without any significant Irish presence.[74] Michael O'Halloran also managed to hold on to his seat in Parliament until 1983. But, as in the 1960s, there was very little working together for Irish issues, and no official grouping of Irish councillors came about until the mid-1980s. Even when the Labour Committee on Ireland was founded in 1980 by the left of the party, it seems as though it was mostly the 'old guard' of various groups such as the CDU, the Campaign for Social Justice and groups of various left-leaning MPs, rather than any Irish-led force.[75] Thus, the pattern of Irish involvement in politics in London in the period 1969–81 was one of silence on the Northern Ireland issue, interrupted by brief expressions of outrage at internment and Bloody Sunday and Gaughan's funeral, and small electoral successes without any work for specifically Irish needs.

EXPLAINING THE 'HEADS DOWN' PHENOMENON

In explaining the general lack of political involvement by the Irish in 1970s, one must first take into account the backgrounds and social situations of the immigrants. The great majority of the Irish in London were of lower-class, rural origin and, while they undoubtedly improved their material condition, they ultimately remained poorly educated and in the lower strata of society during their lives in Britain. Many Irish, therefore, simply did not possess the political knowledge or language to involve themselves in any kind of politics. For most of those involved in Irish political and community organizations, this was one of the primary reasons given by peers for a lack of involvement. David was involved in the Federation of Irish Societies during the 1980s when it was under increasing pressure from newer Irish groups to involve itself politically. He was irritated by the suggestion that all the Irish should be 'political animals': 'If they'd stayed at home they wouldn't have been involved in politics so why should they be here? ... That always annoyed me very much.'[76] Likewise, the politically active Diarmuid, who had spent summers working on building sites in Britain in the early 1970s, put a lack of political involvement among his countrymen primarily down to their background:

> Those 70 year old guys in the demob suits speaking Connemara Irish ... are not going to get involved in politics, for obvious reasons. And many of the younger Irish working on the building sites had left school very early, they weren't politically motivated, they'd get Irish nationalism like almost every Irish person would but they'd be going to places ... [for] the 'country Irish' like the Garryowen and the Galtymore.[77]

Ciara, who became involved in her county association in the early 1990s, still found a lack of confidence among the 1950s emigrants who still ran the association when she was interviewed:

> I find that sometimes the older Irish people will be outspoken, but in their own comfort zone, in their own culture. And then if they have to be outspoken in meetings, more formal, they're not sure, they either say nothing or they are not sure how to put themselves across because they might not be very able to do that. Education was different in Ireland so they wouldn't be articulate.[78]

It is unsurprising that three of the most politically involved of the interviewees, Diarmuid, Eoin and Ultan, were more educated and in better employment than average, and that Declan, also involved in left-wing politics, educated himself in Britain and eventually studied at Oxford University.

Chapter One has highlighted that there was a strong myth of return among the Irish that was beginning to fade by the 1970s but nevertheless still had an emotional hold over some of the Irish community. Furthermore, it has been shown that many of the Irish in London had overwhelmingly Irish social circles. Considering oneself transient or being uninterested in wider society due to a lack of interaction with the host community can be seen as inhibiting the political urges of the emigrant to become involved with British political matters or even in groups based in London concerning Northern Ireland. One striking example is that of Miriam James, who was involved in left-wing republican politics in Dublin to the extent that she was interned for almost three years during the Second World War. When she moved to London in 1949 at the age of 31, she 'shut up about politics' simply because she felt that she was only a temporary emigrant, 'a sort of guest'.[79] Christopher of the Connolly Association saw such feelings of being only a visitor as an important reason for the sustained lack of success in attracting the Irish-born into political movements:

> You take any migrant getting off a plane coming to London. In all probability he will not start reading a local paper for 10 years ... It'll take the best part of 20 years to be part and parcel of the locality. And then to be asking people to be involved in the body politic of this country; it's something more attuned to the second- and third-generation Irish.[80]

As noted above, the Irish-born in London were moving into middle age by the 1970s, and by 1981 59 per cent of the Republic-born population of Britain were over 45 and only 6 per cent of the Republic-born female population in London were aged 15–24, the usual age group in which recent emigrants would be found. It was only by the beginning of the 1980s that many of the second-generation were reaching maturity – in 1981, 23 per cent of females born of Irish parents in London were still under 16, and 33 per cent were aged 16–24.[81] While growing older and starting a family has been seen to have contributed to the compromising of hopes of return and a greater acceptance of life in England, this was not necessarily a process that would have led to a push for political involvement among most of the first-generation. Middle age meant young families for a great many of the Irish in London, and a higher fertility rate for Irish women than their British or New Commonwealth counterparts meant bigger families.[82] The effect of this on political involvement was significant among the interviewees. Peter, involved in Sinn Féin in the 1960s, had stopped attending meetings by the time of the Troubles, although apparently not through any loss of sympathy with the cause, as he explained:

> SS: Why did you stop attending Sinn Féin meetings?
> Peter: Well of course it's like everything else now, when you have family commitments it's not very easy to go back. And I'll tell you something, you had to keep your head down[i.e. work hard] to try and keep a house and keep a family together.[83]

Likewise, one of the reasons Timothy found people fell away from republican activism was due to the difficulties of balancing it with family life. He noticed that many of the most committed were unmarried: 'The amount of time [spent protesting] back then, they were on the road all the time. They'd have to take time off work to support various things, it wouldn't be that easy.'[84] It is perhaps notable that two of the three interviewees who remained politically active from the 1960s and throughout the 1970s were childless. Thus, the demographics of the Irish population in London meant that there was a relative absence of what one may term 'protesting age' – that is, young adults – during the late 1960s and early 1970s when the potential for a widespread movement surrounding Northern Ireland was apparent. It is telling that in the 1980s the newly mature second-generation, partly inspired by the hunger strikes, were influential in many of the new organizations and issues which came to the fore, particularly in the unashamedly nationalist Irish in Britain Representation Group (IBRG), which campaigned for greater ethnic recognition, against anti-Irish jokes and prejudice and had a policy of pushing for a united Ireland.[85]

The social profile and divisions among the Irish in London made the community as a unit an unlikely candidate for political involvement. The rural backgrounds of most of the post-war Irish emigrants contributed to a lack of active involvement in trade unionism and the Labour movement. It has already been noted that, by and large, the Irish in London did not articulate a working-class identity in interviews. Involvement for the rural-born emigrant required inno-vation on the part of an individual to take on a political tradition that was not part of his or her own past. This was exacerbated by the fact that large numbers of Irishmen worked in the almost entirely non-unionized building trade. As Timothy, a politically minded builder originally from Connemara, pointed out, he was something of an exception in his views:

SS: Did you find many of your peers were involved in unions or other political movements?

Timothy: A very small number would be involved because the building trade was all subcontracted, they paid you less and it was in the hand. That type of person then ... they're not into unions at all. They came from areas, apart from cities like Dublin, Limerick, Cork and Galway I suppose, where you didn't have unions.[86]

It is no surprise, therefore, that the County Dublin-born Christopher, a member of the left-wing Connolly Association since 1958, remembered Dublin being the best-represented part of Ireland in the association, followed secondly by those from the (also more urbanized) 'six counties'.[87] The hostility of the Church is also of relevance, particularly to involvement in the far left, which was the mainstay of the groups working on Northern Ireland issues. Certainly, Bob Purdie of the AIL felt that the Church was working against the group due to its left-wing emphasis, saying that Irish people were 'offended and frightened' by his Marxism and that the Church involved itself to prevent meetings at the Irish Centre in Camden.[88]

The social divide noted between the Irish professional class and the working class played a key role in inhibiting political development because it left the core community without the middle-class leadership that had been crucial in the mobilization of the ethnic vote elsewhere in the diaspora. This was a strong theme among interviewees who had tried to get professionals involved in matters regarding Northern Ireland. David, part of the leadership of the Federation of Irish Societies, expressed disbelief that he was left to deal with media questions and to issue statements on behalf of the Irish community when he knew that 'there were so many guys out there who were far better qualified to speak on television and radio than I was, but they wouldn't bother to do it'.[89] David's self-deprecating tone emphasizes that even those at the pinnacle of Irish organizations suffered from a lack of confidence in their ability to express themselves politically, due to their low levels of education. Fr Gilmore spoke of the trouble of involving the middle-class Irish even in the campaign to free the Birmingham Six: 'the leadership from that group was not there, with few exceptions'.[90] Sister Sarah Clarke, who worked on a number of causes to do with Northern Ireland also found this: 'I met opposition where I might have expected cooperation amongst middle-class Irish people in Britain.'[91]

One can only speculate, since several interviewees were sympathetic enough to the nationalist and Labour causes, some attending meetings when asked by associates or expressing sympathy with republicanism, that if effective leadership had been provided they may well have become more involved. Paul, for instance, attended republican political meetings when asked to by workmates but nothing ever materialized in the way of long-term involvement, in spite of his continued nationalist opinions.[92] The middle-class Irish were affected by similar factors to their lower-class compatriots with regard to reasons for a lack of high-level involvement in either Northern Irish or domestic British politics. Their more natural attraction to the Conservative Party, as evidenced by the launch of the (admittedly short-lived) Irish Conservative Association in 1971, also prevented any mainstream Irish Labour movement emerging.[93] John Walsh summed up the political beliefs of his father, who was a doctor and patron of the Irish Club, as being motivated by his social milieu: 'As an anglicised, middle-class Battersea doctor, he was ardently Conservative.'[94] Perhaps the most important reason for the Irish professional class's lack of ambition to provide ethnic leadership regarding any political cause was the fact that they were not in a social environment that was overtly hostile to them, as their predecessors in Protestant America and sectarian Liverpool had been.[95] Thus, they had no need to look to ethnicity to maintain their interests.

For over half the Irish in London, gender played a large part in their not being politically involved. Politics, like many other aspects of life in the Irish community, was a male-dominated space. In the 1970s there appears to have been only one very small group that specifically looked to involve Irish women in the Northern Ireland issue, named 'Women and Ireland' and founded in 1972.[96] Irish women in interviews for this project and in the volumes of interviews carried out by others generally displayed a remove from politics, even in terms of holding opinions. For instance, whereas Danny held strong opinions regarding Northern Ireland and support for the Labour Party, his wife Victoria was rather apathetic.[97] Likewise, Brigid

1. First Holy Communion, mid 60s

2. Second-generation children on the boat to Ireland for the summer, 60s

3. Second-generation boy on his uncle's farm in Ireland in the summer, 60s

4 . Catholic high school in North London, late 70s

5. Second-generation dancers, 1980

6. Second-generation dancers, 60s

7. First Holy Communion, 60s

8. Big Tom (famous country and western singer very popular at the Galtymore)

9. Irishmen in an Irish pub with the Sam Maguire trophy (the All-Ireland winning Kerry team were visiting London)

10. Second-generation in Ireland in the summer

11. Second-generation in Ireland in the summer

12. Garryowen Gaelic football team, 1964

said that her husband was very pro-Sinn Féin but she displayed no political opinion except anger over Margaret Thatcher's treatment of the Hunger Strikers.[98] Comments about *The Irish Post* were also telling.[99] A great many of the male interviewees mentioned the political slant of the paper, whether in a positive or negative way, including those in no way involved in political or community groups. However, of ten female first-generation interviewees, only one, the well-educated Evelyn, had any opinion on the paper's politics.[100] Brenda's experience of having frequently bought the paper for news of where the best dances would be that weekend but having no recollection of the political viewpoints was commonplace.[101] The gender divide with relation to the strength of political opinion can be largely put down to the society from which Irish women came: that is, a rigidly Catholic one with emphasis on the woman's place in the home.[102] Indeed, it was only in 1973 that women working in publicly funded jobs in the Republic of Ireland were permitted to keep their jobs upon marriage. The possibility that there was greater integration among women than men meant that having more English friends and, often, non-Irish husbands could have removed some women from an interest in Irish politics. It should also be noted that women simply did not have much to relate to in the generally masculine world of mainstream British politics. This was even more the case with the extremely gendered Irish national story of armed resistance and the contemporary situation of paramilitary warfare in Northern Ireland.

The fact that the Troubles were a *Northern* Irish phenomenon and that 85 per cent of the Irish in London came from the Republic contributed to the low level of involvement in nationalist politics. Earlier conflict, which had engulfed the whole island, saw a greater, although not hugely significant, engagement of the Irish in Britain.[103] Some Republic of Ireland-born interviewees showed a certain remove from Northern Ireland in spite of a simultaneous nationalist sympathy. John found himself bemused at English people characterizing the violence as a phenomenon from the whole island: 'I mean we were from the south of Ireland, it didn't matter to us.'[104] Likewise, Brenda said about Northern Ireland: 'We were quite removed from that to be honest, being in southern Ireland a long way from the border.'[105] Some people from Northern Ireland observed the little concern about the North from those southerners whom they met in London. Mary Walker, a Catholic originally from County Tyrone, complained that 'They knew nothing about King Billy: there were a lot of southern

Irish that I met who knew nothing about King Billy, but I grew up with him.'[106] Victoria found a negative attitude towards the North among those she met in Irish clubs and her husband Danny noticed different attitudes among some of the southerners he met: 'I found that some people from the south of Ireland couldn't care less what happened in the North. Yet others were every bit as much interested as I would have been.'[107] Even within marriages a divide sometimes appeared, with the Omagh-born Evelyn saying that her husband sometimes showed a lack of understanding: 'I had to say that to him once, "be quiet, you sound like an Englishman." '[108] All of the eight Northern Irish Catholics interviewed spoke of discrimination in the North and five recounted either personal or familial experiences of violence, including the deaths of family and friends. All, apart from Victoria, displayed a high level of concern with the situation in Northern Ireland.

This north/south divide was reflected in the actions of the county associations. The southern associations ceased any involvement in Northern Irish issues after the early 1970s but the northern ones continued to sponsor some nationalist events. The minutes of the Fermanagh Association showed continual interest in the Northern Ireland issue from its inception and through the Troubles, with such motions including: a protest to MPs about internment of republicans involved in the Border Campaign in 1960; the sending of money to the Republican Prisoners Fund in 1975; and inviting Owen Carron MP (who replaced Bobby Sands after his death) to a function in 1981.[109] In comparison, the minutes of southern counties such as Kildare and Tipperary show no such motions passed. This split was recognized at the time, as Fr Tom McCabe recalled: 'There was one particular county association, Armagh, that people felt had an undue degree of IRA influence within its membership ... Many of the county associations from the north did have their quota of [such] people.' Yet in his own Cavan Association the matter of Northern Ireland simply 'didn't feature', in spite of it being a border county.[110] In 1981 the AGM of the Council of Irish County Associations was the subject of controversy as the six northern counties came together to push through official calls for the withdrawal of British troops, to improve conditions in the H-Blocks and to set in motion an Anglo-Irish conference to negotiate peace, and in the following year the Antrim Association was the sole county to sponsor a national demonstration in support of the hunger strikers.[111]

This is not to say that the Irish originally from the Republic were not concerned about Northern Ireland – just not as concerned as they might have been had the violence directly affected more of them. There is evidence that many were sufficiently emotionally involved for it to affect their political behaviour and opinions towards the mainstream political parties. While one must not read *The Irish Post*'s articles as necessarily indicative of general Irish opinion, MacLua's writings at least highlight the thoughts of one Clare-born emigrant of republican heritage. His columns often read as if voting for politicians who were 'sound on Ireland' was the singular concern of the Irish in Britain. For instance, on 23 February 1974 the 'Dolan' column listed all those MPs who were doing 'their bit' on Northern Ireland and those who were in the 'second division' of positive activity on Northern Ireland. Doing their bit on Northern Ireland even led MacLua to recommend his readers to support two Conservative MPs in the midst of a generally viscerally anti-Tory tirade.[112] Similarly, in the lead-up to the 1979 general election MacLua wrote an article suggesting ethnic voting: 'who we, the Irish in Britain, should vote for'. His article again obsessed with the situation in the North, although this time he at least admitted that the decision on who to vote for 'doesn't *entirely* have to do with Northern Ireland'.[113]

Some interviewees originally from the Republic answered positively when asked if their voting was affected by the Irish policies of the parties. Peter, from Leitrim, reflected on the general support of Irish people for the Labour Party: 'Oh I'd say it had a lot to do with the Tories' policies in Ireland … the Tory policy was anti-Irish.'[114] Ultan registered his distaste with the Conservatives by characterizing them as 'the old imperial party'.[115] But by 1979 the Northern Ireland policy of the British government had been characterized by bipartisan agreement and it is perhaps illustrative that *The Irish Post* poll of that year for the first time found a distinct drop-off in support for the Labour Party, with only 22 per cent claiming that they were going to vote Labour and 53.5 per cent either undecided or intending to abstain.[116] While this reflects a general move towards the Conservatives in the 1979 election, it does present a stark contrast to the 80 per cent of Labour voters found in 1970, also a Conservative-won election, when the Labour Party had yet to tarnish its Ireland-friendly reputation.[117] Letters to *The Irish Post* and the almost unanimous sympathy towards a united Ireland among the Irish in London suggest that were there to have been a party making real progress on the Northern Ireland situation, it may have experienced a groundswell in Irish support.[118] Several letters in the run-up to the 1979 election urged abstention from the election due to both parties' poor records on the North, and one contributor demonstrated a severe disillusionment with Northern Ireland policies, which led him to vote on other issues:

> I am as concerned as the next rational person for the situation in Northern Ireland ... [but] whether I vote Tory or Labour has no bearing on Northern Ireland ... It was the Tories who introduced internment and who whitewashed Bloody Sunday ... It was Labour which sold out Sunningdale .... and has since given us Castlereagh and the H-Blocks. The Liberals don't matter ... [so] I am going to vote for mundane bread and butter.[119]

Regardless of feelings on Northern Ireland, it was ultimately 'bread and butter' issues that predominated in the thoughts of most of the Irish in London from both sides of the border. For instance, Brenda said that she had switched between parties based on issues from election to election and did not recognize Northern Ireland as an issue; Fr Terence's opinion on his parishioners was that 'There was nobody in Labour jumping out and down saying we'll solve the Irish problem ... they [the parishioners] were Labour anyway.'[120] Some working-class voters felt that their future welfare was best placed in the hands of the Conservatives, as with both Fr Liam's parents and the Birmingham-based Maura Murphy who were motivated in voting Conservative in order to buy their own houses.[121] Even those north-erners who displayed antipathy towards ever voting Conservative also recognized the pragmatic side of their vote. Danny said: 'I just couldn't vote Tory ... It used to be the Conservative and Unionist Party ... I wouldn't vote unionist and I wouldn't Tory either', but he also spoke of the need to vote Labour because 'we're working-class people'.[122] Gerry remembered his father's similar feelings: 'He perceived the Conservatives to be hand in hand with the Unionists, so that made him particularly distrustful of the Conservatives.' However, Gerry put his family's voting Labour down to 'pragmatic reasons'.[123]

The Irish in London were largely poorly educated, from rural backgrounds in the Republic of Ireland rather than the North, and some still considered themselves as only temporarily resident in Britain. As an emigrant group they were largely heading into middle age by the 1970s and were divided along class lines, and more than half were females. These features made the Irish as a whole very unlikely to involve themselves politically, whether it be within mainstream British parties, working on issues specifically for the Irish in Britain or involvement in the Northern Ireland issue. Nevertheless, one could argue that it is surprising that their instinctive nationalism, which, as shown, was aroused in the early 1970s, did not lead to more constructive comment through the Troubles. One of the major reasons for this was that nationalism had to be re-evaluated by Irish people in the context of continued IRA activity.

Interviewees almost unanimously expressed disgust at the violence emanating from Northern Ireland and several highlighted that it caused the collapse of any sympathy that they and their compatriots in London had with militant republicanism. There was a particular focus upon events, such as the Birmingham bombings, that had happened in Britain, which of course directly affected the Irish in Britain as much as the native population.[124] Fr Terence saw the people in his parishes turning away from tacit support of the IRA after the Guildford and Birmingham bombings of late 1974, which together killed twenty-six people: 'that became a watershed and people were saying "we're not supporting anyone who does that." '[125] After Stephen telling me about the huge marches and sympathy for the 'cause' after Bloody Sunday, I asked him whether the sympathy lasted, and he replied: 'No, it evaporated. The Birmingham thing was very counterproductive; it sort of cancelled out [Bloody Sunday]. And there were some other hugely horrendous killings that turned people [away from republicanism]. And there was a kind of war weariness as well; it seemed to go on and on and on.'[126] Declan went as far as to say that the first decade of the Troubles 'destroyed the whole great thing of a united Ireland, except for the sentimentalists'.[127] While those entirely pushed away from any interest in Irish unity appear to have been in the minority, people who may have been involved in political issues about Northern Ireland certainly were discouraged. For instance, Timothy fell away from political activism by the mid-1970s once the Official Republican Movement had become overshadowed by the more violent Provisionals. Robert spoke of a fall in willingness to buy republican papers in pubs or donate to funds related to Northern Ireland, due to the realization that the proceeds were going to buy guns and bombs that killed innocents.[128] Likewise, Fr McCabe said: 'A lot changed as time went on. In the early days there was a certain innocence about things [funds] that were started up. I think later on more questions were asked about Noraid for instance.'[129]

In addition to genuine disgust at the actions of the IRA, there was a feeling of guilt by association, or embarrassment, present among many of the Irish, that inhibited any likelihood of coming out in support of nationalism of any hue. As will be discussed below, this was partly due to the rhetoric of the British media and government who tended to equate any nationalism with the IRA, but it was also due to the inescapable fact that IRA activity was couched in the rhetoric and symbols that all the Irish had grown up with and many still sympathized with on some level, if only romantically. There has been much commentary on the stark contrast between the celebrations in Ireland of the fiftieth and seventy-fifth anniversaries of the 1916 Rising, the former characterized by an outpouring of uncritical nationalist celebration and the latter by self-doubt and embarrassment over republicanism's contemporary incarnation in Northern Ireland.[130] The Irish in Britain were not immune to such feelings. This is evident through the fact that even interviewees who recollected no anti-Irish comments and had no opinions on the media or police sometimes still said that they would rather not speak on public transport so as not to reveal their Irishness, to 'shrink a bit' as Brenda put it.[131] David remembered: 'I felt uneasy going into work [but] I couldn't put the blame on the work colleagues for it, it was an impression that I had in my own mind that wasn't stemming from anything that had been said before, it was just there.'[132] On occasion, English people had to console their Irish neighbours, so upset were they by the violence, as with one letter writer to *The Times* in the wake of the Birmingham bombings, who spoke of how an Irish neighbour of hers performed a religious act of 'reparation' after any republican attack because she felt 'so dreadful'.[133] Similarly, after the Birmingham bombs, one English policeman bought his Irish neighbour a box of chocolates because she had 'felt awful' after what had happened.[134] The following comment from Phyllis Izzard sum up such feelings:

> But, when the Troubles at home heated up a bit and transferred here, it did become uncomfortable. Hand on heart, I've never felt ashamed to be Irish, but there were times when I didn't want to shout it from the rooftops ... People were disgusted by it [the violence]. Irish people here were disgusted by it and did not want in any way to be associated with it. A lot of English people were very understanding about that, I have to say. They understood that it was only a minority. But it did make you hang your head a bit.[135]

The coverage of the Northern Ireland issue in *The Irish Post* provides, through its editorials and letters pages, an invaluable source for showing an innate nationalism compromised over the course of the Troubles due to violence. The great majority of the interviewees claimed to have regularly bought *The Irish Post* around this time. Under its editor MacLua, a Fianna Fáil republican who, before emigrating to Britain, had written a book in favour of the GAA ban on 'foreign games', *The Irish Post* provided a consistently non-violent but very firmly nationalist viewpoint. This level of nationalism does mean that *The Irish Post* is a problematic historical source, being far more consistently sympathetic to republicanism and damning of British policy than oral history reveals was evident across the Irish in London. Indeed, the interviewees showed a range of reactions to the *Post*'s political commentary. While some simply could not remember it in any detail, others were enthusiastic. Danny mentioned the Dolan column without prompting, saying that MacLua was 'a man after my own heart', and Peter said that 'I agreed with practically everything he said ... there weren't a lot of people prepared to say things like that, and he was prepared to say it.'[136] Others, such as Declan and Robert, were highly critical of the paper's overtly nationalistic stance, with the former saying that it provided a warped view of the Irish in Britain by portraying them as obsessed with Northern Ireland.[137]

In the early 1970s the paper was uniformly critical of the British and Irish governments in their failure to do enough to solve the Northern Ireland problem, as well as frequently criticizing the actions of British troops. John McCaughey, who worked with *The Irish Post* in its early years, has commented that its political articles were 'written in a kind of Machiavellian code translatable only by the politically sophisticated reader'.[138] Indeed, the articles often did not explain fully what they were saying, but the code was never particularly sophisticated in its veiling of sympathy for the nationalist community's use of force in Northern Ireland, as shown in 1971: 'Nationalists ... look upon the small arms which they hold for defensive purposes as vital to their lives and properties. They will naturally resist these arms being taken from them but when searches for arms are accompanied by brutality, destruction and arrogance, then they naturally react in the only way they can.'[139]

Following Bloody Sunday the rhetoric of *The Irish Post* reached a zenith of republicanism. The first editorial following the events called on Irish people who were members of the Conservative Party to resign and the end of the Northern Ireland statelet was anticipated: 'After Derry there can be no going back; no half-way measures; no truck; no compromise; no deals. Those who died on Sunday last must not have died for a compromise.'[140] The same edition contained an article about an Irish-born chemist based in Hammersmith who had been jailed for sending arms to the IRA. The tone was entirely sympathetic, saying that he and his fellow defendant were 'men who felt something had to be done in the wake of the savage pogrom which had been launched against the Catholic community in August 1969. Guns had to be procured to defend what was a defenceless community.'[141] A week later the editorial was again fiercely nationalist in rhetoric:

> The Irish nation has regained its soul in the short period of time that has elapsed since the Derry killings ... Not even the War of Independence commanded such unity. If it holds, we will win, and win decisively ... Ireland is in the road to victory. Provided unity is maintained and the final objective always kept in sight, we cannot lose.[142]

In the same month an editorial attacked Fianna Fáil's inaction in pushing to end the Stormont regime and the IRA was implicitly praised as having done the most towards this aim.[143]

In the following years *The Irish Post* did not lose its nationalist stance; indeed, it continued in its policy of advertising and reporting all political activity in London to do with Northern Ireland and producing frequent comment on the situation. However, it was increasingly anti-IRA and it took on the role of negotiating a path for moderate nationalism in the light of IRA attacks in Britain, and Fr Gilmore admired it for carrying this out successfully.[144] The paper continually reassured its Irish readers that they 'should not be burdened with a sense of association because of their nationality', and David, when interviewed for this project, reluctantly praised the paper because it 'did stand up for the Irish and made a lot of comments that the rest of us were able to use in our places of work'.[145] Nevertheless, the paper's editors realized the difficulty of their task in maintaining a voice sympathetic to the aims of the IRA – for instance, following the Guildford bombings which killed five people in late 1974: 'How can Irish people here pursue legitimate avenues of concern for the North when acts of this kind sully the entire issue? ... [These bombings will] persuade more Irish people here that disassociation from such acts requires the abandonment of the advocacy of Ireland's cause.'[146] After the Birmingham bombings the following month, the Dolan column told Irish people that they had nothing to be ashamed about and reassured them that 'our aspirations for Ireland remain no less valid'. The column also labelled the IRA actions 'evil' and 'sick', a real contrast to opinions in 1972.[147] By 1979 even MacLua had become weary of what he labelled 'this bloody and needless war' following the MP Airey Neave's assassination. The editorial following Mountbatten's killing and the Warrenpoint attack was more a resigned whimper that there needed to be an unspecified 'political solution', a different tone indeed to the confidence in the imminent realization of the nationalist dream in 1972.[148] Although the hunger strikes reinvigorated MacLua's republican spirit, when he praised the strikers as heroes, the instinctive, in hindsight naive, nationalism of the early 1970s could never be regained.[149]

The paper also gave some idea of the opinions of its readership through its letter pages and polls. In 1972, when Dolan's column was fiercely nationalist, a survey of the paper's readers found that, with 83 per cent of those surveyed reading it, it was the most popular part of the paper.[150] Some indication of the sympathy among readers for the aims of the IRA in 1972 was the result of a poll of readers for the paper's 'Man of the Year' award, which was topped by Fr Michael Connolly. Connolly, a Wolverhampton-based priest who raised money for Catholic victims in Northern Ireland, had caused controversy the previous year by making speeches that called for the Irish government 'to hand over guns which are going rusty to the freedom fighters of the north' and had described the IRA campaign as 'a holy war against pagans who have no respect for human dignity'.[151] By 1972, the letters section had become an entire page with vibrant debate often spanning a number of weeks. A specific Northern Ireland section of the page was introduced to cope with the volume of letters on the topic, which had grown to the extent that following particularly notable incidents, editorial notes appeared apologizing for only being able to print a tiny selection of those submitted.[152] Letters were usually moderately nationalist, with those from political groups often being more forceful in their convictions. There was disagreement, however, with some displaying sympathy towards what was seen as defensive violence by the nationalist community of the six counties, and others, as early as 1972, being alienated by republicans' use of violence. Over time, letters to the paper showed a definite move away from earlier sympathy for the Provisionals. This became truly pronounced at the height of the bombing campaign in England.[153] For instance, after Birmingham one contributor contended that the IRA had become 'a mad-dog operation' that had wiped out any previous 'sneaking admiration' that the Irish had for republican militants.[154] Even during the hunger strikes, when real anger was expressed and repeated calls were made to set up a political organization representing the Irish in Britain, which eventually led to the IBRG, no sympathy for the IRA's killings was evident.[155] While *The Irish Post* was more nationalist than much of its target market, giving enthusiastic support to small political organizations concerned with Northern Ireland, the evidence it provides tallies with what oral research has shown: that an initial sympathy for the PIRA vanished in the wake of its increasing use of violence, especially after attacks in Britain.

Hostility from the British state towards anything associated with Irish nationalism, and Irishness itself, has often been seen as preventing the Irish in Britain from exercising an effective political voice. The PTA and resultant police harassment has been pointed to as introducing a large element of fear into the Irish population in Britain, which stifled political activity. Introduced in the wake of the Guildford and Birmingham bombings in late 1974, it outlawed the IRA, allowed police to arrest people without warrant and hold them incognito for up to seven days without charge or even proof of reasonable suspicion of terrorist offences. At ports people could be examined for up to twenty-four hours without being officially detained.[156] Paddy Hillyard characterized the Irish in Britain as constituting a 'suspect community' due to the PTA.[157] He interviewed 115 people who were arrested under the act and claimed that this police activity alienated people from the British system and curtailed involvement in legitimate politics.[158] Hickman and Walter, in their 1997 report for the Commission for Racial Equality that urged the inclusion of an 'Irish' ethnicity option in censuses, contended that the successful operation of the PTA hinged on the suppression of political activity among Irish people through the use of fear.[159] These concerns have been expressed as truisms in some work. For instance, Dooley, without any convincing evidence, has said that the PTA, along with miscarriages of justice, led to 'widespread fear in Irish communities that anyone could be framed and convicted for the most serious crimes'.[160] Again with far from sufficient evidence, Michael

Herbert, in a history of the Irish in Manchester, wrote that once the PTA was introduced, 'many Irish people dropped out of Irish politics while Irish clubs and social centres were terrified of any event – political, social or cultural, which might be connected in any way at all with the war in Ireland'.[161]

Concerns were raised immediately by *The Irish Post* upon the PTA's introduction, with the need for the police to maintain a 'delicate balance' between countering terrorism and 'harassment of the Irish community' being expressed.[162] These worries were based on previous complaints that had emerged from within the Irish population even before the act was in place. In September 1973 the Irish Civil Rights Association had protested to the British government, the EEC and the UN that 'police harassment of Irish people living in Britain during the current wave of bomb attacks has reached serious proportions'.[163] Indeed, in February 1974, prior to the act's introduction, *The Irish Post* reported a raid by forty armed policemen on four homes in west London, all belonging to people from Derry with young families, none of whom were 'politically active in any way'.[164] As the 1970s progressed *The Irish Post* frequently reported police harassment under the PTA and carried stories of the groups protesting about it.[165] The paper was not alone in its concerns. The Connolly Association argued that the PTA 'turned the Irish in Britain into second class citizens', and protested by lobbying parliament.[166] The Troops Out Movement magazine carried a page in the summer 1976 edition of its magazine headed 'POLICE GAG THE IRISH COMMUNITY', which claimed that the PTA was used to 'intimidate and deter people from daring to hold political opinions about Ireland'.[167] Irish groups in the 1980s protested about the PTA to a great extent. A central aim of the IBRG was the repeal of the act, which it saw as a 'racist weapon which is used unjustifiably and indiscriminately against the Irish in Britain to stifle our political development'.[168] The report from the first London Irish Women's Conference in 1984 asserted that 'The most oppressive thing affecting Irish people in Britain is the PTA which is used to intimidate and harass the Irish community ... The PTA makes Irish people afraid to become involved in any political work around Ireland and most of us live in fear that we are going to be arrested.'[169] Even the normally quiescent Federation of Irish Societies in 1982 spoke up over the PTA: 'The Act has stifled healthy political comment by the Irish community in Britain and has inhibited a vital and valuable contribution being made in discussion pertaining to Northern

Ireland and Irish affairs in general. Innocent people have been arrested, frightened, stressed and stigmatised by the application of the PTA.'[170]

There can be little doubt that the PTA did cause some Irish people in Britain hardship. By 1982, 5,501 had been officially detained, yet only ninety-six charged under the act, many of whom were charged with refusing to cooperate at ports as opposed to any involvement with terrorism.[171] Tens of thousands more had been taken in and questioned for less than an hour, figures that did not feature in Home Office statistics.[172] The vast majority of these were Irish.[173] Moreover, there are several horror stories of detention with little or no grounds for suspicion, such as one of Hillyard's interviewees who was detained with her husband for a week because they had given a lift to an Irishman who had been charged with but acquitted of firearms offences.[174] Early-morning armed raids, sleep deprivation, false accusations, threats of jail terms and lack of sanitation have all been complaints among those held.[175]

While none of the interviewees for this work reported being taken in under the PTA, a remarkably high number of stories about police attention were told for such a small sample, even among those not involved in nationalist politics at any time during the Troubles. Robert, who was never involved in politics and was generally very positive about life in London and the English people, recalled being pulled over by the police in the early 1990s without explanation:

> They laid me on the bank and the rifle in the back of my head while they searched the van ... and I said to him, 'You're hurting me with that rifle' and he pressed it bloody more. And he kicked my two feet at the back and he said 'Right now Paddy, take your van and drive it.' And that's my only ever encounter with the police.[176]

Peter and David both remembered (on entirely separate occasions) being unnerved when arriving at ports and finding that police already knew their names when they stopped their cars to be searched, suggesting that the police had information on them and that their registration numbers were on a police database. Peter, after being sarcastic with the officer, was issued with an unfulfilled threat that 'We'll be in your house before you get home.'[177] Fr McCabe said that it was common knowledge that the London Irish Centre was under constant surveillance. This was only confirmed when one night, two days after a known IRA man had pulled up in his car outside the centre but been turned away, he was woken by several armed police officers who pulled apart his bedroom and took away, among other things, his breviary and diary.[178] After starting to teach Irish history in Irish centres, Declan was interviewed by Special Branch.[179] Fr Terence never had any trouble himself with the police but he recalled an episode when he was due to officiate at a wedding in Mayo and the groom, a Derry man living in London who, as far as Fr Terence knew, was never involved in any politics, was held for three days at Holyhead and never told why.[180] By the 1980s such attention also found itself directed at second-generation Irish interviewees. Enda noted the camera surveillance of several of the events he attended during the campaign to free the Birmingham Six.[181] Astoundingly, a party that Patrick had held for visiting Irish cousins was deemed suspicious enough for a neighbour to report him and for the police to follow up:

> We had a party ... and there was loads of Irish music and there were loads of Irish accents. Six months later ... I got a phone call, they said to me, 'Police ... we'd like to speak to you ... we'd like to come and visit you at home' ... it was the anti-terrorist squad. Now I was shitting myself because *The Irish Post* in them days was full of stories about Irish who could be held for seven days ... It wasn't going to do my career any good coming back to the bank saying, 'I've been away for seven days, but I'm innocent!' ... I rushed back to my flat and I removed all signs of Irishness that they could possibly see in the flat, bought the *Daily Telegraph* and left it there on the table and tried to make the flat look as anglicised as possible, removed all my Irish tapes and everything ... They came and what they said to me was, 'Six months ago after [an IRA attack] we asked for people to phone us anonymously about people who they thought might be terrorists and your name came up.' And of course the six months came back to the time I had the party! They said, 'We checked you out at the time ... but we still have some loose ends to tie up.' They questioned me about what my sympathies were ... My response to all their questions was, 'I'm very happy to answer your questions about what I've done and where I've been ... but thought police is one stage too far.' They asked me things like, 'Do you have any Irish connections?' I said, 'I was born in Hampstead.'[182]

Among those involved in politics to do with Northern Ireland during the Troubles, Ultan was interviewed by police and had other encounters with them, which he did not wish to elaborate on.[183] Diarmuid and Christopher, involved in the Troops Out Movement and Connolly Association respectively, told of infiltrators in their perfectly legal groups and police pressure on publicans not to allow meetings to take place.[184] Generally, however, and perhaps surprisingly, those involved in politics through the 1970s either did not have much to complain about or were reluctant to divulge it in interview. Diarmuid, Christopher and Timothy all actually praised the British system for its fairness in allowing them to protest freely and without undue harassment.[185]

It is clear that the police had powers that gave them the ability to target Irish people for very little reason and that this could lead to frightening ordeals. There is some evidence that police pressure and the PTA did deter people from voicing political concerns about Northern Ireland. One interviewee for Hickman and Walter's report, a young Northern Irish man living in London, claimed that he did not attend meetings because he was 'scared of being lifted'.[186] Other interviewees for that report mentioned being aware of police surveillance and not wanting 'attention', but not specifically avoiding political activity because of it. Among interviewees for this project, none said that police powers were what prevented them from engaging in political activity. Three interviewees who were politically active expressed opinions that the PTA was a major deterrent for people who might want to involve themselves in politics. Fr Gilmore said that police attention 'sought to prevent Irish people from expressing those opinions, which were of a political nature, peacefully'. He recounted an episode from the 1980s where a man gave him fifty pounds in private towards the Birmingham Six campaign but would not do anything more active, saying, 'I'm afraid, I have a family, I have a mortgage, I have a job.'[187] Christopher and Ultan similarly thought that people were intimidated, with the latter saying: 'It certainly did [discourage people]. It was an act of real intimidation to give huge powers to the police. You know at that time you'd be frightened to ask a policeman the time with an Irish accent, they were very hostile to Irish people, they used to arrest them for little or nothing.'[188] Christopher, who once became 'paranoid' that he was being watched by police, claimed that 'harassment everywhere' made some Irish people 'so nervous that they wouldn't even buy a raffle ticket; they were frightened that if they put their name down on a raffle ticket they could be done for something'.[189] These three interviewees were involved in campaigns against the PTA. Thus, not only would they be more aware of all the horror stories of people taken in under the act than the non-politically active person, but they had a definite view on the moral wrongs of the act and thus would be inclined to argue for a very detrimental effect on Irish politics.

Given the apparent academic consensus, it is perhaps surprising to note that even among the politically active interviewees, a majority did not subscribe to the idea that the PTA had a major effect on political involvement. Diarmuid was forceful in his views: 'People hype this up a little bit too much that the Irish were running around scared. Try being a black kid growing up in Brixton. Come on, get over it ... I won't stand for any bollocks, people telling me how oppressed they were because they were Irish.'[190] Likewise, the London-born Enda, who sang politically loaded songs and played gigs for the Birmingham Six campaign and some radical left-wing Irish groups in the 1980s, dismissed the police attention as low level and could not see how it would deter people.[191] Peter and Timothy, who were active in nationalist groups at one time, both cited other reasons for their later lack of political activity and said police attention was not a motivation for not carrying on. While this may be partly because of a wish not to admit to being intimidated by state powers, the former had given up actively attending political meetings before the Troubles broke out, due to the difficulty of supporting a young family, and the latter's political protest faded away when violent republicanism eclipsed the communist variety of the Official Republican Movement.[192]

Other than Patrick's experience, Ciara was the only interviewee to express a personal fear of police powers, saying that she often worried after her brother was taken in and questioned simply for his being near the scene of an IRA bomb and speaking with an Irish accent.[193] It is quite possible that others did experience fear, particularly Robert with his personal experience of heavy-handed police behaviour, but either were reluctant to express it or the feeling had faded with time. However, the majority of interviewees had no worries about police attention. A number of interviewees who had little to do with politics or the organization of community activities were unaware of the PTA's powers or had no comments to make. Outside the opinions of the politically involved, those who did talk about police powers tended to focus on delays at ports when going to Ireland and were along the lines of the following:

Stephen: I just found it a pain in the arse. I felt resentful, but that was it.[194]

Danny: Irish people generally didn't like it but they accepted it because they thought it had to be done I suppose.[195]

Brigid: People did used to get wound up by that, a lot of arguments would have happened because of the way they treated the luggage.[196]

Even Declan, who experienced more focused police attention than simply inspections at ports, said that he had fully expected to be interviewed when teaching Irish history to dozens of people, considering the situation with IRA attacks.[197] Likewise, when *The Irish Post* was printing stories and letters about political groups campaigning for the repeal of the PTA in the 1980s, a north London Irishman felt the need to dissent:

I reject Pat Reynold's [an IBRG leader] claim that the 'primary purpose' is to intimidate the Irish. I have never been subjected to such pressure and I'd lay good money that the vast majority of Irish people over here haven't either ... Britain's Prevention of Terrorism Act and the Republic's Offences Against the State Act are – sadly – necessary pieces of counter-terrorism legislation.[198]

The evidence presented here supports the notion that involvement in Irish politics, cultural activities or even, in Patrick's case, simply playing Irish music and having Irish visitors could attract police attention. However, while it is possible that some people were dissuaded from airing a political voice, this has been overplayed. Among the interviewees it was only those who actually did have their 'heads above the parapet' who expressed opinions that it prevented others from following suit and, even among the politically minded, these were in the minority. Furthermore, those involved in political activity generally agreed that police attention was lenient enough to allow protest. As Enda pointed out, the very existence and prominence of groups that formed in the early 1980s and loudly protested about being oppressed proved, in fact, that 'it wasn't that difficult to raise your head above the parapet here really'.[199]

A well-supported consensus has emerged among those who have written about the Irish in Britain, that while a low-level hostility towards them from the British public continued in the post-war era, it was largely overshadowed by concern over the influx of non-white immigrants.[200] However, the submerged hostility is usually seen to have grown into a 'backlash' against the Irish from both the British media and ordinary British people during the Troubles. Liz Curtis and others have written books and studies highlighting what they see as racism, or at least extreme hostility, towards the Irish in the British media.[201] Based on the evidence from interviews with Irish people in London and Birmingham, Hickman and Walter described the 'British reaction' to IRA bombings, particularly the Birmingham bombings of late 1974, as 'an outpouring of hatred against Irish people as a whole, which ranged from physical attack to shunning'. Furthermore, they argued that the 'the Irish response was the adoption of a low profile to avoid recognition'.[202] They saw this as part of a wider anti-Irish hostility that permeated British society. As is the case with the PTA, this 'backlash' has often been portrayed as a truism. Delaney, for instance, whose book terminates at 1969, does not elaborate on his statement that the post-war acceptance of Irish people 'was fragile and subject to rapid renegotiation, as became painfully obvious in the early 1970s when IRA bombings ... reinvigorated long-standing enmities and prejudices'.[203] Outside the academic world this is even more evident. In its obituary for Breandán MacLua in 2009, *The Irish Times* lauded *The Irish Post* for helping the Irish in Britain through a time when they were 'a besieged community'.[204]

There can be little doubt that the Irish and Irish nationalism were portrayed very poorly in the media. It is well documented that there was biased and often distorted reporting of the situation in Northern Ireland in the British media and that the Irish generally were portrayed in cartoons and articles as, in one political cartoonist's own words, 'extremely violent, bloody-minded, always fighting, drinking enormous amounts, getting roaring drunk'.[205] On occasion such sentiments became vitriolic, as with Lord Arran's infamous comment in 1974 in the *Evening News*: 'I loathe and detest the miserable bastards. They are savage, murderous thugs. All of them. Would that a tidal wave were to sweep over that blood-stained island ... May the Irish, all of them, rot in hell.'[206] The *Daily* and *Sunday Express* in particular were seemingly obsessed with the Irish, publishing countless offensive cartoons and being at the centre of controversies when the Irish in Britain were (with no evidence whatsoever) accused of orchestrating a £200 million benefits scam to fund the IRA, and the columnist John Junor opined that he would 'rather be a pig than be Irish'.[207] Pressure was also exerted by the media on the Irish in London, and in Britain more widely, to actively disassociate themselves from IRA violence. Community representatives who had nothing to do with republican politics, such as David, who was involved in the Federation of Irish Societies, and priests at the London Irish Centre were frequently called by journalists to make statements on behalf of the Irish in Britain after an IRA attack.[208] Articles appeared in newspapers investigating the London Irish community's attitudes to the Troubles, which as well as being outrageously patronizing, seemed to begin with the general assumption that they would find extremists. In 1973 one wrote of being in an Irish pub and watching as 'a woman sits drinking with a small group, and quietly sings songs about Ireland and freedom. She seems a part of the heady Irish nostalgia, although, with women now occasionally involved in violent politics, she may be a militant.'[209] Two articles appeared in *The Times*, written by English journalists visiting Irish pubs in north-west London. One in August 1971 unsurprisingly found opposition to the policies of internment and the presence of the British Army in Northern Ireland. Such opinions were dismissed as typical Irish foolishness: 'The London Irish cherish their grievance and their mythology with all the impenetrable obstinacy of exiles.'[210] Another journalist in November 1974, after the Birmingham bombings, found himself 'astounded' in one pub, where 'you can hear republican songs on the juke box', and whose clientele supported the aims of the IRA. The journalist was pleased to report one man in the Irish Club in Eaton Square who suggested that the Irish should 'stand up and be counted' and 'register their names and addresses with their local police stations'.[211] Such reporting reflected a pitifully low level of understanding of the community that the journalists were purportedly investigating and led them to portray those singing patriotic songs and holding the widespread desire for a united Ireland as borderline terrorists holding on to an illogical 'mythology'. Such misunderstanding of Irish rebel songs led some Irish clubs to ban them, due to fear of being branded – as one Irish club was by local media – a 'hotbed of extreme Irish nationalism'.[212] In 1974 the Dolan column in *The Irish Post* complained of this pressure to prove innocence after a rush of articles following the Birmingham bombings condemned the Catholic Church for not excommunicating IRA members.[213] During the 1981 hunger strikes, the *Sunday Express* criticized entertainers from the Republic of Ireland currently 'making a fortune' in Britain: 'Might they not then at this moment of mounting crisis in Ulster show their loyalty to the hand that feeds them by making clear not in private but in public their own detestation of the IRA? Isn't their present silence deafening?'[214] The

Northern Irish-born political cartoonist Mahood parodied this media attitude with a series of cartoons in *Punch*, including one with an epitaph on Michael McMurphy's headstone: 'I am not now, and never have been, a member of the IRA, or the UDA, or any of that ilk.' Two undertakers look on saying, 'I still say they all protest too much.'[215] The media reaction in the early 1980s was fierce when some groups and individuals began to campaign more heavily about Irish issues. After Ken Livingstone invited Sinn Féin leaders to meet him in 1982 he described the media reaction as 'a warning to all others in Britain who dare put their heads above the parapet'.[216]

The great majority of interviewees were aware of the negative reporting of anything to do with nationalism in the media, something that has also been highlighted in previous studies: 'unbalanced', 'disgraceful', 'huge ignorance' and 'smear' were all used to describe British media coverage of the Troubles.[217] Peter was almost amused as he recalled: 'The media ... I think they thought we were all a kind of half loony or animals or whatnot.'[218] While none cited it as a reason for not being involved in nationalist politics, their awareness of how one could be characterized as a terrorist suggests that it may have been a consideration for some. Certainly, Michael O'Halloran, MP, went to great lengths to avoid being associated with nationalism, even to the extent of supporting the council of his constituency in its removal of funding for the Irish Centre, Camden, in 1979–80 because it allowed political meetings (of legal organizations) to take place.[219] Some interviewees spoke of a reluctance to talk about Northern Ireland with English people due to their ignorance of the situation, which they put down to the media. Some of the male interviewees also spoke of *The Irish Post* as providing arguments which they could use to counter those presented to them by the British media.[220]

A 'backlash' from British people was felt sporadically by some interviewees. Generally such incidents happened to those who were in the public eye and thus easy targets for the more extreme elements of British society. All three first-generation priests remembered receiving hate mail, abusive phone calls or being personally verbally attacked after bombings in Britain. Fr McCabe said that 'we were sort of a target, naturally the *Irish* Centre ... So we got lots of abusive phone calls and bomb warnings.'[221] Fr Terence, who was not based at the Irish Centre, had similar experiences: 'When I came to England in 1973 there was a letter bomb campaign and I used to get hate mail saying, "Go back to Ireland, don't be over here." '[222] The politically active found their demonstrations targeted by the National Front, and Christopher was particularly wary of them: 'There was the National Front ... We got this metal grille [*points to the window of the Connolly Association book shop*] because we were afraid the window would be put in, and this box here [*points to the letterbox*], I made that box in case somebody threw in a letter bomb.'[223] Evelyn, whose husband was a medical practitioner with his own practice, recounted the following intimidating incidents:

> When the bombings started and the Troubles started we got a letter from the National Front. My husband was called an 'IRA bastard' and [the letter said] that he'd better watch out for his wife and children. And then we had a bomb scare and I was coming in with two of my children from school or something and [my husband] said, 'quick, get out, there's a bomb scare' ... and we waited for the bomb squad to arrive ... And then we had a few telephone calls. They weren't as scary as the bomb scare and the letter.[224]

Among interviewees, Evelyn's experience was the only one of such magnitude that was aimed at a personal level rather than at an institution such as the Irish Centre or political groups. In the wake of the Birmingham and Guildford attacks there was a small physical backlash in London in the form of two petrol bombs being thrown into an Irish-owned pub in Ealing and a tobacconist's in Streatham, and a window at the Irish Embassy being smashed.[225] The entry in the Carlow Association minute book for December 1974 discussing a surplus after their annual dinner dance showed that this fear was a reality for some:

> £5 of this sum to be kept aside to buy a drink for members of the committee who put a lot of hard work into making the dance a success in spite of the bombings in Birmingham and London [sic]. There were quite a few absentees on this account and it was decided that we return ticket money to those people who cancelled at the last minute through fear.[226]

The Council of Irish Counties Association's proposal to contribute to the Mayor of Birmingham's relief fund for victims was then discussed.

The occasional letter was published in *The Irish Post* from English people showing some hostility. Two came during the 1981 hunger strikes, one saying that the writer's distant Irish ancestry was now 'something to be regarded with shame'.[227] Another from an Oxfordshire English Catholic said that 'I was stupid enough to believe that only a tiny minority of Irish supported terrorism', but that, due to their sympathy with the hunger strikers, 'I feel I can never trust any Irish member of our congregation again.'[228] A small number of interviewees mentioned insults about the IRA thrown at them after attacks in isolated incidents. For instance, after the birth of her child in 1974, Ciara's medical concerns were dismissed by a consultant as follows: 'I haven't met an Irish person yet [who] if they're not throwing bombs they're worrying themselves to death.'[229] Michael, a second-generation interviewee, mentioned his mother buying *The Irish Post* after one attack and being met with the disapproving comment from a woman behind her: 'Wouldn't you think they'd be ashamed coming in here asking for an Irish newspaper today.'[230] Kathleen Morrissey, who lived in Cricklewood, experienced similar low-level hostility as a reaction to republican attacks:

> During the Troubles, perhaps fifteen or twenty years ago, I found even here that our neighbours' attitude towards us changed. We were out in the garden and they said 'You should go back to where you came from' ... At that stage, we'd lived here for thirty-two years, in this same house. It was very hurtful – they'd been our neighbours for about five or six years. I was really upset over that. I found that when people here were talking about the Troubles, it was best to keep my head down and my mouth shut – it was better to say nothing at all. I didn't find it so much in the workplace, because people there knew me well. But outside, I felt that English people were very much against the Irish.[231]

In spite of such incidents, the great majority of interviewees dismissed the notion of a generally hostile British reaction outside an extreme fringe or speculated that maybe it happened elsewhere but not in their localities or lines of work. The following are responses to the question, 'Did you ever experience any backlash or hostility from English people following IRA attacks in Britain?'

Stephen: Very little, very little ... I can't recall ... I can't really think of anything ...

Peter: There wouldn't be that in London now, you see London is very strong with an Irish community and that. But I would say up the country now, if you were up the country ... there would be I'd say.

Brenda: I mean I probably was aware of it on television and stuff, but on a personal nature I can't say I ever felt

	like that, but I was aware that people would defi-nitely think like that.
Robert:	I never had it. I think the lads in Birmingham had it for a short time ... I heard that one or two fellas went out and got into trouble.
Fr Terence:	Not particularly, but you see I was in a very strong Irish community. I don't know what it would have been like if I had been in Kensington, say, where there are very few Irish people.
Brigid:	Only the odd comment, but I never found any personally. Actually in those days I would bring up politics at work more than they ever did. I always felt the attitude was, 'If you want Northern Ireland back, have it, we don't want it.'

Remarkably, even the politically involved, who one might think would have been sensitive to any comments about attacks, struggled to think of any personal experiences:

Timothy:	Not as much as I expected ... Very little. Possibly the work [construction] didn't bring me in touch, you'd probably have to be in an office to know.
Christopher:	There was reaction but I didn't experience it person-ally, and my work [sheet metal work] was always mostly with English people, I worked with very few Irish people ...[232]

Some interviewees were very against the idea that any backlash existed. Eoin said that his own experiences, and in particular his successes in local elections as a Labour Party councillor in a largely Conservative area outside London in the 1970s, 'contradicts the idea that there was a backlash'.[233] David railed against those who speculated about a backlash at the time because the constant talk of a reaction may have actually led to one.[234]

A much stronger theme in the interviews was, in fact, the tolerance shown by the English people towards the Irish through the Troubles, something that was sometimes unfavourably compared to the corresponding lack of such a trait in Ireland. Declan remembered:

Looking at it dispassionately you would have to say that England was fairly tolerant. I mean some shocking things were done [by the IRA]. I remember on the day that the Birmingham bombing went off an Irish friend of mine, who was a trade unionist, was in the east end of London ... He had to address a meeting of 300 shop stewards the following day in his broad Dublin accent and he said he was amazed that nobody ever mentioned what had happened the night before. I'm amazed by that – if that had happened in Ireland after the shooting of thirteen people in Derry ...[235]

Even Ultan, after railing against the British state and media and saying that general hostility made the 1970s 'an horrific time for Irish people living in this country', said that he found only 'a little' anti-Irish feeling outside the 'rougher pubs' and eventually praised the majority of the English: 'By and large I found English people to be very tolerant but you would always get a little element of anti-Irishism.'[236] Those interviewees who were the subject of attacks were also quick to stress that the perpetrators of such attacks represented a tiny minority of the English people that they came across. In spite of the abusive calls and bomb threats at the Irish Centre, Fr McCabe said:

I found English people *incredibly* tolerant in that period. Because what would happen here [in Ireland] if a group from England were over here bombing in Dublin? There'd be hell to pay. At that time, I think, except for a few, you encountered nothing only understanding and people saying, 'well we know these things happen, you can't tar everybody with the same brush.'[237]

Likewise, Evelyn stressed that after the incidents described, 'our English friends were appalled that anybody could sink as low as the IRA because, in a sense, it was as threatening as the IRA sending a letter'.[238] Those who mentioned other insults generally dismissed such attacks as coming from 'yobs' and did not think that such attitudes were pervasive.[239]

It is possible that the low level of backlash that was experienced by the interviewees for this project is due to its London focus. As a number of interviewees said, the Irish in London had become well established and many were intermarried with or friends of the native population. The size of the Irish population of London did give the Irish there particularly deep roots. It is also possible that many interviewees failed to experience any hostility because of the high levels of social interaction within the ethnic community, which provided a protective buffer against any possible contact with those who may have insulted or harmed them. Nevertheless, as has been seen, even those intervie-wees in mainly English workplaces in London did not find themselves targets of abuse because of the IRA. Hickman and Walter's interviews with people in Birmingham following the attacks there do give the impression that there was a higher level of general hostility in the Midlands. There is indisputable evidence of such a backlash in 1974, with firebombings of local families reported in the press, three Irishmen being severely beaten in a pub and videos of English workers walking out of the Longbridge car factory after fights had broken out between English and Irish workers, with banners reading: 'Ban the IRA. Go Home Paddy.'[240] There were also letters in *The Irish Post* from the Irish in the Midlands relating to this, although one was at pains to point out that 'the mass of the British people acted reasonably and intelligently'.[241] It is notable that the one interviewee for this project, who felt that he was subjected to a 'vicious backlash' that included not being served in shops and seeing people demoted at work, was Oliver, who lived outside London.[242] It is also noted that there is a possibility that interviewees played down any hostility that they felt, due to the time elapsed since it happened.

Nevertheless, the fact that any sort of backlash was felt by only a very few interviewees and that the tolerance of the general British public was so highly praised does suggest that the existence of an explosion of anti-Irish sentiment has been overplayed by previous commentators. One suspects that they have placed too much emphasis on incidents that were admittedly unpleasant and frightening but were ultimately quite rare and carried out by a tiny minority of British people. Part of the reason that the 'widespread backlash theory' has gained such currency is perhaps because of the expectation of one that existed at the time, particularly after the worst attacks in Britain that took place in 1974. Various politicians, such as Jill Knight, MP, feared such a widespread and violent public reaction to the Birmingham bombings that they argued that the death penalty should be used against the apprehended 'bombers' to hold back public anger.[243] Harold Wilson, the Prime Minister, made a speech imploring the British public not to seek reprisals against the 'Irish community in this country' and Roy Jenkins, Home Secretary, warned against 'communal hatred' as a reaction to the bombs.[244] Likewise, Irish media frequently seemed to assume that there must have been a widespread reaction against their compatriots in England. Yet the Irish in Britain were often keen to play down the existence of a backlash. As early as 1972 *The Irish Post* complained about the ignorance of the Irish media in holding views that were 'twenty years out of date' with regards to the British public's attitude towards the Irish, pointing to two recent programmes that 'seemingly expected to have found the Irish in Britain already the victims of a massive British backlash'.[245] David recounted that after an attack in the 1980s he told RTÉ in an interview that the Irish in Britain were not suffering from a hostile reaction from British people, but the Irish broadcaster simply did not believe him and did not use the interview.[246]

As well as specific reactions against the IRA, it has been frequently asserted that the Irish in Britain were subject to racism. It has been claimed that such racism was rooted deep within British society and that the attention of the Troubles served to bring this to the fore.[247] Much political noise was made about anti-Irish racism by new, generally left-wing and nationalist-inclined, Irish groups that were being funded by the Livingstone-led Greater London Council in the 1980s. For instance, one published speaker at the London Irish Women's Conference in 1984 spoke of her surprise at finding that the English 'hated us' when she emigrated, and others spoke of the colonialism in the North of Ireland as leading to 'blatant racism' against the Irish in Britain.[248] It is noted that such sources are questionable due to their highly political slant. A flavour of the London Irish Women's Conference can be gleaned from the fact that their publications consistently used inverted commas when printing the word 'police' and spuriously blamed racism by Irish people in Ireland on the malign influence of the British media's 'racist propaganda'.[249]

It is beyond doubt that Irish people in Britain were subject to stereotypes, mocking and jokes. Some interviewees claimed that they had felt stereotyped by English people, usually with regard to stupidity and drunkenness. Danny's comment was fairly typical: 'Sometimes you used to get the stage Paddy. I found it a wee bit sometimes with certain English people they thought you being Irish that you didn't have the same intelligence ... But most of them [the English] treated you very equally ... I thought they were very fair'.[250] Diarmuid found the use of 'Paddy' and 'Mick' as terms of abuse prevalent on building sites in the 1970s, a theme that was quite common among male construction workers, particularly in memoirs of 'navvies' from the 1950s and 1960s:

> I remember one day ... this English ganger comes over and says, 'Oi, Paddy, come over here and shift some rocks,' and everybody would look round and he'd say, 'Yeah, you Paddy,' and he'd point to one of us, he didn't point to me so I turned round and started digging. I heard him shout again, 'Oi, Paddy, I'm fucking talking to you.' ... 'Oi Paddy, you fucking cloth-eared Mick.'

One fella walked across towards the ganger and he said to him, 'I think you must be making a mistake now, me name's not Paddy, me name's Séamus.' This carried on, until the Irish fella whacked him over the head with a shovel 'to help your memory a little bit.'[251]

Every interviewee had heard Irish jokes, which were going through a period of great popularity in the 1970s. The Irish were second only to Pakistanis as the butt of jokes on 'The Comedians' in 1971 and 'Irish joke' books were selling in their hundreds of thousands by the end of the decade.[252] Indeed, when asked about stereotypes, interviewees often brought up such jokes as their point of reference, such as Fr Terence:

Fr Terence: There were people that looked down on the Irish, with the Irish jokes in particular, that Irish people were thick.

SS: Do you think that the image portrayed by these jokes was a perception that English people actually held?

Fr Terence: With some people yeah; the idea that the pig-in-the-parlour was still part of the Irish life.[253]

Some found these jokes highly insulting. *The Irish Post* campaigned against such jokes, as did the IBRG and other such groups in the 1980s. Although some of the interviewees recognized that others found them offensive, none had very strong feelings personally about such jokes and several dismissed them as 'banter' that the Irish engaged in themselves. Ciara said that 'Because the Irish make jokes themselves it didn't annoy me, it really didn't.' Likewise, Robert gave the following reply when asked about whether he had heard Irish jokes:

Oh yeah, but you'd get that anywhere, that happens about every-thing in life ... It's easy for me to take it because I'm from Kerry and with the Kerryman jokes I'm well used to it. That never bothered me. I used to get one or two of the lads saying, 'Who the fuck does he think he is,' but I used to say to them not to worry about things like that.[254]

That there was a high level of acceptance of such jokes and stereotypes was shown by interviewees, and this was evident in the letter pages of *The Irish Post* when a letter complaining about Irish jokes was often followed by one dismissing them as a bit of fun.[255] Most of those who dismissed the idea of a backlash against the Irish did so in spite of having personal experience of being stereotyped and joked about as unintelligent, violent or drunk. For instance, despite Victoria saying that she had sometimes felt stereotyped and had her accent mocked, she also said: 'I can honestly say not once did I ever come up against anti-Irishness or bad feeling ... or that it was there but being concealed. In fact some were very fond of the Irish.'[256] Louise Ryan has suggested that this phenomenon shows that anti-Irish racism is so endemic within British society that the Irish cannot even recognize it when it is staring them in the face.[257] It is certainly true that some race jokes serve to reinforce the superiority of the teller over the subject and that they reflected actual stereotypes held. Yet one might suggest that perhaps academics are too hasty in ascribing their own sensitivities to a joke or comment made that neither party found particularly offensive. The existence of such racial jokes and stereotypes should not be seen to negate the general experience of the interviewees that found very little in the way of serious backlash to the Troubles and found the English generally deserving of praise in their acceptance of the Irish.

One of the themes that emerged from the interviews was that such stereotyping and anti-Irishness was more prevalent in the 1950s and the early 1960s than anything that was experienced during the Troubles era. Every interviewee who emigrated in the earlier period mentioned 'No Irish. No Coloureds. No Dogs.' signs in the windows of boarding houses and routinely told of difficulties in finding accommodation when their nationality was discovered. Some interviewees dismissed these signs simply as people protecting their property from under-standably dirty and sometimes rough Irish builders rather than racism.[258] However, even Evelyn found such difficulties in London, in spite of being there to study as a classical music scholar:

> When I came over and I wanted to get a flat, well it was bedsits in those days, I would ring the doorbell and they would have up 'No Irish. No Coloured.', then sometimes it was children or dogs, but it was always 'No Irish or Coloured need apply.' I would say that I was from the North of Ireland, but as far as they were concerned I wasn't British, I was Irish ... I got a place in a Catholic hostel.

Evelyn eventually found a place with a Rhodesian and an Australian after she 'let them do the talking'.[259] John B. Keane was lucky when his friend convinced a landlady that neither of them was Irish: ' "He's not a Paddy," Murphy said. "He's a Jock the same as myself." '[260] John Healy gave an insight into the attitudes of the 1940s and 1950s. He was born in Kentish Town, north-west London, in 1943 to two Irish parents and he writes of his upbringing in depressing tones: 'Our neighbours on both sides were Londoners and, being immigrants, we were treated as lepers.' He also speaks of being beaten up as a child while being called 'You fucking Irish cunt' and always feeling alien among his young peers.[261] Likewise, John Lydon wrote of his childhood in the late 1950s and early 1960s in a run-down part of Finsbury Park, north London:

> When I was very young and going to school, I remember bricks thrown at me by English parents. To get to the Catholic school you had to go through a predominantly Protestant area. That was most unpleasant. It would always be done on a quick run. 'Those dirty Irish bastards!' That kind of shit. Now they transfer it onto the blacks or whomever ... We were the Irish scum.[262]

Such open and blatant racial discrimination was not a feature in the interviews of emigrants who arrived in London later than the early 1960s. Some of these, such John and Brigid, said that racism must have been worse in the 1950s when they compared what they had heard from family and friends to their own experiences.[263] It seems that the anti-Irishness of the 1970s, in London at least, was much less wide-spread than that of the 1950s. While the Irish were still seen as 'other', being stereotyped, joked about and vilified in some of the right-wing media, by the 1970s the Irish were more acceptable than previously and were making progress on their way to becoming 'white'.

Hickman and Walter asserted that one of the effects of police activity and British hostility was to push people away from Irish community activity.[264] While a few of their interviewees mentioned it, none of those for this project did. The only suggestion of this was with regard to the Irish middle class. David was of the opinion that 'it would have been a more joined up community without the Troubles', due to the middle class steering clear of the wider Irish community for fear of association with nationalism.[265] More evidence seems to support the alternative conclusion, that the cumulative effects of all these factors hastened the development of a community identity in the 1970s. The fact that several interviewees mentioned their own discomfort around English people after events during the Troubles also suggests that this may have caused the community to become slightly more introverted. A letter to *The Irish Post* from a west London Irishwoman, two weeks after the Birmingham bombings, shows that Irish institutions were certainly looked to as a source of comfort during these times: 'I have never been so appreciative of *The Irish Post* as I was last week. It was something to cling onto ... The Leading Article message that: "We are not involved in these bombings and we should not allow ourselves to be frightened into acting as if we were," must have struck a chord in many frightened Irish people.'[266] When reflecting on 1974, *The Irish Post*'s editorial also suggested that 'There are already some indications that the bombings and their aftermath may result in a more conscious and unified Irish community.'[267] Such guilt by association continued throughout the Troubles and did have a negative impact on individual and community identity. Even as late as 1987, when the Irish had endured nearly two decades of watching the violence in Northern Ireland and on the streets of Britain, MacLua still felt the need to remind the readers of *The Irish Post* that the guilt was not theirs:

> Condemnation of what occurred at Enniskillen is without dissent. But I do object to those who would put upon all of us a sense of collective guilt.
> The Irish are a sentimental people. Hence we had, for example, in the days after the bombing, some people telephoning the popular London radio station LBC declaring that they were 'ashamed to be Irish'...
> The Enniskillen atrocity was the work of the IRA, whose political wing, Sinn Fein, received less than 2 per cent of the vote in the Republic earlier this year...[268]

The constant association of Irishness with violence was something that caused introverted behaviour among some of the Irish and, perhaps, the community as a whole. Just as some interviewees, such as Brenda and Fr Terence, admitted feeling nervous about speaking in their own accents on public transport, the community as a whole was nervous of expressing itself on a large scale in view of the wider public. The voluntary cancellation of a large St Patrick's Day parade through central London for thirty years from 1972, something mirrored in Birmingham, was reflective of a whole community keen to keep itself to itself.[269] The London Irish Festival, held in Roundwood Park from 1977 in the highly Irish Borough of Brent, became the greatest display of Irishness in the capital for many years. In spite of attracting several tens of thousands of people, as one documentary pointed out, it was 'virtually unknown outside the Irish community'.[270] It was aimed solely at Irish people and their children and contrasts greatly with the modern-day St Patrick's parades through central London that invite all and sundry to 'be Irish for a day'.[271] The impact of the Troubles certainly had a negative effect on Irish identity and held up what has been a remarkable progress from a vilified and derided people in the first six decades of the twentieth century to the height of 'cool' in the twenty-first.[272] A major part of this progress was the reaching of maturity of the second-generation Irish who had often been brought up to take pride in Irishness through cultural activities, such as Brendan Mulkere's music lessons: 'In the early '70s I started teaching Irish music because of the impact of the Troubles ... [which had] a very negative impact on the notion of Irish identity ... [Second-generation children] needed something that they could latch on to that was cheerful, positive, that would contribute to a more positive image of who they were themselves'.[273] Just 'who they were' for the second-generation was never any easy question; it forms the topic of Chapter Three.

CONCLUSION

During the first decade of the Troubles the Irish in London generally kept their heads down when it came to politics. However, this was not primarily due to a hostile British state scaring a community of budding politicians into submission. The evidence provided in this chapter suggests that the Irish in London, in spite of being generally nationalist in sympathy and at times motivated enough by this to take to the streets, did not constitute a community whose general background, social structure and demographics made them likely candidates for either mainstream or nationalist political involvement. While the shock of internment and Bloody Sunday briefly brought the Irish on to the streets of the capital, more in anger than political conviction, the horrors of the IRA campaign, particularly when it struck Britain, caused a re-evaluation of traditional nationalism and made them far more cautious about expressing sympathy for any nationalist cause. Nevertheless, there continued to be widespread passive concern with the situation in Northern Ireland that could at least influence voting patterns. Police activity and the PTA undoubtedly dissuaded some Irish people from being involved in nationalist politics. Media attention, coupled with jokes and stereotypes from the British population in London, also caused some heads to be lowered beneath the proverbial parapet. However, these factors, which have been seen by many as central to stifling the Irish political voice, seem to be relatively insignificant when analysing a community that in all likelihood would never have involved itself in politics to any great extent anyway.

CHAPTER THREE

'How can you be Irish with an accent like that?' The Second-Generation in London

In an interview with *The Irish Times* in October 2010, the Republic of Ireland footballer Liam Lawrence spoke of the strength of patriotism he had witnessed among the second- and third-generation Irish players while representing the country for which he qualified to play through one of his grandmothers. He recalled an episode involving Gary Breen, a north-west London-born child of two Irish immigrants and regular Irish international, reacting to dressing room 'banter' about his national identity:

> I remember one of the lads [at Sunderland AFC] taking the piss out of his cockney accent. He said something about: 'How can you be Irish with an accent like that?' And he (Breen) just went totally off the lid. Breeny was going to kill the lad, he'd crossed a line that no one knew was there. I suppose I can understand that a lot better now. Because once you feel that sense of pride it means a lot.[1]

Breen's team-mate had unwittingly hit a nerve by asking a question that, no doubt, Breen will have asked himself a number of times through his life. The facts of birth in England and Irish ancestry have not been easy to reconcile for many among the second-generation. The painting that adorns the cover of this book, by second-generation Irish artist Michael Cahillane, shows a London-born boy separated from the main group of people by a railing, on the outside looking in. For the artist, this represents the uncomfortable world that the second-generation inhabit, not able to fully participate in the Irishness of the scene (listening to the All-Ireland final) but not quite removed from it either. His painting represents one of a plethora of accounts that one hears when listening to second-generation interviewees speak about their identities. This chapter focuses largely on the children of the post-war Irish immigrants who were brought up within the core of the Irish community, with a large bias towards those who lived in north-west London. It looks to analyse the extent to which they have been involved in this ethnic community during their lives. It then explores the abstract notion of identity, the factors and actions that have affected it, how it is expressed as adults and how intervie-wees remember how they have expressed and related to their iden-tities over their lives.

Eleven second-generation Irish people who were brought up in London were interviewed. Eight were born of two Irish Catholic parents, two of one Irish and one English parent, and one of an Irish Catholic father and a Northern Irish Protestant mother. This focus clearly excludes a great swathe of the second-generation who were born outside the Irish community in London or who are mixed race, and thus there is no claim that this sample can be representative of the second-generation Irish generally. Nevertheless, it is hoped that some insight can be offered in to how second-generation Irish people assess their own identities. In 1971 there were 1,303,000 people with a Republic of Ireland-born (ROI-born) parent living in Britain. The great majority, 942,000, of these had only one ROI-born parent. However, given that in 1971 the 1 per cent longitudinal survey in London reported that 46 per cent of married ROI-born women had an ROI-born husband, it is quite reasonable to assume that a majority of the second-generation in London had two Irish parents after allowing for North–South marriages. In 1971 over half of the second-generation in Britain were under the age of 17, showing the majority were born of post-war emigrants. In 1974 only 16 per cent of the second-generation in Britain lived in Greater London, although this rose as time passed and those from older communities, in Scotland and Liverpool in particular, passed on, meaning that by 1988–89 Greater London had 21 per cent and the wider south-east of England had a further 20 per cent.[2]

The memory of the Irish community in which they were brought up was strong among most interviewees and clearly played an important role in the formation of their identities. If brought up in areas of concentrated Irish settlement in London, second-generation children experienced a high level of everyday interaction with their peers and first-generation Irish people. Gerry remembered his child-hood as being distinctly Irish due to the area he lived in: 'Well, Kilburn's Kilburn. It was, for all intents and purposes, another county of Ireland. So it meant that you were living with your own.'[3] Rory's memories highlight how social interaction could take on a distinctly Irish flavour even outside organized cultural activities or religious structures: 'We used to spend Sunday afternoons when we were kids up at Old Reading because that was the highest point in Harrow. It'd be, "We think Limerick won but the radio made a funny noise." All my friends would be up there and we'd play football [soccer] ... and then run over and see what the score was.[4]

Rory's comments are strikingly similar to the imagery of Cahillane's painting, as the London-born children play soccer and occasionally run over to check on the Gaelic games to which their parents are devoted. Interestingly, outside the north-west London 'heartland' of the Irish in London, a comparatively small number of people could still create a 'Little Ireland' feel for second-generation children. Enda remembered the south London of his childhood being one inhabited by many Irish people: 'Although that [north-west London] was the heartland, at that particular time the whole of London was full of Irish people. Even in south London in Tooting; Tooting was an enormous Irish area. They used to have an Irish shop in Tooting selling all Irish music, videos, rosary beads and whatever and there were several Irish pubs.'[5] This was in spite of less than 4 per cent (545 people) of the Tooting electoral ward's population being ROI-born in 1971, far below the numbers recorded in the north-west of the city.[6]

Several academics have recognized the home as a key location of Irish culture and identification for the second-generation. This was a strong theme among interviewees and second-generation writers.[7] Anna May Mangan found her parents' house a bubble of Irishness in a London life and she reminisces in her autobiography about listening to aunts reliving stories of Irish dance halls, reading stories from Irish county newspapers to her parents, the entertaining of visiting Irish priests and gazing upon the customary pictures of the Sacred Heart and John F. Kennedy.[8] Enda similarly remembered how his father's siblings would come round and 'have a party and a sing song, a bit of Kevin Barry, a bit of Big Tom, whatever it might be. And the thing is, if you grow up with Irish songs, the history's attached to them.'[9] Catherine characterized the homes of her family as distinctly Irish places and similarly focused on music, a common theme among interviewees:

> The music we listened to, you know, my auntie used to have an [Irish] music shop ... we used to go to her house on a Sunday

and listen to the latest album she'd bought, whether it be Big Tom or Danny Doyle or whoever it was ... Our house was very busy, and my auntie's house as well, there was lots of people around ... and, mostly, everybody that came to our house was Irish.[10]

The home as a location of Irishness became particularly apparent to the London-born Irish when they had experienced the world outside of the ethnic community, something that several interviewees noted when they first went to work. Given his slight removal from the core Irish community as a result of being the son of a doctor, it is notable that the home is a particularly major subject in John Walsh's account of his upbringing. His parents' house represented a place where the English world of his south London school, which in spite of being Catholic was seemingly not attended by many second-generation Irish, and Oxford undergraduate life collided with a Celtic otherness. At school his weapon of choice was a cricket bat while at home his father bought him a hurley stick; at school he encountered English people but at home it was Irish people. This gave him a sense of not really belonging in either place:

And so I gazed on the exiled Irish as they all came drifting by our Battersea retreat, wave upon wave of them, some with English spouses, some with Irish ... some with wholly acclimatised English children, some with confusedly half-Irish offspring christened Breffni or Aoife.[11]

At home I was the small Englishman, regarding the Irish hordes with curiosity and some alarm. At school, by contrast, I was the class 'Mick'.[12]

As with their parents, for most second-generation children the structures of the Catholic Church provided ethnic spaces in which they interacted. For some interviewees this simply involved the habitual Sunday mass: 'We all went to mass, so our religion was very Irish in terms of that's what everybody did, but we didn't consciously think that we were different from anybody else.'[13] Others found the Church more central to their lives. Rory remembered his childhood social life in Harrow revolving around parish clubs, which were overwhelmingly patronized by Irish people:

We had a social club attached to the church and it was just part of your social life. You used to arrange to meet when you were going out on a Saturday night after six o'clock mass, good Catholic kids! ... They used to have family discos ... [Sometimes] we might have a change and go to another Catholic club somewhere else.[14]

Anne remembered the Church as being even more central to community life when growing up. Later, as a teenager, it provided an arena for Irish cultural and national expression through *céilí* dancing.

SS: Did the Church play a big role in your life when you were growing up?

Anne: Oh God yeah! I was thinking about this the other day. Everything revolved around the church when we were growing up! St Agnes' [Cricklewood] is such a big church anyway, and the school is just behind the church, and you were always in and out of the church when we were at primary school. It was all to do with my dad really because he used to put on shows in the school hall for the OAPs, which we were involved in. And he used to organise trips to Walsingham and Aylesford and they used to be great, it was lovely, and all the kids were together. And yes, we had to say the rosary going and coming back. Everything revolved around the church, everyone was down there every Sunday.

SS: I suppose even the *céilí* dancing was in the church hall?

Anne: Well yeah. And the thing about events then, they always used to play the Irish national anthem at the end and you all had to stand for that ... that was a big, big thing wherever you went.[15]

As well as the churches themselves, where 'the priests were almost exclusively Irish', most second-generation children, in north-west London at least, attended Catholic schools, where their teachers were Irish too: 'the nuns were all Irish or Irish descent, all the teachers were'; 'not all the teachers were Irish, but the majority of them were.'[16] Of the eleven second-generation interviewees, nine attended Catholic secondary schools. Hickman has argued that the Catholic school system in Britain has historically made a concerted effort to denationalize the children of Irish immigrants and make them good British Catholics.[17] While several interviewees noted of a lack of Irish history, there were some limited expressions of Irish identity at a number of the interviewees' schools. Most notably, on St Patrick's day,

Irishness was even encouraged. Patrick remembered an annual Ireland versus England football match being played among the boys and Gerry recalled the ubiquitous shamrock in school blazer pockets.[18] Stephen, a first-generation teacher, recalled his time at a Catholic school in west London that he worked in from the 1970s onwards:

> All sorts of things like, one thing I do remember was the kids would come in wearing St Patrick's Day badges and it was encouraged as well. And yes, there would be for example concerts or that sort of thing, kids who were involved in Irish dancing, involved in [Irish] music and whatnot, they would be brought to the fore. Yes, it [Irish identity] was expressed reasonably well.[19]

More important than outward expressions of Irishness in the narratives was the sheer number of fellow pupils from similar backgrounds. Rory remembered his Catholic schools in Harrow in the 1970s and 1980s:

> I went to a Catholic [primary] school where probably 95 per cent of the children were of Irish background and then the same again [at secondary school]. I always remember at [secondary school] when I went there, on St Patrick's Day the new deputy head asked people to put up their hands if they had an Irish background, and literally, no word of a lie, 95 per cent of the school put their hand up.[20]

For others the Irish contingent was not quite as dominant but constituted a majority in the mini-diaspora space of a Catholic school:

> I was in this kind of vacuum. I went to a Catholic primary school that was predominantly Irish and the pupils who weren't Irish were Goan-Indian, Lithuanian and Italians and very, very few English ... By the time we were at secondary school, again it was even more predominantly Irish. The catchment area of the grammar school I went to captured people from Kilburn, Cricklewood, right the way across.[21]

Such domination of schools by Irish pupils and teachers led to the schools becoming distinctly Irish ethnic spaces. John Lydon notably referred to his experiences in 'Irish Catholic schools' in north London.[22] George, an entirely anglicized third-generation interviewee brought up in Kilburn, showed that these schools were seen as such from the outside: 'I can't recall mixing with any Irish people at my [non-

Catholic] school. My Irish mates used to jump on the bus and go to Cardinal Hinsley, which was essentially all Irish.'[23]

As noted in Chapter One, with the realization of 'some degree of permanency' in London, the post-war emigrants began to take a concerted interest in giving a sense of Irish culture to their children.[24] Brendan Mulkere said that his music lessons, which became increasingly popular through the 1970s, were specifically designed to instil a sense of pride in Ireland, to make the children think, 'it's all about us and our background'.[25] *The Irish Post* expressed such sentiments strongly in its tenth anniversary issue, which featured a large picture of a second-generation girl in an Irish dancing dress:

> The single greatest achievement of the Irish who came to this country is their children. They are a great source of pride.
>
> To a far greater extent than at any other period in the history of the Irish in Britain, the children of this generation are growing with a balanced cultural duality ... there is probably more Irish dancing activity in Britain right now than in Ireland ...
>
> So here's to the kids – our children ... May they retain, even expand on, the sense of Irishness which their parents have given them ...
>
> To ... all of our children we say; the world is yours, but never forget your roots.[26]

Brendan Mulkere found that his classes became increasingly popular through the 1970s and eventually concerts played by the children were staged. Such developments were noted by *The Irish Post*, as in 1977 when a report on the Liverpool *fleadh* (festival) praised 'the great wealth of Irish traditional music talent which now exists in Britain – particularly among the children born in this country of Irish parents'.[27] In 1980, Terry Bowler's regular Irish dancing column was expressing near amazement at the expansion seen over the decade:

> The year just gone ended a decade of expansion, consolidation and development for the whole Irish dancing fraternity in Britain. With the tremendous increases in the number of teachers and schools, the proliferation of *feiseanna* [competitions] and an ever increasing number of young pupils ... I don't think Irish dancing has ever endured such a popularity through the country ... As long as parents trouble to foster a sense of Ireland and things Irish in their children, Irish dancing and activities generally will never be threatened with extinction.[28]

No second-generation interviewees for this project were heavily involved in music or competitive step-dancing, although several had attended lessons as children. For those who did take a sustained interest, cultural activities were of paramount importance in providing forums in which young second-generation Irish people interacted with one another. While such activities did provide Irish spaces for the post-war emigrants, music and dancing became distinctly second-generation parts of the community, with *The Irish Post* noting that even by 1980 many of the Irish dancing teachers in the country were second-generation.[29]

There were other cultural expressions outside of music and step-dancing that also provided forums of Irish interaction for the second-generation. Anne described how her participation in *céilí* dancing enhanced the strength of her interaction within the Irish community: 'Well after my mother died we started going to the *céilís*, my poor father didn't know what to do with two teenage girls. We went to Kilburn, Highgate, Percy Road, everywhere … and through that we got a group of friends, again second-generation and their parents.'[30] While the GAA was not as developed in youth structure in the 1970s and 1980s as it would later become, it was also an important arena for interaction with fellow second-generation children for some in London. Orla, the daughter of Peter, a first-generation interviewee, found a social scene through Gaelic football even before she was even old enough to play and later became heavily involved in the club of which her father was a member:

> It was a very Irish, Gaelic football, background. It wasn't compulsory, but it was just part of your life ... We would just naturally just go with my dad every Sunday to New Eltham and there'd be X amount of players in the car, we would head off early morning on a Sunday and come back late at night ... I just remember seeing all of Dad's friends, all of their children, they would also be at New Eltham ... It was a real social scene then.

Orla's parents seemed particularly keen to encourage Irish activity, with her brothers learning the Irish language at *Aras na nGael* in Kilburn and going on an excursion to the *Gaeltacht* (Irish-speaking region), her having some music and dancing lessons, and all the children playing Gaelic games.[31]

Throughout Britain, Irish festivals aimed at families were established and gained great popularity by the late 1970s. As noted in

Chapter One, the London Irish Festival was seen as particularly important to provide the second-generation with a place to express their identities. Videos that were filmed of the festival in the early 1980s show that there were many young people in attendance, usually replete with green clothing and tricolours. The second-generation also formed a central part of the entertainment with their dancing and musical performances.[32] Several interviewees remember going to the London Irish Festivals and smaller, shorter-lived alternatives: 'It was all Irish festivals in Roundwood Park and Harrow Irish Festival and all that. That was our social life.'[33] The enthusiasm amongst the Irish in London for Irish cultural forms led to a commonly expressed opinion that the Irish in Britain were becoming 'more Irish than the Irish', that they were 'the true Irish', 'the true keepers of a heritage'.[34] An interview with a group of second-generation girls at the London Irish Festival in the early 1980s touched on this:

> Girl One: That's what we say in our club – we're more Irish than the Irish.
> Girl Two: We are, because we go to Ireland and we get up and do Irish dancing and they're all amazed that we can do it because nobody over there can do it, they don't bother.[35]

Paul, who has long been involved in Irish music, said: 'The boys from home, the fellas that we meet and play the music with, they can't understand that the [second-generation] lads here are more Irish than the fellas are in Armagh.'[36] These sentiments were echoed by Fr McCabe, who found himself astonished at the success of Irish music during his time in London in the 1970s:

> I was always amazed with the level of interest in Irish folk music, the competition between dance groups – most of them second-generation but so Irish identified it was incredible ... I never saw that amount of interest here [in Ireland] at all ... The popularity of *Comhaltas Ceoltóirí Éireann* – I'd lived here for 27 years then and never been aware of them here.[37]

Campbell has highlighted the occasional forays that music magazines made into the Irish dance hall world in London, with one noting with some surprise in 1985 that the second-generation were regularly out in force.[38] This was not a universal preference, with Brian Keaney expressing his alienation from his parents by contrasting their love of dancing to musicians 'scraping away on fiddles and screeching through tin whistles' to his penchant for 'semi-darkness, coloured lights, an insistent beat'.[39] However, given the possibilities of London night life it is perhaps surprising that so many among the second-generation in the capital preferred nights at the Galtymore or National to the discos and punk gigs that their British-parented peers were attending. These dance halls featured regularly in narratives of interviewees' teenage and early adult years. Catherine's memories of attending them show how they were of great importance in the continuity of an ethnic community among the second-generation beyond the confines of dancing lessons or Catholic clubs: 'It was all second-generation Irish. My cousins used to go to the Galty so I used to go with them a lot and I mixed with their friends who were all second-generation Irish. Having said that, some of them married first-generation Irish as well so I suppose I did mix with them in those days.'[40] When asked whether he had felt part of an Irish community growing up, the dance halls were Gerry's first point of reference: 'Yeah, we would have. If you took what we were doing socially, you know we were going to Irish dance halls, we weren't going to discos particularly ... we'd go to the Galtymore. There'd be lots of discos, nightclubs to go to but that wasn't where we went. That [the Irish dance hall scene] was what we felt part of.'[41] Orla's memories of the dance hall world touched on the theme of the second-generation Irish in London being 'more Irish' than those living in Ireland due to their participation in Irish activities and positioned her, at least in one respect, as more authentically Irish than those born in Ireland.[42] In her case the dance halls provided a link with the dancing culture that her parents brought with them from Ireland, something that she found her Irish-born cousins did not appreciate: 'We socialised in an Irish circle so, particularly myself and my two older sisters, we would go with Mum and Dad to the National and the Galtymore – we knew how to jive, we knew how to waltz ... whereas some of my Irish cousins who lived in Ireland can't jive.'[43]

In much the same way that Campbell has portrayed the Pogues' concerts as being events at which a hyphenated 'London-Irish' identity could be celebrated, the appearances of the Wolfe Tones at the National dance hall were occasions on which the second-generation could express an exaggerated form of romantic Irishness that was impossible to shout about quite so loudly on the streets of London. As with Gerry, Anne's first points of reference when asked if there was a feeling of community among the second-generation were the dance halls and the overtly republican songs of the Wolfe Tones: 'Oh yeah there definitely was. We went to the Galtymore, the National. Again in those days if you went to the National and they used to have the Wolfe Tones and that used to be absolutely packed! And they'd be singing all these nationalist songs and we used to go mad for them!'[44] As well as bringing the second-generation together at the same events, music could help the youth form and express their identities. Michael remembered listening to the Pogues as being 'the first time I thought I'd heard that part of my identity coming out through the radio speakers ... the London-Irish experience', and Enda called the Wolfe Tones 'a great identifying force', who played songs 'we could relate to'.[45] The enthusiasm of the second-generation for a night of rebel songs was noted in *The Irish Post* in 1987: 'A Wolfe Tones concert in Britain in the mid-Seventies was a comparatively low-key affair with audiences almost entirely Irish-born. Nowadays, the second-generation turns out en masse and the atmosphere is somewhat different ... The Wolfe Tones ... have responded by dedicating a song –My Heart is in Ireland – to the second-generation in Britain.'[46] The theme of being 'more Irish than the Irish' was expressed in relation to such music by Rory:

> When we were kids and going to see the Wolfe Tones ... in London it used to be absolute bedlam and we went to see them in Limerick once and it was a load of old Bids clapping politely ...I guess over here, because of our parents and stuff, you declared your identity, declared who you were, by listening to Irish music.[47]

It is notable that Kevin Rowland of Dexy's Midnight Runners picked the Wolfe Tone's favourite London venue, the National, to express his Irishness in a forceful manner by donning a republican-style beret on their final tour date in 1980, underlining again how such dance halls were spaces in which ethnicity could be expressed in exaggerated ways, away from the general British public.[48]

Many second-generation Irish in London spent their childhood and young adulthood within an Irish community that formed through residential areas, churches, schools, cultural activities and dance halls. For them, this meant that childhood and adolescence was often remembered as the most distinctly Irish-oriented period of their lives. For instance, Rory said that 'I can honestly say that I didn't know an English person until I was 18.'[49] The term 'community' was used frequently throughout the interviews in reference to the milieu in which they grew up. Michael described it thus:

> A lot of your mates were Irish. You'd grown up in this community, you'd gone to school with a whole lot of people from this community, had shared backgrounds. It wasn't the case that all your friends were Irish or that everyone you knew was Irish but it was certainly the case that a huge number were and the most influential body of people that you knew were from an Irish background.[50]

For some interviewees this sense of community has continued unabated throughout their lives. Catherine said that the area in which she lived had been described as 'our own little village in Ireland' and that she felt 'very much that I belong to this community here where I was born and where I grew up'.[51] Patrick's response, when asked whether he felt part of an Irish community when he was young, brought out the extent to which the feeling has lasted:

> 100 per cent. And I think even more so as I've grown older. And I think from a purely pragmatic point of view it's kind of fed through to my daughter just how beneficial, forget the feelings about being Irish or whatever, just how beneficial it is to her it is being part of the Irish community. It's an advantage, with the contacts you have if you wanted something done, or whatever, or you want a job, there's always somebody who will come up.[52]

Patrick's words also show that Malone's and Dooley's conclusions that the London-born Irish have failed to form a community of practical help that impacts 'their contemporary existence' do not apply in all situations.[53]

For many of the second-generation, the ethnic community in which they were brought up lived on through their marriages. While this sample is in no way representative, it is still notable that of those who were or had been married, four interviewees married first-generation Irish people, three married second-generation Irish and two married British people. From asking the interviewees about their siblings' and peers' spouses it seems that there was a high level of marriage within the Irish community. As Gerry, who married a British woman he met at university, said, 'You were likely to meet your future partner in the Galty or the National. And if not there, then it would be at university.'[54] The bonds formed have often lasted until the present day and the children of the post-war generation have often continued to engage with the structures of the Irish community in which they were brought up. For instance, Catherine's children have always been heavily involved in Irish country and western music, Orla's sons have played Gaelic football and most interviewees sent their children to Catholic schools. Anne remarked how the Catholic school system perpetuated the ethnic network: 'You're sort of cocooned. Even at [the local Catholic primary school] people are the same as you. I remember walking in with [my son] on his first day and half of [my secondary school] was there!'[55] There was also often concern among the second-generation, as there was among their parents, that a sense of Irish heritage and cultural identity should be passed on.[56] Even John Walsh, whose relationship with Irishness was fraught with difficulty, described how his 'vestigially Celtic heart leapt in its bosom' upon hearing his daughter say that she liked the Pogues because they were 'Irish like me'.[57]

Nevertheless, it is true that the nature and sense of community changed for the second-generation. They became more residentially dispersed – for instance, while four of the interviewees were brought up in Kilburn or Cricklewood, only one now lives near those areas. The second-generation have proved to be very socially mobile. Hornsby-Smith and Dale were able to conclude through sampling of educational attainment statistics that 'by the second-generation, Irish immigrants [sic], both men and women, have been able to equal or exceed the educational qualifications held by their English counterparts'.[58] Likewise, in spite of their parents being largely clustered in low-skilled work, the second-generation were more likely than the rest of the English population to be in high socio-economic groups in the General Household Surveys of 1979–80.[59] These statistics support the qualitative evidence from interviewees and memoirists who often, although not uniformly, stressed the importance that their parents placed on education and social mobility.[60] This social mobility is likely to be a contributing factor to the lack of expression of class identity among the interviewees. While historically the Irish have become a part of the British working class as the generations have passed, the children of the post-war generation had more access to education and thus to social advancement than their predecessors.[61] The second-generation Irish usually found themselves working in environments in which there would be few Irish people. Thus, as everyday interaction became less of a feature of second-generation lives, the community became less tightly knit and more of a cultural community that was there for those who chose to engage with it. While London-born interviewees did often have several links with cultural and religious aspects of Irishness, they portrayed far less of a need to socially ghettoize themselves as they outgrew school and Irish dance halls. Several continued to have many second-generation Irish friends from their youth but this was in no sense as strong a theme as among first-generation interviewees, who often exclusively had socialized with Irish people throughout their time in London. It is notable that organizations such as the county associations failed to attract continued interest among the second-generation when they reached adulthood, in spite of it being clear from minute books that several associations had attempted to form 'Junior Associations' for their children.[62] David expressed disappointment that his children did not feel the need to join Irish associations in spite of their identification with being Irish and his best efforts to encourage them.[63]

EXPRESSING IDENTITIES

A limited number of investigations have been carried out that have explored how the second-generation Irish define their own national identities. As early as December 1970, *The Irish Post* reported on a survey of over 100 boys carried out by a teacher at a Catholic school in north London. Labelling them 'mixed up kids', it reported that they saw themselves as 'neither Irish [n]or English, but as a mixture of both nationalities', although most (62 per cent) would support Ireland over England in a game of soccer and thought that Northern Ireland should become part of the Republic. When asked to define their nationality, given a choice between 'Irish', 'English' or 'a mixture of both', the results were 24 per cent, 24 per cent and 52 per cent respectively.[64] A more academic investigation was carried out in the 1980s by Philip Ullah. Using groups from two Catholic schools in Birmingham and one in south-central London, he again found widespread results, with the middle ground the most popular choice – 'Completely Irish' scored 0 per cent, 'Mainly Irish' 20 per cent, 'Half and Half' 56 per cent, 'Mainly English' 13 per cent, 'Completely English' 9 per cent.[65] Hickman's study in the 1980s found that 81 per cent of her sample of London schoolchildren gave their identity as 'Irish' or 'Irish descent' – which is also notable for the fact that nearly a fifth denied the facts of their descent in describing their identity.[66] What is clear from such surveys is that defining oneself as a second-generation Irish person has never been a straightforward task. More recent studies, such as the 'Irish2' project's outputs have focused more on the complexities of identity rather than asking people to tick a defined box.[67]

Campbell's work on second-generation Irish musicians has explored in great detail the complexities of identity formation and expression and he has argued convincingly that we should pay more attention to the agency of the second-generation's cultural agency in impacting the host culture, rather than focusing attention on a range of narrow issues such as diasporic identity formation.[68] It is nevertheless felt that an exploration of how individual second-generation people have described their identities throughout their lives and the influences on their visualizations of their identities is useful and is an important part of the story of the Irish community that was formed by the post-war emigrants. Moreover, the study of the process of diasporic identity formation does not necessarily assume cultural passivity and does not simply tell a story of the Irish resisting or embracing assimilation. Rather, the process of forming an identity for the London-born Irish has been a dynamic one whereby choices are made that allow Irishness to be re-imagined in a modern, anglicized, urban milieu.

The interviewees' descriptions of their identities differed enormously. While it is probably unhelpful to generalize, one might divide them into four wide categories that inevitably overlap: 'Irish', 'London-Irish', 'English and Irish' and 'English'. The majority of interviewees could be said to be within the middle two categories. While 'British' and 'English' were usually used interchangeably, the former was occasionally preferred as a more inclusive version of the latter, which was seen as having ethnic connotations, and being 'European' was also mentioned twice.[69] Below is a selection of the discussions with various interviewees that highlight the range of identities expressed, the nuances that exist even within the broad categories noted and how they have changed over time.

THE IRISHMAN

Patrick was born of two Irish Catholic parents and has always lived around north and north-west London. The way in which he expressed his identity, and those of his Irish-born wife and London-born daughter, was remarkably straightforward:

Patrick: I don't use London-Irish, I don't use anything, I just use Irish. Down to the voting forms that come through, all three of us are down there as Irish.

SS: I suppose it's hard to have a hyphenated identity, like Irish-British?

Patrick: Yes, they're mutually exclusive ... There's a lady next door called [a very Irish name] and she said to me 'I'm half Irish, half English.' So I said to her, 'I've met your father, he's Irish, is your mother English?' She said, 'Oh, no, she's Irish as well.' [*pause*] So, anyway, that's up to them.

Patrick was very comfortable with his 'pure' Irish identity. He said that he had never felt any differently and, as already noted, he was very attached to the idea of belonging to an ethnic community in London. This is not to say that he did not recognize some differences between the Irish-born and the London-born Irish. When arguing that living outside Ireland heightened the importance of one's Irishness, he mentioned how his daughter knew details of episodes in Irish history that her Irish-born cousins had not heard of. He also noted how the London-born Irish were very sensitive to other cultures due to their growing up in what Brah would term a 'diaspora space':

Patrick: Growing up in north London we had exposure [to other cultures] ... Going to school in [north London], the number of Italians there were! ... You went to the restaurants of the Italians in the class, I had a job waiting in one. So you learned how they did things differently, like they got married on Sunday, which we didn't, all the little cultural differences, so you were much more open to people doing things in a different way ... We were well ahead of the game. I managed [bank] branches ... where it was totally Jewish and I knew their customs inside out and then later in my career ... I had the same thing again with the Muslims ...

SS: I suppose you're more inclined than the Irish-born to be tolerant?

Patrick: That's right, those things become second nature.

Patrick's ability to speak of Ireland as somewhat of an outside observer is notable. When discussing the changes in Ireland that have taken place since his childhood, he reminisced about the 'intimacy' between people, in terms of how 'everybody knew everything' about neighbours' affairs, that he found 'so funny'. When speaking of long summer holidays spent with his grandparents in Ireland he said: 'The marked difference was what made it so fun. So all the kids came back with the stories at primary school and the Italians and others wanted to go!' Ultimately, while Patrick recognized differences in outlook and attitudes, for him being Irish as a nationality was achievable in its entirety regardless of place of birth and upbringing.[70]

'I'M IRISH'/'VERY MUCH LONDON-IRISH'

Rory was born of two Irish Catholic parents and has lived in north-west London all his life. The following conversation took place with Rory regarding his definition of his own identity:

SS: In terms of your national identity, how would you describe yourself now?

Rory: Irish, nothing more complicated than that. I really dislike the label second-generation, third-generation Irish.

SS: Why?

Rory: Well I'm Irish. There's no second-generation, third-generation about it, I'm Irish.

SS: Was there ever any confusion?

Rory: No, I never would have called myself English. It sounds a weird thing to say, when I first travelled abroad I was 21 and I got my Irish passport ... I just remember, you know that bit on the passport where it says nationality and underneath it says 'Irish' and it was just, I just remember being so happy having my passport, now it's official, I'm Irish!

Rory seemingly has a 'pure' identity without any dilution of his Irishness, similar to Patrick's. Nevertheless, his answers reflect that he has had to consciously reject other possible labels, such as 'second-generation'. He also, like several other interviewees, placed great symbolism in his Irish passport, which he used to prove both to the world, and perhaps himself, that he was entitled to hold an unadulterated Irish identity.[71] Later in the interview it also became clear that Rory constantly had to negotiate a path that could accommodate his

Irish identity and the fact that he was born and has always lived in London. Without prompting, Rory came back to the issue of his identity, describing how he had tried to express it through symbols and how passing it on to the next generation was troubling for him:

> Rory: You know you have your kind of county identity about where your parents are from? I remember getting a London GAA shirt and wearing that to Ireland so as kind of to prove a kind of difference in identity …
>
> SS: Would you say that you had a London-Irish identity then?
>
> Rory: I wouldn't describe myself as second-generation Irish, because I'm Irish, but I would describe myself as London-Irish … I'm very much London-Irish. I mean I can't stand the game of rugby but I have every London Irish [RFC] shirt going just to kind of say, 'This is who I am,' sort of thing. But I don't like the differential that there is more Irishness because of the generational thing … I must admit though, this is one of my great dilemmas: Me and my wife, please God, will have children one day and what the hell do I bring them up as? Because they'll be, for want of a better label, third-generation, and they'll be that much more detached from it.

While Rory had that 'county identity' and the attachment to specific places in Ireland formed during summer holidays that most interviewees expressed, he looked to acquire symbols that he could use to accommodate the facts of his London birth. Rory's use of sports teams and symbols as repositories of identity was commonplace among interviewees. As Holmes has pointed out, sporting events are recognized as being 'occasions when members of a national grouping can truly feel they are part of a larger imagined community'.[72] Supporting the Irish soccer team, who play a sport that many of their parents would have regarded as a poor man's Gaelic football, represents a form of identification that was picked up and developed by the second-generation, often entirely independently from their parents. For the interviewees in this project who expressed a purely Irish identity, the Republic of Ireland soccer team certainly appeared to offer opportunities to 'perform' ethnicity.[73] The only two interviewees who professed a purely Irish identity, Rory and Patrick, were both committed supporters of the Irish soccer team, and could both reel off the names of the many British-born players who have represented the Republic.[74]

The 'London-Irish' label is something that Rory was comfortable with, although its suggestion of a 'difference in identity' did not quite match his earlier concern that he not be labelled 'second-generation'. This tallies with other studies and memoirs that have shown an attachment to places and regions within England alongside a rejection of being 'English' or 'British' in an abstract sense.[75] Pete McCarthy, for instance, said that he and other second-generation Irish peers in Lancashire were relieved when England versus Ireland sports games were over so that 'we could return to the simple eternal truths that nobody in Lancashire ever need question – you know – all southerners are bastards. So are Yorkshiremen. That kind of thing.'[76] Rory was certainly attached to his wider 'community' in the place that he has always lived. When asked if he would ever live in Ireland he replied: 'No. It's a very bizarre thing. I love going to Ireland on holiday and I go to Ireland maybe six/seven times a year but I don't think I could live there ... This is my community really; I've been born and brought up in this area and I've got no huge desire to leave it ... It's a very different way of life in Ireland.'[77] The fact that in spite of an attachment to his locality Rory could not envisage himself as 'English' in any way highlights that, for many, the two monolithic nationalisms have remained diametrically opposed. The use of a London GAA shirt is particularly significant in that it imagines London-Irishness within a specifically Irish frame – Rory equated London with an Irish county to mirror the county identities that the first-generation held on to. London almost becomes imagined as another county of Ireland, accepting but minimizing Rory's distinctiveness from the Irish-born. This concern to incorporate a London identity marked a slight difference from Patrick's lack of concern for place of birth.

THE LONDONER OF IRISH BACKGROUND

The 'London-Irish' label appears to have only gained widespread currency relatively recently and was something that only a few interviewees actively identified themselves as being. Certainly the term did not appear in *The Irish Post* as a term of identification in the 1970s and seems to have become popularized by some of the second-generation and the Pogues in the 1980s.[78] When I posed the possibility to Catherine (whose reply to a question about identity neatly avoided a label: 'my parents are Irish but I was born here') of a London-Irish identity, she replied: 'That's a terminology that I find is growing recently. My children, and I, recently have said "London-Irish" but it's not something that we would have grown up with ... [it's] a good way of putting it.'[79] It is a label that can have nuances. Enda, born of an Irish father and an English mother (albeit a Catholic with two Irish grandparents) and brought up in south London, was comfortable with his London-Irish identity at the time of interview:

> You see the thing is, being London-Irish is a perfectly kosher identity as far as I'm concerned. I'm a Londoner of Irish background, I'm not Irish in the same sense as somebody who comes from Ireland, and neither would I want to be, I am who I am ... I find it quite amusing that I've got a grandfather who was in the British Army and the other grandfather was in the IRA.

'London-Irish' meant something slightly different to Enda than it did to Rory. The former's use of the phrase seemed a more comfortable one than the latter's, in that it was his primary description of identity rather than a sub-identity of 'Irish'. Being Irish for Enda was a flexible phenomenon, something that he could be comfortable with and enjoy without it restricting other features of his personality that was formed growing up in a cosmopolitan London. A break from old-fashioned Irishness was apparent when he showed annoyance at the frequent conflation of 'Irish' and 'Catholic'. He also opined that 'a lot of London-Irish people tend to be a bit more broad minded because they're living in a city and have a different perspective and a broader horizon about things'.

In spite of Enda's currently well-expressed identity, one of the strongest themes of his interview was that comfort in a London-Irish identity was not always the case. His memories show the fluid nature of identity and the tendency some have to overcompensate for their English birth with an exaggerated Irishness at times in their lives:

> I think with a lot of people in my situation, what we tend to do is over compensate by becoming more Irish than we might be, by thinking that if we're more outlandish or more expressive about being Irish, whether it's about our football, our historical or political opinions or whatever it is. I mean when I was a kid I had pictures all over my wall of Kevin Barry, James Connolly and a tricolour and all that stuff – it's all about trying to be Irish I suppose.

An even more dramatic set of swings between identities happened with Michael, who saw himself as English until his teens and felt he had to defend the English against the xenophobia of his family in Ireland. Later he began 'to think about having an Irish identity'. Irishness proceeded to take over, dominating to the extent that he broke up with a girlfriend due to his uncompromising republicanism. That stance then gave way to a more comfortable acceptance of both strands of his identity.

As with Rory, Enda's attempts at expressing a pure Irish identity were never truly satisfactory. He spoke of how he felt that had to deny his own self in order to hold on to his Irishness:

> Years ago if someone came up to me at a gig and said to me, 'Where are you from?' And instead of saying, 'I'm from London,' I'd always say something like, 'My dad is from Ireland,' or whatever. But they weren't asking me where my dad was from, they were asking me where I was from. And I suppose I was in denial of the fact that I was a Londoner.

Enda's denial of any English identity again brings to light the theme of the diametrically opposed historical nationalisms that make it hard for a London-born Irish person to express an identity. This led to what he described as an 'identity crisis':

> Growing up in London with an Irish background is not the same as growing up in America with an Irish background for many reasons. But the main reasons are that we have the accent and the birthplace of the country that is the oppressor of our fatherland, or whatever you want to call it. So I suppose identity crisis is the thing that comes up.
>
> I think if you go around saying I'm half English half Irish it doesn't really work, I don't think it does.

It is notable that even though Enda now embraces the fact of his birth in London and his part-English ancestry, the phrase 'London-Irish' is still essentially an uneasy formulation used to avoid the seeming impossibility of being an 'Irish-Briton' or an 'Irish-Englishman'.

Enda's 'journey' to being comfortable in his own skin as an Irish Londoner is also significant because it supports what Walter and colleagues have found – that having only one Irish parent does not necessarily dilute a sense of Irishness and in fact it can serve to highlight the distinctiveness of the Irish part of a person's upbringing.[80]

Enda's case is a perfect example of this, as he found himself caught between an England represented by a south London 'slum' and the history of an 'oppressor' and an Ireland represented by his father's village, which was 'like something out of Walt Disney', and an heroic history of fighting in spite of the odds, 'a David and Goliath history'.[81]

THE 'MIXED UP KID'

The Irish2 project has argued for a move away from the model of the second-generation being caught between two cultures. Nevertheless, some of the London-born have clearly envisaged their identities in this way.[82] *The Irish Post* might have labelled Anne, who was born of two Irish parents and has always lived in north-west London, a 'mixed-up kid'. When she described her identity it appeared to fluctuate over the course of a number of sentences, going from 'half and half' to using the England sports team as an analogy of how she is perhaps more English to saying that her Irishness is now 'more dominant than it was':

> Anne: I think it changes as you get older. Probably now I'm half and half. I do like stupid things like the English footbal team and the English cricket team. I watch Ireland but it doesn't compel me passionately.
>
> SS: Do you support England more than Ireland?
>
> Anne: Yeah, I probably do. Not that I'm not interested in Ireland. I think as you get older you want to pass things on to your kids ... your background, you start passing that on. And I've recently started to look into my father's family to try and find out things. When I was there [Ireland] in September I went to the grave yard in Bandon and got some dates and stuff. So I think my Irishness is more dominant at the moment than it had been say ten fifteen years ago ... So yeah it [identity] fluctuates, at the moment it's more of the Irish.

Anne appeared to see her identity as fluctuating between two poles of 'English' and 'Irish', with no hybrid terminology used at all. Her family graves and history represent personalized *lieux de mémoire*, repositories of Irish identity that she could explore when her sense of Irishness was paramount in her mind, such as when trying to pass it on to her children. Pierre Nora's terms are particularly useful here:

while Anne was still relatively attached to the structures of Irish interaction, such as the Catholic Church and schools, and she is married to a second-generation Irish man, she felt that she had 'removed' herself from the Irish scene as she had grown older; she had left the *milieu de mémoire* of the Irish community and now looked for sites of memory through which she could explore her Irish identity. Such exploration of Irishness as an adult was common among the interviewees. Catherine had also looked into her family history, and several interviewees spoke of events and characters in Irish history that they had learned of through books read as adults. The motivation to explore Irishness by the second-generation was a major factor behind the rise of centres and journals of Irish Studies in Britain in the 1980s as many of the children of the post-war emigrants reached maturity and wished to study Ireland, a subject on which the British education system has been found wanting.

THE ENGLISHWOMAN

Kimberley was born of an Irish Catholic father and a Northern Irish Protestant mother and described her identity as follows:

> I say 'English with Irish parents' if anyone asks but I don't say it as a matter of course ... I am English, I will always write that on forms. If I meet someone who is Irish then I'd say, 'Oh my mum and dad are from Ireland.' I don't think I'm Irish in any way, shape or form, never have done ... It's just, they're Irish and I'm English. Strange.

Kimberley represented one of two interviewees for whom the question of national identity was straightforward, the other being Patrick who was simply 'Irish' with no caveat. In spite of her regular visits to Ireland as a child and her close relationship with Irish relatives engendering fond feelings for Ireland and its people, she said that she has never felt any need to explore her Irish background or anything about Irish history or culture. It appears that her description of identity was not a conscious rejection of Irishness but a bald statement of fact: 'I'm proud of my parents and their background. I don't know why, it just comes from me that I say I'm English, I was born here.'[83]

INFLUENCES ON IDENTITY

What is clear from the above examples is that the second-generation have significant agency in creating and deciding the identities that they proclaim through their lives. The first four examples all had very similar backgrounds: all attended Catholic schools, socialized within Irish circles throughout their lives and had married first- or second-generation Irish people. Yet the ways in which they described their national identity differed in terminology and the nuances of their usage of terms. Kimberley was the only example used who was brought up largely outside the Catholic Church and school system, although she did visit Ireland every year as a child and her parents have always socialized within Irish circles. Perhaps the most striking way to illustrate the personalized nature of Irish identity and the unpredictability of how a second-generation person will identify his or her self is how interviewees characterized other second-generation people that they knew. Michael told of a family of second-generation Irish brothers he knows and used the common allegory of support for national sports teams: 'I know a family of four fellas – one of them is a mad keen English rugby fan, another is a mad keen Irish rugby fan, [the other two] are in the middle.'[84] Rory's comments about his relations, all born of two Irish parents and brought up in largely the same manner as him, are telling:

SS: Do you know any second-generation people who would see themselves as English?

Rory: Some of my cousins even ... My uncle for instance, he's got three kids and they've all got British passports, all support England, and they live [in north-west London] as well ... A real schizophrenic family in a sense – another uncle who lives [in north-west London], he's got five children, three of whom have English passports and consider themselves English, two of them have Irish passports and consider themselves Irish.[85]

This variation in perceived degrees of Irishness within families was common. Orla and Anne both characterized their sisters as 'more Irish' than they were, with one of the former's sisters having taken the decision to live in Ireland permanently. Even Kimberley, among whose family questions of national identity were seemingly never raised, said that her older sister was more inclined towards attending Irish events and 'if any of us would say we were Irish it would be her'. Several first-generation interviewees also spoke of their children as identifying with Ireland to differing degrees, or having perceived national traits that were more Irish or English. Evelyn, for instance, said that one of her daughters was 'getting more English'; the other, who now lives in Ireland, was more Irish-identified and her son was 'very British', albeit with some Irish identification. Ciara felt that 'my elder daughter is more English [and] I'd say my younger daughter is more Irish'.[86]

In spite of the unpredictability of how a second-generation person will look upon their identity throughout their life, it is interesting to explore the influences that interviewees remembered as having an effect on how they have viewed themselves and how these influences were incorporated into visualizations of what being Irish means. It has already been noted that Catholic churches and schools played an important role in creating Irish spaces and extending the ethnic community into the second-generation. The frequent interaction that such spaces engendered in itself was important to a sense of being Irish – it is notable that Kimberley specifically pointed to the fact that she 'didn't go off to a Catholic school and have an Irish social circle' as a possible reason for her lack of identification with Ireland.[87] However, Catholicism in itself was important in creating a sense of 'otherness' among the second-generation. It was seen as something that included Irish people but excluded English people, and several interviewees spoke of Catholicism being an integral part of their Irish identification. Anne's narrative of her Irish identity was tied up inextricably with Catholicism. The communal aspect of Irish Catholicism in particular was part of what set her apart, even from her English co-religionists:

> SS: How did Catholicism 'fit in' with being Irish for you?
> Anne: There was no difference. Again it was only really when I went nursing and I was away from home that you had the choice to go. Up to then it wasn't an option, you just went, everybody went! So I didn't go for a while ... but that can't have been for long ... Again that set you apart from the people you were training with. Although some were English Catholics, they had a different ethos ... they were very different to us. To us it was a community, you knew everybody, whereas [theirs] was different.

For one young woman interviewed in the 1980s as part of an Irish video project, Catholicism was an integral part of being Irish and the key identifier of English 'otherness':

Interviewer:	When you were growing up in east London were you aware that your parents were Irish?
Young woman:	Yes, very.
Interviewer:	How did that come across – did that make them different, did you see them as different?
Young woman:	Yes, it made us different to our neighbours because most of our neighbours were English. And we were different in every way, because we were Catholic, because my parents were Irish, because we were involved in our parish and the [Catholic] school and we were just totally different. The English were just sort of outside our lives. In particular it was religion, Catholicism, and a strong emphasis on family life. We all went to children's mass together on Sunday mornings and processions once a month. In October we also did the rosary every evening. Your religion was tied up with your relationship with your parents as well.[88]

Patrick, like the first-generation Evelyn, preferred to place 'Irish' rather than 'Roman' in front of 'Catholic'. While he separated Irishness from Catholicism, Rory said that Catholicism is 'as much a part of your cultural identity as the Irish bit'. Likewise, Fr Liam, who did not attend a Catholic school, separated the two but again mentioned them in close proximity: 'Our identity, I suppose, was given to us through our parents as Irish people but also as Catholics.'[89] While some interviewees had fallen away from Catholic belief and practice, all acknowledged the large role it had played in making their Irishness distinctive in Britain.

Fr Liam's mention of his parents as passing on their sense of identity also shows the importance of the direct influence that the words and encouragement of parents could have on children. While Campbell notes the often pivotal role played by mothers in the encouragement of participation in Irish cultural forms, many memoirs and interviews have pointed to fathers in particular stressing to their children that they were Irish in an abstract sense and, perhaps just as importantly, not English. Anna May Mangan remembered her father saying 'He's you, son, and be proud of him', when her brother asked who 'Paddy' was. After being on the receiving end of some football-hooligan abuse, he also said to his daughters that 'we're just visitors here.

Remember that.'[90] When speaking about his identity, Gerry said: 'The strongest identity would be Irish and I think that would have come very much more from my dad. He would have been very Irish, and almost anti-English, so that would have been a very strong influence on me.'[91] Rory spoke of his father as 'very much the driving force behind our Irish identity':

> My dad was a very big sports fan ... when we watched it with him as kids, if Ireland were playing we supported Ireland, if England were playing we supported whoever they were playing against ... It's been beaten into me from an early age!
>
> He had a strong sense of Irish history ... I remember reading Irish history books when I was 11 or 12 and there was that programme by Robert Kee, the history of Ireland, stuff like that we used to watch ... When we used to go to places like Armagh he used to love going to places like Armagh Cathedral for the history and in later life when we started to go to Dublin we'd go to places like Kilmainham Gaol.[92]

Maude Casey's novel, *Over the Water*, inspired by her own Irish upbringing in London, focuses on the protagonist's father as the parent who tried to get her to empathize with Irish history: 'the rulers of England took it all away ... They took our land away, and then made us till it for them, made us grow the waving corn for their own use ... Mary, I'm telling you this so that you'll never forget how it was that your people first had to leave their land.'[93]

Irish history often featured in interviews and seemed to be a strong influence for some, especially males, in their sense of Irish identity. The very masculine Irish national story of fighting against the odds during centuries of persecution undoubtedly appealed to men more than women. As Walter and colleagues found, this history need not necessarily be the general Irish national story but could be extremely personal.[94] Enda said that he had kept his grandfather's IRA medal and, when he visited Ireland in the summers, he listened to his grandfather's stories of the civil war, which he 'was still fighting in 1971'. This appears to have had a significant impact on his identity as he 'was mesmerised' by the stories he heard and found Irish history 'intoxicating'.[95] Likewise, Joe showed how such stories seep into a person's identity when, in a general discussion about his background, he recounted how his grandparents' house was a republican safe house during the War of Independence and how he had been told a story of the shooting by the Black and Tans of a young brother of one of the republican fighters hiding in the house.[96] Such stories were not always to do with nationalism, with sentimental tales of Ireland also being passed down from parents.

Enda's memories of going to Ireland when young were typical among interviewees, most of whom spent significant periods there every year. Frequent trips to Ireland were undoubtedly important in creating a deep sense of attachment to Ireland. Joe, whose identity is currently 'leaning more towards Irish', spoke at length of his summers in Galway as a child: 'When we went on holiday for the summer we just thought it was a wonderful thing, we'd be crying coming home you know.'[97] Gerry spoke similarly of how going to Ireland was 'a big part' of his identifying primarily with Ireland through his life: 'We used to really look forward to it. Even now, you know, seeing the house we used to stay in, it could still make your heart skip a beat.'[98] Several second-generation memoirists mention the long holidays in Ireland that caused it to become 'an extension of home'.[99] Buckley has described trips to Ireland as 'anchoring the identity of the second-generation children in experiences of the Irish mainland ... [This] can be so intense that some second-generation Irish speak of growing up with a constant sphere of oral reference to another location that was called "home".'[100] Indeed, one interviewee, Patrick, routinely referred to Ireland as 'home' and several interviewees had a strong identification with specific places in Ireland where family are based and which they regularly visit.[101]

Cultural activities played a part in the development of identity for those who took part. In a focus group of second-generation children that was recorded at a west London Catholic school in 1984, one girl described the importance of dancing to her, her parents and many others in expressing an identity: 'My mum and dad introduced me to Irish dancing just to remember our Irish identity ... There's thousands of other people from America and all places like that and their parents are Irish and they just want to keep their Irish identity by doing something like Irish dancing and Irish music, to remember they've got an Irish background.'[102] Orla's involvement in Gaelic football and her exposure to music and dancing as a child clearly impacted her vision of her identity, which she described as 'culturally Irish'. Anne spoke of *céilí* dancing as reinforcing her sense of having a distinctive cultural heritage, something that was heightened when she left home to train as a nurse and her course-mates 'didn't know what the hell it was!'[103]

Anne's memory of people not knowing about *céilí* dancing was part of her general culture shock when she left home. Mixing with non-Irish people on a regular basis for the first time brought issues of identity to the fore:

SS: Did you realise that you were Irish when you were a child?

Anne: When I was little I didn't really know. I knew I was Irish background but I didn't know any different and most of the people we mixed with were Irish. It was only really when I went nursing that I realised that we had a different upbringing from other people really.

SS: So when you left school?

Anne: Yeah, because at school really the majority of people had Irish backgrounds.. .... but when I went nursing I met people who had very English upbringing and that's when you realise what your identity is I suppose. I felt when I went nursing they thought I was very Irish but when I came home I became very English, and it was quite difficult really ... I felt conscious that I was of a different, not class, a different level and I felt that I had to change to be accepted I suppose with them.

SS: Did you change?

Anne: Yeah, I think I did, you want to fit in don't you?[104]

Anne's experience emphasizes the peculiarly strong nature of the Irish community in north-west London. Several other interviewees, as already noted, spoke of their being 'cocooned' among Irish people during their youth. The realization of otherness took place earlier for some and created pressure for the second-generation to choose between identities. In the 1984 documentary already mentioned, the following conversation took place:

Girl One: We was given the choice, either to go English or Irish. And I think if I did go English I wouldn't fit in with my family, I wouldn't get on as well ... If I did go the other way I wouldn't be comfortable because they always go to an Irish club and I like being with my parents all the time. So if I did go that way I wouldn't be as friendly or as close to my mum and dad. So I'm glad I've gone Irish you know.

Girl Two: The way that came across to me. It seems like, because if you're gonna choose to be Irish with a big 'I' you don't have the freedom to think the way you want to, you've just got to be traditional, and I don't think that's being Irish. Being Irish is being able to have different views on things. Being Irish isn't being traditional and saying, 'Yeah mum, that's right,' and, 'Oh I wouldn't think about that,' and 'No, that isn't in the Church,' d'ya know what I mean? I don't think that's being Irish, maybe that's being Irish fifty years ago or before, I don't know, but to me that's not it.

Girl One: Yeah, but if I was sort of English, if I, say, did everything that English kids did my parents, I mean, I just wouldn't get on with them at all, no way. That's what I mean when I say I prefer to be Irish, go to Irish clubs, listen to Irish music, try and act the same as my mum and dad, because if I acted like English girls there's no way that I'd fit in at all.[105]

An Irish home in an English world threw light on the differences between the two for many among the second-generation and created pressures to identify with one or the other. The above conversation shows 'Girl One' visualizing 'Irish' as something entirely separate from 'English' in music, social interaction and, it is hinted, morality. Her Irish home and social life pressured her to feel that there was a simple choice to be made between what she saw as two mutually exclusive nationalities and modes of behaviour. Her argument that she would not get on with her parents if she 'acted like English girls' touches on a theme in some of the memoirs of the second-generation, whose identification with English culture left them alienated from their parents. The English-oriented life of the teenage John Walsh left him 'longing for modern, London parents'.[106] Keaney's father's preference for clothing that Shane MacGowan might call 'Paddy Chic' led the memoirist to write that he had 'wanted a father who behaved normally, like the other kids'.[107] Maude Casey's novel also portrays the adolescent girl as feeling distant from her parents.[108] The only suggestion of such a feeling among interviewees was with Michael, who found himself having to defend what he saw as his country, England, against the attacks of his relatives:

A debate, let's say, took place between me and my massed

assembled relations ... who left me in no uncertain terms that being English was not a very nice thing to be. Now that didn't make me think I don't want to be English, it made me feel the reverse. I thought that I wasn't having that, I'm going to stick up for myself here.[109]

Thus, for some, particularly those who did not grow up fully within the Irish community, growing up in an English cultural milieu created a pressure to be English that grated against the pressure from the home to be Irish. 'Girl Two' had apparently gone a long way to reconciling this clash. She visualized her Irish identity as something more flexible that could be expressed in the more cosmopolitan English world; Irishness was a characteristic that allowed her to 'have different views on things', it gave her a different perspective on life to the British person. In spite of this revision of Irishness for use in the modern London world, 'Girl Two' still recognized the pressures to adhere to traditional Irishness of strict Catholicism and social conservatism.

This debate was set against the backdrop of a sometimes hostile media, negative stereotyping and Irish jokes that could feasibly have pushed the second-generation Irish away from their ethnic heritage.[110] Casey's novel features jokes and stereotypes being directed at Mary by English schoolchildren, which she partly takes on board and she is depicted as slightly rejecting conservative Ireland in favour of mini-skirt London.[111] As was noted in Chapter Two, both John Lydon and John Healy mentioned vicious anti-Irish abuse being directed at them as children. Ullah's research found the experience of anti-Irish racism 'a major issue' in the lives of the children in his focus groups.[112] Similarly, one second-generation schoolboy spoke of how he regretted revealing his Irish heritage: 'Even your friends tend to distinguish you when you declare that you're Irish. I made the mistake of declaring I was Irish and they took the mick out of me afterwards. Before they knew I was Irish they treated me as one of them.'[113] While it is accepted that such anti-Irishness existed, it is significant that very few second-generation interviewees for this project remembered much anti-Irish feeling. Indeed, some such as Enda said that he would have looked upon being called an 'Irish so and so' as a compliment.[114] A few interviewees mentioned that when they were growing up 'it wasn't fashionable to be Irish' and noted a 'cultural shift' that has meant Irishness is now 'something to be displayed' in Britain.[115] That Ireland was perhaps not the height of fashion may well have pressured young people to express a British identity, although none of the interviewees for this project remembered feeling that. Any actual expressions of anti-Irish feeling from British people that they remembered never extended beyond jokes or low-level negative stereotyping and it certainly did not represent 'a major issue' in any of their lives. It could be argued that the positive images of Irishness experienced over the past two decades have erased old memories, although one suspects that if anti-Irishness was a serious factor in their lives they would remember it. It could also be argued that this highlights the extent to which the heavily Irish spheres in which those in north-west London moved provided a buffer against anti-Irish sentiments that featured in the lives of the second-generation elsewhere or that English accents saved them from abuse. Nevertheless, the fact that most interviewees dismissed any sustained or serious anti-Irishness in spite of their varied working lives does suggest that it has perhaps been exaggerated. When asked about anti-Irishness, some second-generation interviewees contrasted their own experiences growing up with what they had heard from their parents about feelings in the 1950s:

> Orla: I mean my parents would remember the times when they came over here and they weren't welcome. It had obviously changed by the time I'd come around.
> Enda: The worst anti-Irishness from what I can gather was in the 50s after the war ... I've heard people say it was terrible here in the 70s. I dunno where they were living but I was in London myself and I don't remember it.[116]

A small number of interviewees mentioned pressure from British people to drop an Irish identity, although this seems to have been a small feature of life in a multicultural London inhabited by countless cultures. Enda mentioned being asked why he 'was pretending to be Irish'; Patrick's bugbear was the British media continually questioning the right of second- and third-generation Irish players to play for the Republic of Ireland soccer team; and Rory mentioned that a workmate had repeatedly ribbed him by calling him 'English'.[117] However, Patrick revealed the source of most pressure to reject or modify Irish identities in his answer to the question, 'Were you ever put under pressure by normal English people to conform to an English identity?':

> Yes. But it's more annoying when you get what I call 'Free State Irish' who try and imply that you're somehow not Irish and then I can point to them to the declaration of independence

... Connolly, Clarke ... And in sport – Ronan O'Gara wasn't born in Ireland ... David O'Leary was born in England but because he's got an Irish accent he's Irish. But Joe Kinnear was born in Dublin and has a cockney accent so he's English.[118]

This pressure applied by the Irish in Ireland to reject or modify their own Irish identities was the most consistently aired grievance among the interviewees and was surprisingly often brought up in answer to unrelated questions. Rory's unsolicited thoughts on the topic are illustrative:

Rory: I think the only time that I ever considered myself English was when I went to Ireland, ironically enough. I suppose that no matter how Irish we may be, we're always going to speak with this London accent I guess. And we never used to think about it when we were here; all our friends were Irish ... And then you went to Ireland and they called you English ...

SS: Have you ever got that following the Irish football team?

Rory: Yeah a little bit, but not from those that live in London ... The one time that happened, not to do with football, was when I took a group from my school to World Youth Day, the Catholic event, in Sydney and the idea is that you bring your flag and you wave your flag and I had an Irish flag ... This group from the Dublin diocese came over, 'Oh, you're Irish, where're ya from?' And I opened my mouth ... And this girl had such a go, 'The problem is all you people think you're Irish and you're not Irish and you've got to get effing over it.' ... You get a bit of a ribbing about it following the football, they'll call you a Plastic Paddy and similar derogatory terms that they can come up with.

SS: How do you take being called a Plastic Paddy?

Rory: I don't find it particularly pleasant. I find it a bit offensive actually ... I know it's just a little bit of ribbing sometimes, but when you have an identity that's as strong as a London-Irish identity and then there's people who you think should understand what your identity is and then don't and rib you about it, it's quite hurtful really.[119]

The label 'Plastic Paddy' was attacked by several interviewees,

Catherine calling it 'disgusting' and 'derogatory'.[120] After Fr Liam
said that the term had often been directed at him when in Ireland,
he protested, 'I'm not a plastic anything ... What is that? A replica, a
fake, a remould? I didn't feel like that at all.'[121] Similar sentiments
were expressed periodically in letters to *The Irish Post*.[122] Scully has
argued that the second-generation have dealt with the term 'Plastic
Paddy' in a number of different ways, such as adopting it as a valid
description of those who are seen as being overly Irish; rejecting it
as offensive; and using it as a term of endearment.[123] While one
would agree that different views of the term exist, and that the use
of the term as one of endearment has been come across, the vast
majority of interviewees for this project reacted against such a term
as deeply offensive. In some circumstances the term has become
acceptable for Irish-descent people in London to use with reference
to each other but is offensive otherwise, as Orla said to me: 'I think
if you used it to me or I used it to you, I wouldn't be insulted by it.
I think I'd be more insulted if it was an Irish person saying it.'[124]

For some, the frequent denials of their identity from those whom
they thought of as compatriots seem to be a major reason behind
them not being able to fully express an Irish identity with any confidence. This appears to have been the case with Enda, who experienced being called a 'Plastic Paddy' to a great extent when he moved
to Ireland for a number of years and continued to play the live music
he had first played in the pubs of London. His move was motivated
by 'that romantic dream' about Ireland but he was 'heartbroken' to
find that he was not accepted as Irish:

> The thing is, when you live in a very rural part of Ireland, a
> very isolated part of Ireland, you're never going to be accepted
> by the locals really because you've got an English accent, you're
> defined by your accent. It doesn't matter if your name's
> Séamus Paddy O'Hooligan or whatever, it doesn't make any
> difference ... I got called some terrible things when I was there
> ... I've got some friends over there who changed their accents,
> took on an Irish accent ... But why would I change my accent,
> it's part of who I am. If I changed my accent I'd be doing it to
> accommodate morons, narrow-minded ignorant dickheads, so
> I'm not going to do that.[125]

One of Scully's interviewees underwent a similar process, saying: 'I
never wanted to be London-Irish' but identifying as such became

necessary because of the refusal of 'new wave' 1980s emigrants to accept her as Irish. To Scully this represented a defensive diasporic claim on authentic Irishness.[126] However, it could be seen, and appears to be the case with Enda, that rejection by the Irish-born has forced many of the London-born to face up to genuine differences that they had previously attempted to deny. Orla's difficulty in describing her own national identity stems from being called 'Plastic Paddy and worse' on the Gaelic football pitch and the reluctance of Irish officials to issue her with an emergency passport due to her birth place: 'I would see myself culturally as being Irish because that's what I do – I play Gaelic football, I'm involved in Gaelic football, it's such an integral part of my life. But I don't know that I'm accepted by the Irish ... I'm not Irish when I go to apply for my passport ... To the Irish I'm not Irish.'[127] From John Healy being called 'Black and Tan Swine' in the 1960s to the Hehir brothers, London-born and raised County Clare Gaelic footballers, being greeted by 'Brits Out' graffiti in the 1990s, the biggest barriers to the second-generation Irish who have wished to express themselves as Irish has seemingly been the rejection of such attempts by some of the Irish in Ireland.[128] It is worth noting that this rejection of Irishness by the Irish-born was not a figment of the second generation's collective imagination; Gray's and Kell's pieces of research among young first-generation emigrants in the 1990s found frequent rejection of the Irishness of the second-generation in London and an aversion to what they saw as an old-fashioned Irishness characterized by staunch Catholicism and republicanism.[129]

The children of the post-war emigrants grew up with the Troubles in Northern Ireland. It is certainly conceivable that the events may have played a part in turning people away from identifying with Ireland. One young second-generation woman from east London, filmed in the 1980s, said that people around her were being affected by the bombings: 'People say to them, "oh you're Irish; it's your lot who are doing all that bombing," and I think the majority of people are more keen to deny their Irishness now, or perhaps to say I'm Irish but ...'.[130] While she did not say that the Troubles dissuaded her from Irish identity, Kimberley, daughter of a Catholic father and Protestant mother, did say that the events in Northern Ireland gave her a negative view of religion and she never identified with the Catholic faith, which played a key role in the Irish identities of other interviewees.[131] However, a great many of the second-generation, if they were affected in any way beyond being appalled by the violence, seem to have been pushed towards Irish identification by the Troubles. Males in particular found that anger at the British Establishment increased their sense of alienation with the country in which they lived. Enda spoke of the Hunger Strikes of 1981 being 'a modern Easter Rising' to him, Bernadette Devlin being a 'hero', and being horrified at seeing 'the B Specials beating the shit out of the Catholics'. While Enda said that he did not see the Troubles as having any definitive impact on his favouring an Irish identity, they certainly fitted into his general narrative of the importance of Irish history to his identity. Others have been more explicit in saying that the Troubles were a major factor in their early identities. Gerry said:

> When I was very young we'd always support the England football team. I think from the time of the Troubles, from the early 70s, I think we became more sort of anti-English and I think also because there would have been things to do with the family. My dad's family down through the generations would have had connections with republicanism; I had cousins who were interned ... The identity was partly to do with the Troubles, it became more entrenched.[132]

Gerry articulated something that was common among his peers; in Free's study of second-generation Republic of Ireland soccer fans he found two London-born supporters who went to the same school as Gerry reminiscing about an incident during the Troubles that highlights the effect that events in Northern Ireland could have on young people's expressions of identity: 'When British army soldiers visited for publicity/recruitment purposes during the 1981 IRA Hunger Strikes, some lads wore balaclavas in the schoolyard while others wrote IRA in reverse on their palms, imprinting them on the soldiers in handshakes.'[133] Steve Brennan of the IBRG remembered his father reacting to Bloody Sunday by proclaiming that he would join the IRA. This had a large impact on Brennan, who developed republican views and identified solely as Irish:

> I was going to join the IRA if he did, that was the logical thing if people were going to be killed because they were Irish Catholics and you were just waiting for your turn. I was only 14. It certainly made me think and in many ways is responsible for the way I think now. It made me realise that you had to make a decision to be English or Irish, that there was no middle ground.[134]

Michael found that the Troubles and sympathy with republicanism gave him 'a way in' to the masculine and anti-English world of the Irish labourers' pub:

> You had to have a damn good reason to be in that pub, you needed to have something to give you a position in it, a space in it. You could argue that, 'my parents are Irish,' but you got, 'but where were you born?' So how do [you] get round that? You adopt the Irish banner and start talking about the IRA ... that gives you right to be there. Some of those Irish boozers back in those days were not the place for an Englishman.[135]

Growing up within an Irish community that revolved around the Catholic Church and its schools; parental enthusiasm for passing identity on; the wonders of Irish history, often brought alive through holidays to Ireland; involvement in cultural activities; hostility to expressions of Irishness, most virulently from those living in Ireland themselves; the Troubles – all these played significant influences on the identity formation of the children of Irish parents in London. Yet none can be said to be a panacea for the predicting how a second-generation person will describe their national identity. For instance, Patrick had never been involved in Irish cultural activities when young and self-identifies as entirely Irish; Orla danced and played musical instruments as a child and has been heavily involved in Gaelic football throughout her life but has trouble in seeing herself as totally Irish because of the rejection of her Irishness by those in Ireland, and also because she sees and identifies herself as a 'Londoner'; Anne *céilí* danced for several years but recognizes an English side to her identity. The variety of visions of identity that people from largely similar backgrounds expressed shows that it is something that has been engaged with on a very personal basis.

Malone and Dooley have suggested that the basis for this personalized attachment to Ireland among the second-generation has been focused on 'an idyllic but mythical "homeland", the rural Ireland of long ago'.[136] Gerry admitted that at times in his life he had been overly nostalgic about the Ireland of the past:

> I remember in the late '80s when we first got married and we used to get people round for dinner, quite often the people we'd invite round to dinner would be second-generation Irish people. And over the next ten years after that, as the economy in Ireland was taking off, we'd quite often chart how things

were changing in Ireland, and they did change remarkably. But it was almost, we were bemoaning the changes, this increase in prosperity and what was being lost and we were sort of locked into a particular caricature of Irish, you know the half doors and the thatched cottages and cutting turf and the honesty and integrity, as we saw it, being lost in favour of greater materialism. As people became more affluent social identity was being diluted. A lot of nonsense talk really over many years. But somehow we felt we were losing the Ireland we knew, but I'm not sure if the Ireland we knew ever existed.[137]

Yet Malone and Dooley's view, in spite of its truthfulness in some cases, is too stereotypical of the Irish abroad. The fact of being in close proximity to Ireland has meant that most interviewees have travelled there frequently throughout their lives, continue to have family there, do not begrudge Ireland its modernity and take an interest in the Ireland of the present: for instance, some mentioned following the news in Ireland through newspapers or the internet. While Rory did criticize the 'Celtic Tiger' years, he did so in a considered way and actually expressed distaste at the romanticized images that some of his father's generation held:

St Alban's Irish Club has this appalling mural of a cottage at the back of the stage ... I think my father in particular would have [had] this romantic image where he'd go back and work the farm and stuff. I never had that ...

I think with the growth of the economy, the Celtic Tiger, and maybe it's easy for me to sit here and say having had a relatively easy upbringing, that Ireland lost its soul a little bit during the Celtic Tiger. It's very easy for me to say because I didn't have to worry about emigrating because I didn't have a job or anything ...[138]

There was some nostalgia exhibited among interviewees but being Irish meant far more to them than a simple 'yearning' for old Ireland. As the second-generation reached maturity, they generally exhibited a determination to see Irishness in their contemporary worlds as something to be proud of. While interviewees did criticize aspects of Ireland, with matters such as overbearing Catholicism and the history of poverty featuring, the picture of being Irish was unanimously a positive one, represented by, among other things, the Irish dance halls of London, the Pogues, Jackie's Army and U2, as well as a slightly rose-tinted view of Ireland created by summer holiday experiences. Catherine's comments on the Troubles were simply that she found herself upset at the negativity surrounding Ireland, because she 'was always fairly passionate about thinking of Ireland as a good place, a nice place'.[139] Gerry could almost understand the phrase 'Plastic Paddy' in the sense that his Irishness and that of his contemporaries was so positive:

> You know the phrase 'Plastic Paddies', there was a sense that ours was the Ireland of the summer holiday and the weather was generally pretty good and you could run through the fields or it was the Irishness of the dance hall and the show bands and having a good time. Or flirting a bit with music or literature ... It was no surprise that it was our generation that created that 'Irish is cool' type, superficial Irishness ... I think with the older generation there was a darker side to their Irishness, ours was resolutely upbeat.[140]

The children of the post-war generation were often university educated, self-confident and had grown up in a diverse city in which the doctrine of multiculturalism was becoming increasingly accepted. In the 1980s, Enda became involved in the Birmingham Six campaign and attended some events of the more left-wing and radical groups of the 1980s, such as the Irish Freedom Movement. He eloquently captured the self-confident attitude of the London-born Irish of the time that contrasted so much with the 'heads down' approach of their parents' generation: 'I was born here, I've got an Irish dimension to me but I can say what I fucking want because I come from London. I can say what I want.'[141] The second-generation Irish, as a speaker at the London Irish Women's Conference in 1984 said, 'want to reclaim the part of our identity that is Irish for our own understanding of our lives'.[142] The 'Irish element' has not always been easy to express in words and incorporating it into a modern, urban and anglicized life caused difficulties. Yet for most, Irishness was re-imagined as an overwhelmingly positive feature compatible with their contemporary lives.

CHAPTER FOUR

Epilogue
The 1980s: The Community Comes of Age

The 1980s marked the beginning of another Irish story in London, that of the 'new-wave' emigrants. From 1981 to 1991 the Republic of Ireland experienced a net outflow of 206,000 people, about two-thirds of whom left for Britain. A majority of these were young and headed for London. These new-wave emigrants, leaving an Ireland that was increasingly being 'constituted as "modern" ', have been seen by academics as a different phenomenon from those who came before them.[1] No longer were the emigrants overwhelmingly poorly educated and from a rural, west of Ireland background; a significant minority were university educated and emigration affected all parts of Ireland.[2] These new emigrants to some extent posed a problem for the existing Irish in London, with the Federation of Irish Societies having to battle criticism that the older community was not welcoming the newcomers.[3] In her research among middle-class Irish emigrant women in the 1990s, Kells found that 'Middle class attitudes to Kilburn or other Irish localities are of distaste', and Gray found similar aversion to the forms of Irishness that the post-war emigrants and their children expressed. As one of her interviewees told a post-war emigrant in the London Irish Centre: 'that is the difference between you and me, because not only are we from different generations but we actually come from a different Ireland'.[4] New social structures emerged for young emigrants, independent of existing organizations, such as the London Irish Network in 1989.[5] In spite of these developments, a significant portion of the 1980s emigrants were not well educated and many did slot into the structures of the established Irish community, as highlighted by the fact that several second-generation interviewees married 1980s emigrants after meeting them in Irish venues. While Donal, a 1980s emigrant from Northern Ireland, found the county associations 'a bit too old fashioned for the '80s mob', he otherwise welcomed the 'warmth for new people coming into the community' and soon settled into the existing structures of the community, marrying a second-generation Irish woman, sending his children to Catholic schools and involving himself in the Irish dance hall music scene.[6]

As well as being changed by new emigrants, during the 1980s the Irish community in London flourished culturally and politically. This was partly to do with the funding provided by the Greater London Council (GLC), led by Ken Livingstone, that funded about thirty Irish groups by 1985 and bankrolled them to the tune of £3,000,000 from 1983 to 1985.[7] While the GLC funding provided the means through which the Irish could form various interest groups and a conducive atmosphere in which to do so, the changes in the community in the 1980s were more than the results of politically motivated cash injections and had already begun to take place before Livingstone gained control of the GLC in early 1981. The growth of the self-confident and culturally aware second-generation, an even greater acceptance of the permanency of habitation in London (enhanced, surely, by the renewed difficulties in the Irish economy in the 1980s) among the first-generation, and a 'new wave' of emigrants arriving in the English capital came together and allowed the Irish in London to express themselves culturally and politically in new ways.

In 1980 the 'Sense of Ireland' festival took place. This looked to showcase Irish culture to London, largely through imported musicians, dance troupes, literary figures and artists. A major aim was to 'make a significant contribution to improving understanding and relations between the people of these islands'.[8] By 1985 a more 'indigenous' cultural festival, *Síol Phádraig*, began with the financial aid of the Greater London Council (still under Ken Livingstone's leadership). The films, concerts, art exhibitions and a book fair were being run 'almost entirely of the Irish in London themselves'. *The Irish Post* praised the venture as a 'Remarkable London Irish Renaissance' and noted the great involvement of the second generation.[9] The London-born Irish continued to heavily involve themselves in Irish dancing and music and some literary flair began to be shown through the Green Ink writers' group and publications such as Casey's *Over the Water*.[10] In fusions of the influences of Irish heritage and a London upbringing, the comedian John Moloney incorporated the accordion-playing skills he learned with Brendan Mulkere into his 'Irish cabaret' that was designed to undermine the stereotypes portrayed by Irish jokes in Britain, and James McNally brought his Irish music into

Afro-Celt Sound System.[11] As the Irish in London became more accepting of their own permanence in Britain and the second-generation grew without any formalized knowledge of their ancestors' country, the community became more interested in itself. The Irish in Britain History Group was set up in 1980; the *Irish Studies in Britain* journal was established in 1981; lecture series were held, notably the controversial 'Terence MacSwiney Memorial Lectures' that several revisionist historians from Ireland declined to attend; and the academic-based British Association for Irish Studies (BAIS) came together in 1985.[12] The BAIS specifically noted the interest in 'their home culture' among 'the Irish communities in Britain' and the 'popularity of Irish music among the young' as reasons for its foundation.[13] In addition to academic interest, several groups emerged that were interested in the welfare needs of the Irish. The first, the Brent Irish Advisory Service, was formed in 1978, and began work providing help to Irish people with subjects such as citizens' rights, as well as promoting cultural activities and lectures of Irish interest.[14] During the 1980s others were founded, such as the London Irish Women's Centre in December 1980 and the Cara Housing Association in 1984.[15] All this was taking place alongside the London-Irish cultural phenomenon of the largely second-generation Irish band the Pogues, who in 1988 recorded a song, 'Streets of Sorrow/Birmingham Six', that admonished the British Establishment for arresting people for 'being Irish in the wrong place at the wrong time' and referenced the misuse of PTA powers. In this song the Pogues mixed their distinctly London-based form of Irish cultural expression with a political cause. In this they reflected the new-found political voice of the Irish community that mixed with the cultural, academic and welfare advances in the 1980s.

The growth of a political voice was sparked by events in a prison in County Down. The hunger strikes in Northern Ireland caused 1981 to be a tumultuous year for the Irish worldwide. The strikes radicalized opinion in the North, with support for Sinn Féin growing among moderate nationalists.[16] Nationalist feelings in the Republic of Ireland also experienced somewhat of a revival, with the election of two H-Block prisoners as TDs, and marches and riots taking place in Dublin. Black flags were hung across Ireland 'as Nationalist Ireland, North and South, vented its anger at Mrs Thatcher'.[17] The Irish in London, along with their American cousins, joined in this national outpouring of grief and outrage.[18] *The Irish Post* in 1981 covered the hunger strikes extensively from their beginning in March, and MacLua's political column went into overdrive. Articles appeared that were hagiographic in their praise of the 'heroic' Bobby Sands ('People will be writing about and recalling Bobby Sands for as long as there is an Irish race or while heroism continues to be revered') and Joe McDonnell, 'the bravest of them all'.[19] By July, MacLua was seemingly on the verge of outright support for the IRA, saying that Thatcher's stance may well be regarded 'as her only achievement', as the increased support for the IRA would in the long term 'almost certainly be to Ireland's benefit'.[20] MacLua's tone was generally matched by letters to the paper, although the occasional dissenting letter was published.[21] Several were written by people who were not frequent letter writers and were apparently not particularly politically active. Mrs O'Brien from Tottenham proclaimed that she would never vote Labour again because of the party's backing for Thatcher, and T. Quinn from Watford derided the hypocrisy of the British press, who, he said, would have been hailing the hunger strikers and freedom fighters had they been in a Soviet jail.[22]

Anger over the hunger strikes was evident in several interviews with people who generally had no strong political views. Stephen remembered that 'There was a tremendous feeling of pro-hunger strikes, or anti-Thatcher.'[23] Even the otherwise apolitical Brigid said that 'to this day I have this hatred of only one person on earth, that's Maggie Thatcher because of how she dealt with all that'. She proceeded to show me a twenty-fifth anniversary candle that she had bought in 2006.[24] These feelings affected the second-generation as well. As noted above, Enda saw the events as a 'modern Easter Rising'.[25] Brian Dooley, Enda's fellow south-Londoner, portrayed the hunger strikes as pivotal to his identification with Ireland: 'the weekend of my 18th birthday, Bobby Sands began his hunger strike, and I chose an Irish passport'. One of Dooley's interviewees, the London-Irish Jimmy Murphy, who was in the same IRA 'cell' as the London-born Diarmuid O'Neill when he was killed by police in 1996, cited the hunger strikes as the major motivation for his physical force republicanism.[26] *The Irish Post* for the period March to October 1981 reported an extraordinary number of meetings and demonstrations, including twenty-four-hour fasts, torchlight processions, vigils outside Westminster Cathedral and Westminster Abbey and political meetings at the London Irish Centre.[27] Some interviewees saw the long summer of 1981 as a time of great activity: Diarmuid saw it as 'the

biggest mobilisation that I ever saw in my time' and as a time when
'people did start to put their head above the parapet'. Likewise, Fr
Bobby Gilmore, of the Irish Emigrant Chaplaincy Scheme, and
Christopher, of the Connolly Association, remembered it as a time
when usually non-political people came out in protest.[28] Certainly, the
pages of the organ of the Connolly Association, the *Irish Democrat*,
show that it was a frantic period.[29] Some of these protests were specifically aimed at encouraging the Irish population. Demonstrations
were held in Kilburn, where there was fighting with police on
Sunday 26 April, along with vigils every time a hunger striker died.[30]
In this vein, the Troops Out Movement invaded the Irish Club in
Eaton Square in order to try to wake the Irish middle class from its
slumber. Diarmuid, who took part in this, saw the club's clientele as
'a load of Uncle Toms sitting there drinking and ignoring what was
happening in their own country ... and trying to keep their heads
well down and noses clean. So we thought we'd go in there and
shake them up a bit.'[31]

However, while the number of demonstrations was impressive,
none appeared to be particularly large – the greatest numbers
recorded in newspapers were about 2,000. To put this in perspective,
April 1981 saw a protest of 15,000 people against new citizenship laws
and 50,000 during the People's March for Work. In addition to this,
most of the protests were carried out by groups that were not
centred on the Irish community.[32] Unlike Bloody Sunday, the hunger
strikes only persuaded one usually non-politically active interviewee
to go on a demonstration.[33] The events of 1981 did not turn the Irish
in London into political protestors on the streets but they certainly
encouraged significant numbers to begin to express themselves
politically as Irish people in Britain. Through the summer of 1981 the
pages of *The Irish Post* came alive with letters and articles debating
whether and how the Irish in Britain should begin to organize as a
body. By June, letters began to be published complaining about the
lack of Irish representation at protests: 'I notice the demonstration [at
Finsbury Park] is sponsored by only one county association – Antrim.
Where are the rest? Where is the Federation of Irish Societies? Why
must it be Ken Livingstone, an Englishman, who speaks out?'[34]

A full-blown argument was launched about the role of the Federation of Irish Societies, with one of its estranged founder members
deriding its lack of political voice – 'What sort of Irishmen are you?'[35]
The Irish Post's editorials followed these letters, wading into the

debate: 'Every Irish community throughout the world has spoken out on the hunger strikes. The exception is the Irish community in Britain. The elected leaders of that community, the officers of the Federation of Irish Societies, have stood idly by and in doing so have gravely embarrassed our community.'[36]

By August, the continued wrangling over the role of the Federation was joined by suggestions for a new organization for the Irish in Britain.[37] The *Irish Democrat* picked up on this feeling among the Irish and began to call on MacLua to form a group, in spite of the Connolly Association's usual stance that it was the only necessary group for the Irish in Britain. In August, under the headline, 'TIME FOR THE IRISH IN BRITAIN TO SPEAK WITH ONE VOICE', was written:

> Irish prisoners are dying one after another, as Tory politicians openly gloat ...
> What humiliation, to stand powerless and watch this happen! ...
> Whatever the measures, the Irish must be able to speak with one voice, and act as one body. Then we'll be a political force ...
> There is one man who might be able to give a lead ... Mr MacLua.[38]

While MacLua did not take the initiative himself, his paper gave support to such suggestions and continued to attack existing Irish organizations for sticking to the 'non-political and non-sectarian' line.[39] *The Irish Post* praised a proposal for 'an Irish political organisation which, while deeply concerned about the situation in Ireland, would also derive its raison d'être from the social and political needs of the Irish in Britain'.[40] This proposal eventually led to the formation of the IBRG in October along with another, shorter-lived and apparently unnamed, lobbying group formed at the Irish Club.[41]

Over the next decade, sections of the Irish community expressed themselves politically to a great extent. The IBRG was particularly significant in that it was, according to Hickman, 'very much a second-generation initiative'.[42] The group campaigned on a number of issues, were unrepentantly nationalist and, although they would claim otherwise, were firmly left-wing.[43] The IBRG represented something very different from anything that the Irish in Britain had produced before. As one can see from a selection of its demands, the group were very much the product of those who grew up as Irish within a modern urban milieu: 'Equal rights for the Irish in Britain', 'Equal rights for Irish women, lesbians, gay men and Travellers', 'An end to all racism including anti-Irish racism', 'An end to the racist PTA laws', 'Recognition for the Irish as an ethnic minority', 'Irish unity and self determination and the ending of British Imperial interference in Ireland' and 'The promotion of Irish culture and language in Britain.'[44] The group made much political noise during the 1980s, lobbying the Labour Party and Irish politicians over issues, which included delegations to Dublin that met with senior members of the main parties, and taking up specific causes such as the provision of social welfare in Islington and the provision of an Irish element to education in Britain.[45] The GLC-funded organizations all had a ethno-political edge to them. The Ireland Commission, which organized Síol Phádraig, lobbied extensively on the introduction of Irish Studies to the school curriculum, while the LIWC described itself as a 'feminist collective' and joined campaigns for the repeal of the PTA, attended trade union marches and protested over Northern Irish issues such as the treatment of republican prisoners.[46] Likewise, the Newham and District Friends of Ireland promoted Irish language classes, held dances and put on exhibitions campaigning against anti-Irish racism.[47] Irish councillors across London also began to work together on issues affecting the Irish community for the first time, in the London Irish Councillors Group from the mid-1980s.[48]

This period was one of controversy as the Irish community adjusted to its new-found political voice. Strong opinions were expressed on the IBRG in particular as it consistently tried to act as the self-appointed representative body of the community. While *The Irish Post* was generally supportive of such groups and covered their campaigns extensively, letters to the paper often railed against them as unrepresentative and too left wing. One running debate took place in the summer of 1988. One London-based former secretary of the Federation of Irish Societies attacked the IBRG:

> Its appalling behaviour and wheeling and dealing with the GLC resulted in the possibility of the Irish Commission losing its grants ... The people involved in the early days of establishing the IBRG are now gone. John Martin was pushed out, as indeed have many others who had a real feeling for the community. What is left is an organisation operated along Militant Tendency lines ... If the IBRG is attempting to establish credibility in the community ... it should abandon its role of giving the IRA cred-ibility...it should abandon its narrow political role ...[49]

The pushing out of the first-generation founder, John Martin, on ideological grounds was indicative of the divide that the IBRG embodied. Another letter writer from Manchester, who was accused of being 'anti-second-generation', specifically said that the organization had 'alienated many first-generation Irish' and accused them of despising 'people who play safe on political issues'.[50] Tensions also arose between the IBRG and the London Irish Festival when the latter continually refused the former a stand at the event throughout the 1980s. Later in the decade the Festival continued its aversion to anything remotely political by refusing the Birmingham Six campaign a presence.[51] On a smaller scale, the everyday tensions and nervousness about political issues generally was highlighted by an argument over the decision of some Gaelic footballers for the Guinness team to hold a minute's silence for Bobby Sands. Their actions led to their being banned from Guinness premises.[52]

The controversy caused by the new political voice was evident in a number of interviews, with even politically minded interviewees characterizing the IBRG as having 'departed from reasoning'.[53] David also criticized the IBRG for their uncompromising stance on many issues: 'rather than being pro-Irish they were anti-Brit'. He went on to dismiss the 'crazy notion' that Livingstone's GLC helped the Irish community, pointing out quite rightly that very few of the Irish groups set up and funded in the period remain in existence today.[54] Nevertheless, it cannot be denied that the atmosphere that pervaded in the 1980s was one in which Irish people felt they could speak out about issues. This included the Federation of Irish Societies, which began to change following the criticism that it received during 1981. Eventually, in October 1981 it was decided that the Federation should meet to discuss a policy on Northern Ireland. By November, issues such as releasing a statement on the use of plastic bullets were being discussed, in 1982 a new campaign against the PTA was launched, and eventually its constitution was changed to read 'non-*party-political*'.[55] In a stunning turnaround from the Federation's impotence during the hunger strikes, by 1987 its chairman was urging Irish organizations to 'break away from the misguided assumption, which has existed for far too long, that the Irish should not be politically active' and delegations were sent to Dublin to discuss action over Irish prisoners in Britain.[56] Even the Council of Irish County Associations (CICA) was forced into issuing a statement about Northern Ireland in late 1981. The statement first dealt at length with how it was decided that a political statement could be made and went on to call for a united Ireland, withdrawal of British troops and the repeal of the PTA.[57]

While a great many of the Irish in London continued to be quiescent and unsure about the Irish having a political voice, the events of 1981 undoubtedly represent a turning point as groups claiming to represent the community began to speak out about a variety of issues on a regular basis. By 1983 Steve Brennan of the IBRG was hailing 1981 as a turning point:

> I think the deaths of the hunger strikers have really changed and certainly for the better Irish people's attitudes to politics, Irish people living here anyhow. I think stemming from that people were dissatisfied with the old way of representation, if it could be called such ... Generally they have ... suppressed political activity within their community. They have consistently apologised for the acts of other Irishmen and Irishwomen and have refused to take a strong stance against the acts indeed the atrocities of the British state ... We do want a British withdrawal from Irish affairs, we do want to see a united Ireland in our time ... We've deluded ourselves that we're going somewhere, we're not, we're permanent.[58]

Hearts and Minds, a perceptive booklet that accompanied a photo exhibition about London's Irish community in 1986, praised the left-wing GLC for funding a great number of Irish projects, studies and groups. A confident tone was struck in the conclusion to the booklet:

> The past ten years has seen the Irish community change from being a mainly immigrant group whose main focus was towards Ireland and the prospect of returning there to one where there is an even larger number of London born Irish, the children of emigrants.
>
> The London Irish community of today is very firmly rooted here and feels itself to be one ethnic minority among many. Today's Irish community is more confident and assertive of its rights than ever before.[59]

While the tone of *Hearts and Minds* was perhaps overly confident, the picture it painted represented the realization of an ethnic community identity that began in the dance halls, churches and GAA fields of the 1950s.

Biographies of Interviewees

These biographies are designed to provide some relevant background information to the interviewees. Two priests, Frs Tom McCabe and Bobby Gilmore, and the Irish music teacher Brendan Mulkere, who were prominent enough to be identified if any information was provided about them, agreed to be referred to by their real names. Otherwise, all names are pseudonyms.

FIRST-GENERATION

Abigail
Early life: Born in County Donegal in 1945.
Education: Left school at 16.
Emigration: She left Ireland in 1962 because of the lack of jobs at home. She has always lived in Brent in her time in London. She returned to Donegal briefly in 1971 but found that she could not settle again and so moved back to London.
Occupations: Abigail worked in the post office.
Marital status and children: Married to an Irishman whom she met in Ireland. Has children who went to Catholic schools.
Social, cultural, political or religious activities: While not involved in specifically Irish activity, Abigail has been active within the Catholic Church.

Fr Bobby Gilmore
Early life: Born in Glenamaddy, County Galway, in the 1940s.
Education: Went to secondary school as a boarder before deciding to become a Columban missionary and thus trained as a priest.
Emigration: Fr Gilmore spent much of his working life abroad but is now back in Ireland.
Occupations: After working in the Philippines, Fr Gilmore became director of the Irish Emigrant Chaplaincy, which looked out for the

well-being of the Irish in Britain, from 1979–92.

Social, cultural, political or religious activities: In the 1980s Fr Gilmore was involved in campaigning for the release of the wrongly convicted Birmingham Six as well as against the PTA.

Brenda

Early life: Born in the 1950s into a small farming, and Irish-speaking, family in Connemara, County Galway.

Education: After two years of secondary school as a boarder she returned home and attended a domestic science course, leaving at 18.

Emigration: Joined her sister in London in 1968. Brenda had a job in Galway city but the pay was poor compared to wages in London. In London she lived in Holloway (borough of Islington) and Camden before moving out to Harrow.

Occupations: Worked in an advertising agency for eleven years after emigrating and before having a child and staying at home. The over-whelming majority of the workforce was English and 'absolutely lovely'.

Marital status and children: Married an Englishman, who, to the relief of her family, was a Catholic. Brenda met him because he worked for Murphy's construction, as did one of their mutual friends. They have two children who both attended Catholic schools. Neither speak Irish.

Social, cultural, political or religious activities: When she first emigrated, Brenda's social life was overwhelmingly Irish-orientated and she spent much time in Irish dance halls. One child did Irish dancing when young.

Brendan Mulkere

Early life: Born in the 1940s in County Clare into a family with a long tradition of being teachers. His father was involved in fighting for the IRA during the War of Independence.

Education: A degree from University College Dublin.

Emigration: Moved to London in 1970 for work.

Occupations: Brendan taught in both primary and secondary schools, both Catholic and Anglican.

Social, cultural, political or religious activities: Heavily involved in the Irish community, primarily through his teaching of traditional Irish music, which he began in the early 1970s. In our period he was an important figure in the expansion of Irish music in London. He was also involved in organizing the Síol Phádraig festivals in the 1980s and in promoting an Irish dimension in school curricula through the Irish Commission.

Brigid
Early life: Born in the Donegal *Gaeltacht* in the mid-1950s, into an Irish-speaking family.
Education: Up to leaving certificate, 18.
Emigration: To London in 1972. There was no work near where she was from and so she had to move. As several of her older sisters were in London, she moved there, living in Archway (Borough of Islington).
Occupations: Worked in insurance, with mainly English people, before having children from the late 1970s.
Marital status and children: Married to a man originally from Belfast, whom she met in Ireland. She has four children, of whom only one attended a Catholic secondary school.
Social, cultural, political or religious activities: Brigid has always had Irish friends, but English ones also.

Christopher
Early life: Born in the late 1930s and lived in Bray, County Wicklow.
Education: Left school at 14.
Emigration: To London in the mid-1950s for work.
Occupations: A metal sheet worker, mainly working with English people.
Marital status and children: Unmarried and no children.
Social, cultural, political or religious activities: Christopher joined the Connolly Association in 1958 and has been a member ever since. In our period he was heavily involved in demonstrating for civil rights in Northern Ireland and against the PTA in Britain.

Ciara
Early life: Born in rural south-east Ireland in the 1950s.
Education: Left education at 15.
Emigration: Left in 1971 after marrying and having nowhere to live.
Occupations: Initially stayed at home to look after her children, then went back into education in the late 1970s before entering office work. Later in life she studied more and now works with young people.
Marital status and children: Married to John (below) and has two children, who went to Catholic schools.
Social, cultural, political or religious activities: In her early years in

London she was very much in the Irish social scene but not involved in activities. In the 1990s she became involved with her county association.

Con
Early life: Born in the 1940s, brought up in Dublin city.
Education: Left school at 14.
Emigration: Left at 16 for work in London. Moved to a town near London in the late 1960s.
Occupations: Plasterer.
Marital status and children: Married to an Irish woman whom he met in a dance hall in London. His children did not go to a Catholic school and neither he nor his wife is a practising Catholic.
Social, cultural, political or religious activities: Con was an active physical force republican who spent a decade in jail in England from the mid-1970s for a failed robbery attempt designed to procure funds for the IRA. He was on hunger strike at the same time as Frank Stagg, who eventually died. Since release he has not been politically active but is still involved in cultural activities.

Danny
Early life: Born on the Falls Road, Belfast, in 1934 into a working-class family.
Education: Left school at 14.
Emigration: Danny left for London at the age of 21, more out of a sense of adventure than need for work as he had been working in the shipyards in Belfast. In London he initially lived in Camden before moving out to Barnet in the 1960s. In the 1990s he and his wife moved back to Northern Ireland.
Occupations: Worked with telecommunications companies for most of his career, mainly with English people.
Marital status and children: Married to Victoria (below). They met in London when lodging with her family.
Social, cultural, political or religious activities: While never involved in cultural or political activity, Danny's social circles were always '100 per cent Irish'.

David
Early life: Born in the late 1930s.
Emigration: Left for London in 1957 before moving slightly outside

London in the 1960s.

Marital status and children: Married to an Irishwoman. They met in London. Has children who were involved in Irish activities when young.

Social, cultural, political or religious activities: David was initially prominent in the GAA before becoming involved in the Federation of Irish Societies.

Declan

Early life: Born in a small town in County Longford, in 1944. His family owned a small shop.

Education: Left school permanently by 12 years of age and had only attended intermittently prior to that. However, in the early 1970s he studied at university.

Emigration: Left with his family in 1959 due to the collapse of their shop business.

Occupations: Initially he worked with his father as a labourer. However, through the 1960s he earned a living by illustrating, mainly for left-wing publications, and in the 1970s he was a student, writer, illustrator and artist.

Marital status and children: Has children. They did not attend Catholic schools due to his atheism.

Social, cultural, political or religious activities: Was involved in left-wing politics, but not attached to any group. Declan was part of the growth in Irish studies, leading adult classes on Irish history.

Diarmuid

Early life: Born in the 1950s and lived in Newcastle, Northern Ireland.

Education: He gained bachelor's and master's degrees at Queen's University Belfast before moving to London in 1977 to do a PhD in Engineering at Imperial College. He lived in Brixton for several years after moving to London.

Occupations: Teacher, lecturer.

Marital status and children: Married to an English woman, has children who did not attend Catholic schools.

Social, cultural, political or religious activities: Diarmuid joined the Troops Out Movement soon after arriving in London and was heavily involved in campaigning about Northern Ireland, the PTA and other issues. In 1980 he joined the Labour Party due to the formation of the Labour Committee on Ireland, a fringe group that in 1981 played a large role in influencing the party to make Irish unification by consent its policy. Socially, Diarmuid was entirely removed from the working-class, north-west London Irish community.

Elizabeth
Early life: Born c. 1940s. Brought up in County Meath, the daughter of a solicitor.
Education: A degree in law from UCD.
Emigration: Went to America with her husband in the 1960s and came to England in the 1970s. Has always lived outside London.
Occupations: Worked as a solicitor.
Marital status and children: Married to an Irishman whom she met in Ireland. She sent her children to Catholic schools – one to a boarding school in Ireland.
Social, cultural, political or religious activities: She was a member of the NUI Club in London and chairwoman of the Irish Club, Eaton Square, in the 1980s.

Eoin
Early life: Born c. 1940s and brought up in Ardoyne, Belfast.
Education: A qualified chemist.
Emigration: Came to London to study in the late 1950s, returned to Northern Ireland for a while but could not find suitable work, partly due to his nationalist views, and returned to England. He has lived near Portsmouth since the 1960s but has been involved in Irish activity in London.
Occupations: Chemist.
Marital status and children: Married to an Irishwoman whom he met in England. His children attended Catholic schools, although he is only a 'cultural Catholic'.
Social, cultural, political or religious activities: Involved in a variety of Irish activities in his life in England, including the Irish Literary Society.

Evelyn
Early life: Born c. late 1930s in Dublin. Brought up in Omagh, Northern Ireland. Her father was a dentist and her mother had a degree from UCD.
Education: Educated at a convent school and trained as a classical pianist.
Emigration: Left for London in the mid-1950s in order to take up a

scholarship for her piano playing.

Occupations: Musician.

Marital status and children: Married to an Irishman whom she met at the Irish Club and has children who attended Catholic schools.

Social, cultural, political or religious activities: She was part of the middle-class Irish scene, socializing at the Irish Club and being a member of the Irish Literary Society. She is a practising Catholic.

Jack

Early life: Born c. 1950s and brought up in County Armagh, Northern Ireland.

Emigration: Jack came to London in the 1980s with his band.

Marital status and children: Married a second-generation Irish woman (Catherine, see above).

Social, cultural, political or religious activities: Jack has been involved in the Irish country and western music scene and an Irish golf society.

Joanna

Early life: Born in County Monaghan, in the late 1940s, into a family that owned a shop.

Emigration: Left Ireland for work in 1964 and went to London to live with her sister. Has lived in north-west London since.

Occupations: Housewife.

Marital status and children: Married to an Irishman whom she met in London. Has children who went to Catholic schools. She made a conscious effort to pass on a sense of Irishness to them.

John

Early life: Born in the early 1950s in a small town in south-east Ireland.

Emigration: Left for London in 1971 in order to get work to support his pregnant wife. While he had been working in Ireland, the job was unstable and not well paid.

Occupations: Worked as a labourer with Murphy's and other Irish building contractors.

Marital status and children: Married to Ciara (see above) with children, who attended Catholic schools.

Social, cultural, political or religious activities: No specific activity but social life very much in the Irish community.

Nora
Early life: Was born in Dublin in 1935 into a family that owned a small shop.
Emigration: Nora left Ireland in 1959 for work and joined her sister and friend in London.
Occupations: Worked in telecommunications, as a dinner lady and in a dry-cleaners.
Marital status and children: Married to an Irishman. They met in London. Has children who went to Catholic schools.

Oliver
Early life: Born in the 1930s, brought up in County Cork in a poor rural family.
Education: Boarding school run by the Christian Brothers until the age of 18.
Emigration: Left in 1953 to go to Oxford because he could not find any job better than a porter in Ireland. He feels that his time in England has been characterized by racial discrimination from English people.
Occupations: Psychiatric nurse.
Marital status and children: He was married to an Englishwoman. His children did not attend Catholic schools because he is not a practising Catholic.
Social, cultural, political or religious activities: Since retiring he has completed a degree in Irish history.

Paul
Early life: Lived in rural Fermanagh, born in the early 1950s.
Education: Up to 18.
Emigration: Left for London when 21 due to inability to get a job in Northern Ireland. Lived in north-west London since.
Occupations: A building worker.
Marital status and children: Has children, who went to Catholic schools and who were taken to Irish dancing and music lessons.
Social, cultural, political or religious activities: Heavily involved in a Gaelic football club in his earlier years and playing traditional music up to the present day.

Peter
Early life: Born into a small farming family in Leitrim in 1933.
Education: Left school at 14.

Emigration: Peter left Ireland relatively late, initially migrating to London in 1956 only to do a tailoring course in order to set up his own business back home. He ended up staying and has lived in Cricklewood since the mid-1960s.

Occupations: A tailor and teacher of tailoring at a college.

Marital status and children: Married to an Irishwoman, a nurse, whom he met in London. His children all went to Catholic schools and have been very involved in Irish activities. Father of Orla (see below).

Social, cultural, political or religious activities: Peter has been a prominent figure on the London GAA scene for decades and was on the Provincial Board which covers the whole of Britain. He has also been involved with his county association. In the 1960s he was an active member, indeed one-time leader of his *cumann* (association), of Sinn Féin in London. He fell away from this when he started a family. He is a practising Catholic.

Robert

Early life: Born in a small town in County Kerry, in the mid-1940s. He was a younger child in a large and poor family.

Education: After leaving school at 15 he attended catering college for two years.

Emigration: With no work available locally, he 'hit the gravy for London' at the age of 19. Lived in Kilburn before moving further out, although still within Brent, in the late 1960s.

Occupations: He initially worked with the 'Green Murphy's' construction company as a labourer and later set out on his own as a general builder.

Marital status and children: Married to a second-generation Irish woman from London. Has one child, who went to a Catholic school.

Social, cultural, political or religious activities: Robert has been a very prominent figure in the London Irish scene for decades, being involved in his county association and London Gaelic football.

Rose

Early life: Born in the 1930s, brought up in a fishing village in County Wexford.

Education: Left school at 15.

Emigration: Left Dublin with her husband in the mid-1950s for London when there was a bar workers strike that he could not afford to be involved in.

Occupations: Rose ran a pub with her husband before having children.
Marital status and children: Has children who attended a Catholic
school.
Social, cultural, political or religious activities: She is a practising
Catholic. Has been involved in *céilí* dancing for many years.

Stephen
Early life: Born into a farming family in County Derry, in the 1940s.
Education: A degree and teaching qualification from QUB.
Emigration: After teaching for three years near Belfast he left for
London in 1968/69. He left because he got 'pissed off' with Northern
Ireland at this time. He has lived in the Borough of Harrow since.
Occupations: A teacher in a Catholic school in west London.
Marital status and children: Married to an Irish nurse from Galway
whom he met in London and has children who attended Catholic
schools.
Social, cultural, political or religious activities: Was involved in Gaelic
football when younger and has many Irish friends. However, his
profession provided him with a mixed social circle.

Fr Terence
Early life: Born in 1949 into a relatively well-off farming family in
County Limerick.
Education: Secondary and seminary education.
Emigration: He left Ireland in 1973 to be a priest in Kentish Town,
where he remained for the rest of the 1970s.

Fr Tom McCabe
Early life: Born in County Cavan in the late 1940s.
Education: Secondary and seminary education, ending with ordination
to the Oblate order.
Emigration: He first spent a summer at the London Irish Centre, Camden, in the summer of 1968 or 1969. He then worked as a chaplain
there for two years from 1971 and, after leaving, returned most
summers up until 1981 to cover for chaplains on holiday.

Timothy
Early life: Born in County Galway in the late 1940s, into a small farming
republican family.
Education: Only primary.

Emigration: He first moved to Liverpool in 1966 before spending some time in America and finally settling in London in late 1967.
Occupations: In the building trade.
Marital status and children: Married to an Irishwoman whom he met in London. No children.
Social, cultural, political or religious activities: Timothy was involved in the British-based wing of Official Sinn Féin, Clann na hÉireann, until the group was eclipsed by the Provisionals by the mid-1970s. He has been very involved in a hurling club and prominent within London GAA.

Ultan
Early life: Born in 1939 and lived in Portlaoise, County Laois. He was brought up in a staunchly republican family.
Education: Leaving Certificate.
Emigration: Left for London in 1957 with two friends, seemingly more for adventure than necessity. Lived in west London since.
Occupations: Company accountant for most of his working life. He was also a Labour councillor for many years.
Social, cultural, political or religious activities: Ultan was a founding member of the CDU in 1965. He campaigned heavily for civil rights in Northern Ireland in this period and after the CDU faded away he continued to battle from within the Labour Party for a policy more conducive to a united Ireland.

SECOND-GENERATION

Anne
Early life: Born in the 1960s and brought up in north-west London. Brought up within the Irish community and had an almost exclusively Irish social circle growing up.
Parents: Both Irish-born Catholics, although mother had lived in England from the age of 8.
Schooling: Catholic.
Social, cultural, political or religious activities: *Céilí* dancing for a number of years. Anne is still a practising Catholic and sent her children to Catholic schools.
Marriage: Second-generation Irish man, whom she met at school.
Current description of national identity: 'I think it changes as you get older. Probably now I'm half and half ... So yeah it fluctuates, at the moment it's more of the Irish.'

Catherine
Early life: Born in the late 1950s and brought up in north-west London. Catherine was brought up within the Irish community and had an almost exclusively Irish social circle growing up.
Parents: Both Irish-born Catholics.
Schooling: Catholic.
Social, cultural, political or religious activities: Catherine is still very much within an Irish social scene. She is still a practising Catholic and sent her children to Catholic schools.
Marriage: First-generation Irish (Jack, above), whom she met in an Irish pub.
Current description of national identity: 'My parents are Irish but I was born here.'

Enda
Early life: Born in the late 1950s and brought up in south London. Enda was brought up within an Irish social scene.
Parents: Father an Irish-born Catholic, mother English/third-generation Irish on one side.
Schooling: Catholic, south London.
Social, cultural, political or religious activities: Has played Irish ballads and released some records since his teenage years. He is no longer a practising Catholic.
Marriage: Was married to a first-generation Irish woman, whom he met in an Irish dance hall.
Current description of national identity: 'I'm a Londoner of Irish background, I'm not Irish in the same sense as somebody who comes from Ireland, and neither would I want to be, I am who I am.'

Gerry
Early life: Born in the late 1950s and brought up in north-west London. Brought up in Kilburn within Irish community.
Parents: Both Irish-born Catholics.
Schooling: Catholic, north London.
Social, cultural, political or religious activities: No explicitly Irish activity. Gerry is a practising Catholic and teacher at a Catholic school. His children did not attend Catholic schools due to them not living in a catchment area.
Marriage: To a British woman, whom he met at university.
Current description of national identity: 'Well it's a very difficult

thing. If you take the argument that you have multiple identities, which is probably where I am. The strongest identity would be Irish ... I don't particularly describe myself as British. I mean I carry an Irish passport and if I'm filling in forms I put Irish. But I also see myself as European.'

Joe
Early life: Born in the 1950s and brought up in north-west London.
Parents: Mother an Irish-born Catholic, father an English Protestant (although he later converted)
Schooling: Catholic, north-west London.
Social, cultural, political or religious activities: None.
Marriage: First-generation Irish woman, whom he met at a relative's wedding. Joe is a practising Catholic. His children attended Catholic schools.
Current description of national identity: When asked about sports matches – 'I probably tend to be more up for Ireland to win. Really I sit on the fence you know. At the moment it's more of the Irish.'

Kimberley
Early life: Born in the 1960s and brought up in west London.
Parents: Father a Catholic from the Republic, mother a Protestant from Northern Ireland
Schooling: Non-Catholic.
Social, cultural, political or religious activities: None, never a practising Catholic.
Marriage: Was married to an English man.
Current description of national identity: 'English'.

Fr Liam
Early life: Born in the 1950s and brought up in north-west London.
Parents: Both Irish-born Catholics.
Schooling: Non-Catholic.
Social, cultural, political or religious activities: Nothing explicitly cultural as a child but has always been interested in Irish culture and enjoys Irish music. Liam is a Catholic priest in a London parish.
Current description of national identity: 'European, Irish yes ... I'd say I'm not English ... I could be British, it's not something I'd dismiss because it's more inclusive and it's an amalgam of different cultures and histories, English is more specific.'

Michael
Early life: Born in the 1960s and brought up in west London within an Irish social scene.
Parents: Father Irish-born Catholic, mother a second-generation Irish Catholic (both parents).
Schooling: Catholic.
Social, cultural, political or religious activities: Played Gaelic football as a child. He is currently active in Irish cultural activities in London. No longer a practising Catholic.

Orla
Early life: Born in the 1960s and brought up in north-west London with parents who were heavily involved in the Irish community. Daughter of Peter (see above).
Parents: Both Irish-born Catholics.
Schooling: Catholic, north-west London.
Social, cultural, political or religious activities: Has always been very involved in Gaelic football. Also had lessons in Irish dancing and music as a child. She is a practising Catholic and her children attended Catholic schools.
Marriage: Second-generation Irish, whom she met at school.
Current description of national identity: 'I would see myself culturally as being Irish because that's what I do – I play Gaelic football, I'm involved in Gaelic football, it's such an integral part of my life. But I don't know that I'm accepted by the Irish ... Any team that came over and played [Gaelic football] at Ruislip I would be on the London side ... Could we have it as an extra county of Ireland?'

Patrick
Early life: Born in the early 1950s, he was brought up in north-west London.
Parents: Both Irish-born Catholics.
Schooling: Catholic, north London.
Social, cultural, political or religious activities: Nothing explicitly cultural as a child. Was a founding member of the Republic of Ireland Soccer Supporters Club in London in the 1980s and travels to games regularly. He is a practising Catholic and his daughter attended Catholic schools.
Marriage: First-generation Irish woman, whom he met through work.
Current description of national identity: 'I don't use London-Irish, I don't use anything, I just use Irish.'

Rory
Early life: Born in the early 1970s, he was brought up in north-west London in an exclusively Irish and Catholic social circle.
Parents: Both Irish-born Catholics.
Schooling: Catholic, north-west London.
Social, cultural, political or religious activities: Nothing cultural as a child but has always followed Irish sports and is a member of the Republic of Ireland Soccer Supporters Club in London. He is also heavily involved in his local Catholic church and other Catholic organizations and teaches at a Catholic school.
Marriage: Second-generation Irish woman, whom he met through a Catholic organization.
Current description of national identity: 'Well I'm Irish. There's no second-generation, third-generation about it, I'm Irish ... I'm very much London-Irish.'

Other
George
Note – I interviewed George having understood that his mother was first-generation Irish. In fact, she turned out to be second-generation Irish. Nevertheless, he offered an interesting insight as an English-identifying person living in the very Irish area of Kilburn and so has been included.
Early life: Lived in Kilburn. Baptized a Catholic but never practised.
Parents: English father, second-generation Irish (both parents) mother who identifies as English.
Schooling: Non-Catholic.
Identity: English, he has never been interested in his part-Irish background.

Notes

INTRODUCTION

1. http://www.irishtimes.com/blogs/generationemigration/ (accessed 3 April 2012).
2. It is worth noting that it is not an aim of this work to enter into theoretical debates over terminology, such as whether the Irish can truly be said to constitute an 'ethnic minority', whether 'diaspora' is an appropriate phrase or whether one should refrain from using the suffixes of '(im/e)migrant' – such terms when used are not intentionally loaded.
3. On the Irish in Britain during the nineteenth and early twentieth centuries, see Donald M. MacRaild, *The Irish Diaspora in Britain, 1750–1939* (Basingstoke: Palgrave Macmillan, 2011), pp.110–40 on politics, pp.161–88 on anti-Irishness; Lynn Hollen Lees, *Exiles of Erin: Irish Migrants in Victorian London* (Manchester: Manchester University Press, 1979); Stephen Fielding, *Class and Ethnicity: Irish Catholics in England, 1880–1939* (Buckingham: Open University Press, 1993); Roger Swift and Sheridan Gilley (eds), *The Irish in Victorian Britain: The Local Dimension* (Dublin: Four Courts Press, 1999). For a helpful overview of the historiography, see Roger Swift, 'The Historiography of the Irish in Nineteenth-Century Britain', in Patrick O'Sullivan (ed.), *The Irish Worldwide: History, Heritage and Identity*, vol. 2, *The Irish in the New Communities* (Leicester: Leicester University Press, 1997), pp.52–81.
4. David Fitzpatrick, 'A Curious Middle Place: The Irish in Britain, 1871–1921', in Sheridan Gilley and Roger Swift (eds), *The Irish in Britain, 1815–1939* (Savage, MD: Barnes & Noble, 1989), pp.10–59; Lees, *Exiles of Erin*; Fielding, *Class and Ethnicity*; John Belchem, 'Class, Creed and Country: The Irish Middle Class in Victorian Liverpool', in Swift and Gilley, *Irish in Victorian Britain*, pp.190–211.
5. MacRaild, *Irish Diaspora*, pp.161–88, provides a useful summary of the debate over anti-Irishness.
6. Lees, *Exiles of Erin*; Belchem, 'Class, Creed and Country'.

7. On racism, see Mary J. Hickman and Bronwen Walter, *Discrimination and the Irish Community in Britain: A Report of Research Undertaken for the Commission for Racial Equality* (London: CRE, 1997). On racism and identities, see Louise Ryan, 'Who Do You Think You Are? Irish Nurses Encountering Ethnicity and Constructing Identity in Britain', *Ethnic and Racial Studies*, 30, 3 (2007), pp.416–38. A good article on health and identity is James J. Walsh and Fergus P. McGrath, 'Identity, Coping Style, and Health Behaviour Among First Generation Irish Immigrants in England', *Psychology and Health*, 15 (2000), pp.467–82. Among several studies of second-generation identity construction and expression, a recent and comprehensive example is Sean Campbell, *Irish Blood, English Heart: Second-Generation Irish Musicians in England* (Cork: Cork University Press, 2011).

8. Enda Delaney, *The Irish in Post-War Britain* (Oxford: Oxford University Press, 2007).

9. James Moran, *Irish Birmingham: A History* (Liverpool: Liverpool University Press, 2010); Brendan McGowan, *Taking the Boat: The Irish in Leeds, 1931–81* (Killala: self-published, 2009).

10. Quote from Delaney, *Irish in Post-War Britain*, p.125.

11. See Appendix for biographies of interviewees.

12. On this, see Trevor Lummis, *Listening to History: The Authenticity of Oral Evidence* (London: Hutchinson Education, 1987), pp.117–31; Alan Baddely, 'The Psychology of Remembering and Forgetting', in Thomas Butler (ed.), *Memory, History, Culture and the Mind* (Oxford: Blackwell, 1989), pp.33–60; Mark Roseman, 'Surviving Memory: Truth and Memory in Holocaust Testimony', *Journal of Holocaust Education*, 8, 1 (1999), pp.1–20.

13. Catherine Dunne, *An Unconsidered People: The Irish in London* (Dublin: New Island, 2003); Anne Holohan (ed.), *Working Lives: The Irish in Britain* (London: The Irish Post, 1995); Mary Lennon, Marie McAdam and Joanne O'Brien (eds), *Across the Water: Irish Women's Lives in Britain* (London: Virago, 1988); Rita Wall (ed.), *Leading Lives: Irish Women in Britain* (Dublin: Attic,1991); Pam Schweitzer (ed.), *Across the Irish Sea: An Age Exchange Publication Based on Memories of London Irish Pensioners* (London: Age Exchange, 1989).

14. Donall MacAmhlaigh, *An Irish Navvy: The Diary of an Exile*, translated from the Irish language original by Valentin Iremonger (London: Routledge & Kegan Paul, 1964).

15. Anna May Mangan, *Me and Mine: A Warm-Hearted Memoir of a London Irish Family* (London: Virago, 2011); John Walsh, *The Falling Angels: An Irish Romance* (London: Flamingo, 1999).
16. MacRaild, *Irish Diaspora*, p.6.
17. Alvin Jackson, *Ireland 1798–1998* (Oxford: Blackwell, 1999), pp.69, 83.
18. MacRaild, *Irish Diaspora*, p.12.
19. Ibid., p.30.
20. Enda Delaney, ' "Almost a Class of Helots in an Alien Land": The British State and Irish Immigration, 1921–45', *Immigrants & Minorities*, 18, 2–3 (1999), pp. 241.
21. Fielding, *Class and Ethnicity*, p.27; Lees, *Exiles of Erin*, p.47; Fitzpatrick, 'Curious Middle Place', p.13.
22. Delaney, ' "Almost a Class of Helots" ', p.241.
23. Enda Delaney, *Demography, State and Society: Irish Migration to Britain, 1921–1971* (Liverpool: Liverpool University Press, 2000), pp.162, 231.
24. Michael P. Hornsby-Smith and Angela Dale, 'The Assimilation of Irish Immigrants in England', *British Journal of Sociology*, 39, 4 (1988), p.523.
25. 'Republic of Ireland-born' is used for ease to describe the twenty-six counties of Ireland not part of the United Kingdom – it is recognized that most would in fact have been born in pre-independence 'Ireland', the post-independence 'Irish Free State', or the 1937–49 state of Ireland/Éire.
26. Hornsby-Smith and Dale, 'Assimilation of Irish Immigrants', p.523.
27. P.J. Drudy, 'Migration Between Ireland and Britain Since Independence', in P.J. Drudy (ed.), *Irish Studies 5: Ireland and Britain Since 1922* (Cambridge: Cambridge University Press, 1986), p.116.
28. Note on terminology – 'Irish-born' refers to the entire island of Ireland.
29. The Small Area Statistics (hereafter SAS) for Great Britain, 1971, accessed at http://casweb.mimas.ac.uk/. In 1971, unlike 1981, the SAS contradict the main census figures for London, with the latter giving a few thousand more residents. Where possible the SAS have been used, as they were used in official London reports. Unfortunately, the SAS figures aggregate NI-born figures with 'other', such as Isle of Man and Channel Isles, and so the main census figure has been used for the NI-born. The Birmingham

figure is that recorded under the SAS for 1971 and does not take account of the 1974 restructuring of boundaries. The total for Warwickshire was 70,000.

30. This was roughly the ratio across Britain. Hickman, *Discrimination*, p.20.
31. *Census 1971, England and Wales County Report, Greater London*, vol. i (London, 1973), p.58.
32. For the relative proportions of populations emigrating and total population figures, see *Northern Ireland Census of Population 1961: General Report* (Belfast: HMSO, 1964), p.1; *Census Ireland, 1951* (Dublin, 1952), pp.1–2; *Census Ireland, 1956* (Dublin, 1957), pp.1–2.
33. McGowan, *Taking the Boat*, p.64.
34. Bronwen Walter, *Irish Women in London* (London: London Strategic Policy Unit, 1988), p.9; Bronwen Walter, *Outsiders Inside: Whiteness, Place and Irish Women* (London: Routledge, 2001), p.15.
35. Brendan Caulfield and Ashok Bhat, 'The Irish in Britain: Inter-marriage and Fertility Levels, 1971–6', *New Community*, 9, 1 (1981), p.73; *Census 1971 ... Greater London*, volume 1, p.58.
36. Pauric Travers, ' "There Was Nothing For Me There": Irish Female Emigration, 1922–71', in Patrick O'Sullivan (ed.), *The Irish World-wide: History, Heritage, Identity*, vol. 4, *Irish Women and Irish Migration* (Leicester: Leicester University Press, 1995), p.149.
37. Delaney, *Irish in Post-War Britain*, pp.32–3.
38. Hickman and Walter, *Discrimination*, p.256.
39. *Census NI 1971*, pp.31–2.
40. Walter, *Irish Women in London*, p.24.
41. John A. Jackson, 'The Irish in Britain', in Drudy (ed.), *Irish Studies 5: Ireland and Britain since 1922*, p.130.
42. Liam Ryan, 'Irish Emigration to Britain Since World War II', in R. Kearney (ed.), *Migrations: The Irish at Home and Abroad* (Dublin: Wolfhound, 1990), p.57; Caulfield and Bhat, 'Irish in Britain', p.75; Walter, *Outsiders Inside*, p.180.
43. Delaney, *Irish in Post-War Britain*, p.33. On this, see also Damian F. Hannan, 'Migration Motives and Migration Differentials Among the Irish Rural Youth', *Sociologia Ruralis*, 9, 3 (1969), pp.195–219; John Jackson, *Report on the Skibbereen Social Survey* (Dublin: Human Sciences Committee, 1967), pp.56–60.
44. Ryan, 'Irish Emigration to Britain', p.61.
45. On this, see Hickman and Walter, *Discrimination*, p.39.
46. SAS, 1971.

47. SAS, 1971 and 1981. The Northern Ireland statistics are problematic.
The figures published in the 1971 country of birth tables are consistently higher than the SAS figures for all nationalities. However, in
1981 the published figures match that year's SAS. Therefore I have
used the SAS figures for 'NI etc.', which includes those born in the
Channel Islands and Isle of Man, in 1971 and 1981.
48. On social mobility, see Hickman and Walter, *Discrimination*, p.43.
49. SAS, 1971 and 1981.
50. SAS, 1971 and 1991.
51. Walter, *Outsiders Inside*, p.79.

CHAPTER ONE

1. Part of a song heard by John B. Keane on a crossing to from Ireland
to Britain. John B. Keane, *Self Portrait* (Dublin: Mercier Press, 1964),
p.37.
2. Discussed in Alan O'Day, 'Revising the Diaspora', in D. George
Boyce and Alan O'Day (eds), *The Making of Modern Irish History:
Revisionism and the Revisionist Controversy* (London: Routledge,
1996), p.198.
3. Quotation from Mangan, *Me and Mine*, p.7.
4. Marc Scully, 'Discourses of Authenticity and National Identity
among the Irish Diaspora in England' (unpublished PhD thesis,
Open University, 2010), p.143.
5. Delaney, *Irish in Post-War Britain*, pp.19–21, 26, 39; Lees, *Exile of
Erin*, p.24.
6. Delaney, *Irish in Post-War Britain*, p.10.
7. Rose, interview with the author.
8. MacAmhlaigh, *Diary*, p.21.
9. Oliver, interview with the author.
10. Philip Donnellan, *The Irishmen: An Impression of Exile* (1965).
11. Robert, interview with the author.
12. Interviewee in 'I only came over for a couple of years ...' film, BBC,
Interview with London Irish Elders, Irish Studies Centre, London
Metropolitan University (2003).
13. Quoted in Schweitzer (ed.), *Across the Irish Sea*, p.135.
14. Travers, 'There Was Nothing For Me There', p.159.
15. Robert, interview with the author.
16. Donnellan, *Irishmen*.
17. Declan, interview with the author; Sweeney quoted in Holohan
(ed.), *Working Lives*, p.2.

18. Diarmuid, Evelyn and Jack, interviews with the author.
19. Brenda, interview with the author.
20. Interviewee in 'I only came over for a couple of years ...'.
21. Stephen, interview with the author.
22. Ann Rossiter, *Ireland's Hidden Diaspora: The 'Abortion Trail' and the Making of a London-Irish Underground, 1980–2000* (London: IASC, 2009), p.59. See also McGowan, *Taking the Boat*, pp.67–70, for a number of quotations from his female interviewees who were restless to leave Ireland.
23. Quoted in Wall (ed.), *Leading Lives*, p.78.
24. Quoted in ibid., p.65.
25. Gerry Harrison, *The Scattering: A History of the London Irish Centre, 1954–2004* (London: London Irish Centre, 2004), p.104.
26. Rossiter, *Ireland's Hidden Diaspora*.
27. Quoted in Dunne, *Unconsidered People*, p.135.
28. Ibid., p.104.
29. Eoin, interview with the author.
30. Mangan, *Me and Mine*, p.5.
31. David, interview with the author.
32. The strongest statement of this is made by the collection of essays in Swift and Gilley (eds), *Irish in Victorian Britain*. David Fitzpatrick rails against a concept of Irish community in 'Curious Middle Place', pp.10–59.
33. Mary Hickman, *The Irish Community in Britain: Myth or Reality?* Irish Studies Centre Occasional Papers Series, 8 (London: University of North London Press, 1996), p.7.
34. John Hutchinson and Alan O'Day, 'The Gaelic Revival in London, 1900–22: Limits of Ethnic Identity', in Swift and Gilley, *Irish in Victorian Britain*, pp.260, 274.
35. After Benedict Anderson, *Imagined Communities: Reflections on the Origin and Spread of Nationalism* (London: Verso, 1983).
36. Danny, interview with the author.
37. Fr Terence, interview with the author.
38. In Dunne, *Unconsidered People*, pp.97–8.
39. Joe, interview with the author.
40. Stephen and Paul, interviews with author.
41. Mary Malone, 'The Health Experience of Irish People in a North West London "Community Saved" ', *Community, Work & Family*, 4, 2 (2001), pp.204, 208.
42. Walsh, *Falling Angels*, p.60.
43. Ciara, interview with the author.

44. Timothy, interview with the author.
45. Ryan, 'Who Do You Think You Are?', p.423.
46. MacAmhlaigh, *Diary*, pp.8, 125.
47. Fr Terence, interview with the author.
48. SAS, 1971.
49. Ibid.
50. Fermanagh Association Minute Book, 18 October 1957.
51. Letter dated 1 July 1984 regarding new emigrants; letter dated 7 July 1987 regarding cheque for £684.
52. *Fermanagh Association Annual Report*, 1971. See also the collection of *The Irish Counties Journal*.
53. Anne, interview with the author.
54. Fr Tom McCabe, Robert, Peter and Ciara, interviews with the author.
55. David, interview with the author.
56. Robert, interview with the author.
57. Peter, interview with the author.
58. John Kavanagh, *Irish Post*, 1 June 1974.
59. Harrison, *Scattering*, passim.
60. Ibid., pp.34, 88–9.
61. Ibid., passim; Fr McCabe, interview with the author.
62. Ciara, interview with the author.
63. For report of this boom, see *Irish Post*, 11 January 1975; interview with Breandán MacLua, editor of *The Irish Post*, in Martin Doyle (ed.), *A History of the Irish Post: The Voice of the Irish in Britain* (London: The Irish Post, 2000), pp.19, 35.
64. 'Federation's Growth Year', *Irish Post*, 30 November 1974.
65. Ibid; 'South London Irish Club on the Way', *Irish Post*, 15 February 1975; Rory, interview with author.
66. Mangan, *Me and Mine*, p.116.
67. Brenda, Stephen, Brigid, Ciara and Timothy, interviews with the author.
68. Elizabeth, Evelyn and Diarmuid, interviews with the author.
69. MacAmhlaigh, *Diary*, p.28.
70. Quoted in Dunne, *Unconsidered People*, p.70.
71. 'Damhsa an Deorai' (The Dance of the Exile), TG4, 2002.
72. Mark McGovern, 'The "Craic" Market: Irish Theme Bars and the Commodification of Irishness in Contemporary Britain', *Irish Journal of Sociology*, 11, 2 (2002), p.90.
73. Danny, interview with author (my emphasis).
74. George, interview with the author.

75. Kevin Casey, quoted in Dunne, *Unconsidered People*, pp.57–8. Fr Timothy also called them ghettos, in interview with the author.
76. Robert, interview with the author.
77. Dunne, *Unconsidered People*, p.10; John, interview with the author.
78. Delaney, *Irish in Post-War Britain*, p.169.
79. Quoted in Ultan Cowley, *The Men who Built Britain: A History of the Irish Navvy* (Dublin: Potters Yard Press, 2001), p.227.
80. Timothy, interview with the author.
81. Brigid, interview with the author.
82. Robert Mulhern, *A Very Different County* (self-published, 2011), p.46.
83. Fr Kieran O'Shea, *The Irish Emigrant Chaplaincy Scheme in Britain, 1957–82* (Naas: Irish Episcopal Commission for Emigrants, 1985), pp.37–9.
84. Fr Terence, interview with the author.
85. Ibid.
86. Fr Bobby Gilmore, interview with the author.
87. Casey was mentioned by Brenda, Fr Bobby Gilmore and Fr Terence in interviews with the author, and also by Mary Walker in Dunne, *Unconsidered People*, p.102.
88. Ibid., p.146.
89. Ibid., p.102.
90. Stephen and Kimberley, interviews with author.
91. See Appendix for this information.
92. Brenda, interview with the author.
93. Rose, interview with the author.
94. Robert, interview with the author.
95. Brenda, interview with the author.
96. Timothy, interview with the author.
97. Danny, interview with the author.
98. Peter, interview with the author.
99. Quoted in Dunne, *Unconsidered People*, p.89. A similar theme is expressed through many of the interviews in that book, as it is in Holohan (ed.), *Working Lives*.
100. 'Terry Wogan Denounces the "Ghetto Irish" ', *Irish Post*, 9 January 1971.
101. Transcript of speech by the Bishop of Killaloe at Tipperary Association dinner, 1971.
102. Letters page, *Irish Post*, 23 January 1971.
103. Brigid, interview with the author.

104. David, interview with the author. Other interviewees with mixed friendship groups included Ciara, Joanna, Declan and Nora.

105. Des Cusack of Sussex, British Library Sound Archive, London (hereafter BL Sound Archive), Millenium Memory Bank.

106. Ciara, interview with the author.

107. Danny, Victoria, Ultan, Paul, Peter, Timothy, Nora, Robert and Christopher, interviews with the author. It is acknowledged that this impression may be influenced by the sampling techniques for this project and others that have partly sought out those involved in Irish cultural activities and have used snowballing techniques. However, it also suggests that in areas with large numbers of Irish people, and in north-west London in particular, there was (and is) a strong theme of Irish social networks predominating among emigrants that has led researchers to such interviewees. For examples of Irish people outside London having fewer Irish friends, see interviews in such as Noreen Hill of Leicester in Lennon, McAdam and O'Brien (eds), *Across the Water*, pp.91–102. On the similar picture to London of the Birmingham Irish in our period, see Paul Harrison, 'Culture and Migration: The Irish English', *New Society*, 25, 272 (1973), pp.699–702.

108. Doyle, *History of The Irish Post*, p.42.

109. Diarmuid, interview with the author.

110. Caulfield and Bhat, 'Irish in Britain', p.81.

111. Walter, *Irish Women in London*, p.22.

112. In 1971 137,296 of the Republic of Ireland's population was not born in the state, which suggests a significant number of emigrants may also have been outside the twenty-six counties. Damien Courtney, 'A Quantification of Irish Migration with Particular Emphasis on the 1980s and 1990s', in Andy Bielenberg (ed.), *The Irish Diaspora* (Harlow: Pearson, 2000), p.298.

113. Reported in 'Frank Dolan', *Irish Post*, 9 February 1980.

114. Caulfield and Bhat, 'Irish in Britain', pp.81, 83.

115. Tony Beatty, *From Post to Post: A Memoir* (Dublin: Currach Press, 2006), p.89.

116. Fr McCabe, interview with the author.

117. Walsh, *Falling Angels*, pp.61–2.

118. Evelyn, interview with the author.

119. *Irish Club Bulletin*, February 1971.

120. Evelyn, interview with the author.

121. Elizabeth, interview with the author.
122. Danny, interview with the author.
123. Ciara, interview with the author.
124. Anonymous, interview with author.
125. Timothy, interview with the author.
126. David, interview with the author.
127. Brian Dooley, *Choosing the Green? Second-Generation Irish and the Cause of Ireland* (Belfast: Beyond the Pale, 2004), p.23.
128. Quoted in Holohan (ed.), *Working Lives*, p.118.
129. Eoin, interview with the author.
130. Eoin and Stephen, interviews with the author.
131. See, for example, the contrast with America, in Delaney, *Irish in Post-War Britain*, p.198; Dale B. Light, Jr, 'The Role of Irish-American Organisations in Assimilation and Community Formation', in P.J. Drudy (ed.), *Irish Studies 4: The Irish in America: Emigration, Assimilation and Impact* (Cambridge: Cambridge University Press, 1985), pp.113–41. On nineteenth-century Liverpool, see Belchem, 'Class, Creed and Country', pp.190–211; and Ryan Dye, 'Catholic Protectionism or Irish Nationalism? Religion and Politics in Liverpool, 1829–1845', *Journal of British Studies*, 40, 3 (2001), pp.357–90.
132. Harrison, 'Culture and Migration', p.702.
133. Ryan, 'Who Do You Think You Are', p.423.
134. Victoria, interview with the author.
135. Quoted in Dunne, *Unconsidered People*, p.42.
136. Declan, interview with the author. This was a common criticism of Ireland among interviewee, also being mentioned by Con and Brenda.
137. McGowan, *Taking the Boat*, p.82.
138. Victoria, interview with the author.
139. MacAmhlaigh, *Diary*, p.50.
140. Liviu Popoviciu, Chris Haywood and Máirtín Mac an Ghaill, 'Migrating Masculinities: The Irish Diaspora in Britain', *Irish Studies Review*, 14, 2 (2006), p.177.
141. Fr Bobby Gilmore, interview with the author.
142. Quoted in Dunne, *Unconsidered People*, p.191.
143. Walsh and McGrath, 'Identity', p.468; Hickman and Walter, *Discrimination*, p.59.
144. John Lydon, with Keith and Kent Zimmerman, *Rotten: No Irish, No Blacks, No Dogs* (London: Hodder & Stoughton, 1992), p.43; Ciara, interview with the author.

145. Hornsby-Smith and Dale, 'Assimilation of Irish Immigrants', p.525.
146. Gerry, interview with the author.
147. Campbell, *Irish Blood, English Heart*, p.106, references women taking a leading role in passing on culture.
148. Quoted in Dunne, *Unconsidered People*, p.83.
149. Maírtín Mac an Ghaill, 'What About the Lads? – Emigrants, Immigrants, Ethnics and Transnationals in Late 1990s Diaspora', in R. Lentin (ed.), *Emerging Irish Identities* (Dublin: Trinity College Dublin/National Consultative Committee on Racism and Interculturalism, 2000), p.44.
150. 'Is "Post" Male Oriented?', *Irish Post*, 23 January 1971.
151. London Irish Women's Centre information leaflet, 1985; Walter, *Outsiders Inside*, p.87.
152. Rossiter, *Ireland's Hidden Diaspora*, p.53 (original emphasis).
153. Ibid., p.65.
154. Quoted in Lennon, McAdam and O'Brien (eds), *Across the Water*, p.184.
155. Frank Byrne interview transcript, 2003, HISTORYtalk, Kensington, Irish Oral History Project.
156. LIWC information leaflet, 1985.
157. Diarmuid, interview with the author; interview with Noelle Egan, BL Sound Archive, Hall Carpenter Collection.
158. See Chapter 3.
159. For an example of marriage to a non-Irish spouse leading to someone having fewer Irish friends, see Mary Walker in Dunne, *Unconsidered People*, p.100–1.
160. Brenda and Peter, interviews with the author.
161. Evelyn, interview with the author. She is referencing the frequent talk in 1980s about the possibility of the need to have a British passport being introduced in Nationality Acts.
162. Victoria and Oliver, interviews with the author.
163. Diarmuid, interview with the author.
164. Maurice O'Neill interview transcript, 2003, HISTORYtalk, Kensington, Irish Oral History Project.
165. For a report on the 1916 anniversary, see *The Times*, 11 April 1966. For other incidents, see Chapter 2.
166. Danny and Robert, interviews with the author.
167. Ciara, interview with the author.
168. Fr McCabe, interview with the author.
169. This is particularly high, considering that some interviewees

were specifically sought out for their left-wing political views, and, it is suspected, they would be less likely to have stayed within the Catholic Church.

170. Evelyn, interview with the author.
171. Abigail, interview with the author.
172. Evelyn, interview with the author.
173. Stephen, interview with the author.
174. Eoin and Con, interviews with the author.
175. Declan, interview with the author.
176. Fr Kenneth McCabe, 'A Personal Sort of Column', was a regular feature before an unspecified disagreement led to his departure. For an example of an article, see *Irish Post*, 19 December 1970.
177. Eileen Pollock in Wall, *Leading Lives*, p.38. Non-Catholicism was not explicitly stated by groups such as the Irish in Britain Representation Group and the LIWC, but support for abortion, homosexual issues and radical socialism suggest that Catholicism was not a prominent characteristic.
178. Diarmuid, Christopher and Timothy, interviews with the author.
179. Patrick Kenny, of Kensington, interview transcript, 2003, HISTORYtalk, Kensington, Irish Oral History Project.
180. Brian Keaney, *Don't Hang About* (Oxford: Oxford University Press, 1985), p.95.
181. *Irish Post*, 12 February 1972.
182. 'Frank Dolan', *Irish Post*, 23 February 1974.
183. Letters page, *Irish Post*, 3 January 1981.
184. Fr Terence, interview with the author.
185. Quoted in documentary, 'The Irish in England', Irish Video Project, Channel 4, London, 1983.
186. Con, interview with the author.
187. David, interview with the author.
188. Danny, interview with the author.
189. 'Viewpoint' and 'Are You Qualified to go Home?', *Irish Post*, 13 February 1970. See similar articles ten years later, *Irish Post*, 16 February 1980.
190. Quoted in Doyle, *History of The Irish Post*, p.14.
191. Courtney, 'Quantification', p.298.
192. Enda Delaney, 'Placing Postwar Irish Migration to Britain in a Comparative European Perspective, 1945–1981', in Bielenberg, *Irish Diaspora*, pp.338, 344–5.
193. Con, interview with the author.

194. Fr Gilmore, interview with the author.
195. Rory, interview with the author.
196. Walsh, *Falling Angels*, p.217.
197. Fr Liam, interview with the author.
198. Courtney, 'Quantification', p.296.
199. Walsh and McGrath, 'Identity.'
200. Maura Murphy, *Don't Wake me at Doyle's* (London: Headline, 2004), passim; Mangan, *Me and Mine*, p.37; MacAmhlaigh, *Diary*, pp.11, 26, 62, 73–4.
201. Brendan O'Hara interview transcript, 2003, HISTORYtalk Kensington, Irish Oral History Project.
202. Declan, interview with the author.
203. Letters page, *Irish Post*, 9 January 1971. Similar sentiments expressed in interview with Gary Massey, of Kensington, 2002, HISTORYtalk, Kensington, Irish Oral History Project.
204. Oliver, interview with the author. Mary Allen, in 'Irish in England', said she is 'bitter now' but was not before.
205. J.J. Lee, *Ireland 1912–1985: Politics and Society* (Cambridge: Cambridge University Press, 1989), p.385.
206. Hickman and Walter, *Discrimination*, p.30.
207. Quoted in Dunne, *Unconsidered People*, p.43.
208. Eoin, interview with the author.
209. Ciara, interview with the author.
210. Ultan, interview with the author.
211. Brenda, interview with the author.
212. Evelyn, interview with the author.
213. Stephen, interview with the author.
214. Quoted in Dunne, *Unconsidered People*, p.178.
215. Report in unspecified newspaper, Carlow Association Scrap Book, 1983.
216. G. Gmelch, 'The Readjustment of Returned Migrants in the West of Ireland', in R. King (ed.), *Return Migration and Regional Economic Problems* (London: Routledge, 1986), pp.162–3.
217. Abigail, interview with the author.
218. David, interview with the author.
219. See Walter, *Outsiders Inside*, especially Chapter 6.
220. Brigid, interview with the author.
221. Eoin, interview with the author.
222. Norrie Fox, interview transcript, 2003, HISTORYtalk, Kensington, Irish Oral History Project.

223. Robert, interview with the author.
224. Beatty, *From Post to Post*, p.100.
225. On readership, see *Irish Post*, 14 February 1980, 29 January 1972; Beatty, *From Post to Post*, p.91.
226. Quoted in Doyle, *History of the Irish Post*, p.17.
227. *Irish Post*, 17 May 1975.
228. For an example of a feature on an Irish community, see the feature on the Bristol community, *Irish Post*, 9 November 1974.
229. 'Federation's Growth Year', *Irish Post*, 30 November 1974; 'Irishman of the Year' was a regular feature in early years, followed by the Irish Post Awards.
230. 'Irish Vote Should Be Put to Use', *Irish Post*, 13 February 1970.
231. Transcript of speech by the Bishop of Killaloe at Tipperary Association dinner, 1971.
232. Doris Daly, member of an association, in 'Irish in England'.
233. See Chapter 3 for more on this.
234. Peter, interview with the author.
235. Rose, interview with the author.
236. Paul, interview with the author.
237. See Chapter 3 for more on this.
238. David, interview with the author.
239. See Epilogue.
240. Hickman, *Irish Community in Britain*, p.6.
241. Fr Terence, interview with the author.
242. Peter, interview with the author.
243. Fr Gilmore, interview with the author.
244. David and Peter, both involved in nationwide organizations, mentioned the Irish Community in Britain in this sense, in interviews with the author.
245. Rose and Danny, interviews with author. Also mentioned by Brigid and Ciara.
246. Fielding, *Class and Ethnicity*; Hickman, *Irish Community in Britain*.
247. Diarmuid and Eoin are from Belfast, Christopher from Dublin (albeit from a town outside the city) and Ultan from a fairly large town. Timothy, from Connemara, was the only left-wing politically active person from a rural background, although Declan is from a petit bourgeois background in a small town in the midlands. Peter is also from a rural area but was inspired to join Sinn Féin through nationalism rather than Marxism in the 1960s. Con, a physical force republican, grew up in Dublin city.
248. Rory, interview with the author.

249. Gerry, interview with the author.

CHAPTER TWO

1. M.A.G. Ó Tuathaigh, 'The Irish in Nineteenth Century Britain: Problems of Integration', *Transactions of the Royal Historical Society*, 31, 1981 pp.170–3; Hutchinson and O'Day, 'Gaelic Revival', p.270.
2. Hutchinson and O'Day, 'Gaelic Revival' for information on the ISDL, p.274.
3. Lees, *Exiles of Erin*, pp.213–43.
4. John Archer Jackson, *The Irish in Britain* (London: Routledge & Paul, 1963), p.122.
5. Michael Herbert, *The Wearing of the Green: A Political History of the Irish in Manchester* (London: Irish in Britain Representation Group, 2001), p.155.
6. Danny, interview with the author.
7. Ultan, interview with the author.
8. 'Frank Dolan', *Irish Post*, 5 May, 1979.
9. Rory, interview with the author.
10. Delaney, *Irish in Post-War Britain*, p.192.
11. Kevin O'Connor, *The Irish in Britain* (Dublin: Gill & MacMillan, 1972).
12. Ultan, interview with the author.
13. 'Irish in England'.
14. Peter, Timothy, interviews with the author.
15. Ultan, interview with the author.
16. Christopher, interview with the author.
17. Simon Prince, *Northern Ireland's '68: Civil Rights, Global Revolt and the Origins of the Troubles* (Dublin: Irish Academic Press, 2007), pp.87–99.
18. Connolly Association, What is the Connolly Association? Constitution and Explanation (n.d. [1972]), pp 1, 7–10; Prince, *Northern Ireland's '68*, pp.87–99.
19. Bob Purdie, *Politics in the Streets: The Origins of the Civil Rights Movement in Northern Ireland* (Belfast: Blackstaff Press, 1990), pp.108–9.
20. Ibid., p.103.
21. Timothy, interview with the author.
22. *The Irish Post*, 30 January 1971, carried a double-page spread detailing all the Irish political organizations in Britain.
23. Fermanagh Association Minute Book, 21 November 1967 and 23 January 1969, for sending of delegates to meetings.

24. Christopher, interview with the author.

25. Jackson, *Irish in Britain*, p.125.

26. Purdie, *Politics in the Streets*, p.119.

27. Ibid., p.120.

28. *Irish Times*, 21 October 1968.

29. *Irish Times*, 3 January 1969.

30. *The Times*, 21 October and 28 October 1968.

31. Peter, interview with the author.

32. For information on Gerry Lawless and Brendan Clifford, see http://www.irishtimes.com/ newspaper/obituaries/2012/0128/1224 310862555.html (accessed 28 March 2012).

33. Constitutions of several county associations available at Irish in Britain Archive, London Metropolitan University. Pointedly, the Fermanagh Association was 'free to support any cause deemed worthy' by its members.

34. Eoin and Elizabeth, interviews with the author.

35. *Irish Times*, 12 July 1971.

36. *Anti-Internment News*, 4 (June 1972); Siobhán Maguire, 'The "Anti-Internment League": A Study of an Irish Political Organisation in 1970s Britain' (unpublished MA dissertation, University of North London, 1999), p.6. Note that Maguire's thesis is partly based on the oral testimony of her parents who were active members of the group.

37. Maguire, ' "Anti-Internment League" ', p.12. Ali Renwick, founder of the Troops Out Movement, also stresses the Irish-dominated nature of the AIL and the Irish Solidarity Campaign, in *Oliver's Army: A History of British Soldiers in Northern Ireland and Other Conflicts* (2004), http://www.troopsoutmovement.com/Ultansarmy chap8.htm (accessed 26 August 2009).

38. *The Times*, 1 November 1971, reported that '20,000 hear IRA men at rally'.

39. Maguire, ' "Anti-Internment League" ', pp.17–18. She says that one march started in Kilburn, but, according to a poster in the Irish in Britain Archive (AIL box) it started in Cricklewood – 'Mass Demonstration October 31! Release the internees! Withdraw the troops!'

40. *The Times*, 7 February 1972; *Anti-Internment News*, 2 (February 1972).

41. Maguire, ' "Anti-Internment League" ', pp.18–22; poster, 'Mass Demonstration October 31! Release the internees! Withdraw the troops!', Irish in Britain Archive, AIL box.

42. Ultan, Timothy and Christopher, interviews with the author.
43. Paul and Stephen, interviews with the author.
44. Fr McCabe, interview with the author.
45. *Irish Post*, 1 March 1991 (twenty-first anniversary edition, looking back).
46. *Anti-Internment News*, 2 (February 1972). They were found guilty but this was later overturned. On the ban from Trafalgar Square, see Rodney Mace, *Trafalgar Square: Emblem of Empire* (London: Lawrence and Wishart, 1976), p.231. It was lifted in 1996. See http://www.independent.   co.uk/news/bottomley-lifts-ulster-protest-ban-1326485.html (accessed 6 April 2012).
47. *Irish Post*, 26 February 1972.
48. *Irish Post*, 29 January 1972.
49. *Irish Post*, 4 March 1972.
50. Maguire, ' "Anti-Internment League" ', p.22.
51. *Irish Post*, 1 April 1973.
52. Diarmuid, interview with the author. Further evidence of its largely non-Irish membership is a letter in *The Irish Post*, 14 March 1974, from a Troops Out Movement (TOM) member saying that the membership was 'largely British' and appealing for Irish people to come to a meeting.
53. See *Irish Post*, 2 November 1974, for a picture of left-wing Labour MPs Joan Maynard and Stanley Thorne on a march with the Troops Out Movement in London.
54. Examples of groups with publications in the Irish in Britain Archive and Diarmuid's private collection are: *Big Flame*, Revolutionary Communist Group/Tendency and the IMG (International Marxist Group). For the complaints of the TOM member about lack of sustained involvement from the British Left, see *Ireland Socialist Review*, 1 (Winter, 1977–78) – a publication of Socialist Charter, Haringey TOM and Hemel Hempstead Troops Out Committee.
55. Diarmuid, interview with the author. Indeed, none of the leaders of the group which this author knows of, such as Liz Curtis, Aly Renwick and Mary Pearson, were Irish.
56. Con, interview with the author.
57. *Irish Times*, 8 June, 10 June and 11 June 1974. Connolly was later dismissed from his parish for these comments – *The Times*, 12 June 1974; *Irish Post*, 15 June 1974.
58. Timothy and Ultan, interviews with the author.

59. Robert, interview with the author.
60. According to Fr Tom McCabe. Paddy Mee was renowned for his forthright nationalist views.
61. Such as in Hickman and Walter, *Discrimination*, p.127, and Harrison, *Scattering*, p.12.
62. MacLua pointed this out in the 'Frank Dolan' column, *Irish Post*, 5 September 1981.
63. Fr Bobby Gilmore, interview with the author.
64. Robert, interview with the author.
65. Expression of support from Antrim Association for 1981 hunger strikers in *Irish Post*, 20 June 1981; Fr McCabe quote from Harrison, *Scattering*, p.134.
66. *Irish Post*, 25 May 1974.
67. Robert, Timothy and Peter, interviews with the author.
68. *Irish Post*, 19 October 1974.
69. Information in this paragraph from *Irish Post*, 6 May 1979.
70. There was apparently only marginal difference between the first- and second-generation.
71. Election figures fromhttp://www.politicsresources.net/area/uk/uktable.htm (accessed 19 August 2009).
72. Fr McCabe, interview with the author.
73. Eoin, interview with the author.
74. *Irish Post*, 8 June 1974; Camden Council website, http://www.camden.gov.uk/ccm/content/council-and democracy/whorepresents-you/the-mayor-of-camden/file-storage/bookmark-of mayors. en (accessed 15 August 2009).
75. *Labour and Ireland* newsletter, May 1980.
76. David, interview with the author.
77. Diarmuid, interview with the author.
78. Ciara, interview with the author.
79. Quoted in Lennon, McAdam and O'Brien (eds), *Across the Water*, p.65.
80. Christopher, interview with the author.
81. Walter, *Irish Women in London*, p.13.
82. Caulfield and Bhat, 'Irish in Britain', p.73.
83.Peter, interview with the author.
84.Timothy, interview with the author.
85. Hickman on the IBRG, in Doyle, *History of The Irish Post*, p.52.
86. Timothy, interview with the author.
87. Christopher, interview with the author.

88. Maguire, ' "Anti-Internment League" ', p.16.
89. David, interview with the author.
90. Fr Gilmore, interview with the author.
91. Sr Sarah Clarke, *No Faith in the System: A Search for Justice* (Dublin: Mercier Press, 1995), p.68.
92. Paul, interview with the author.
93. Delaney, *Irish in Post-War Britain*, p.194; *Irish Post*, 9 January 1971.
94. Walsh, *Falling Angels*, pp.5, 135.
95. On America, see P. J. Drudy (ed.), *Irish Studies 1:Irish in America: Emigration, Assimilation and Impact* (Cambridge: Cambridge University Press, 1985). Introduction. On sectarian Liverpool, see MacRaild, *Irish Diaspora*, pp.182–8.
96. Breda Gray, 'From "Ethnicity" to "Diaspora": 1980s Emigration and "Multicultural" London', in Bielenberg (ed.), *Irish Diaspora* (2000), p.73.
97. Danny and Victoria, interviews with the author.
98. Brigid, interview with the author.
99. The fact that the interviewer was male might have deterred some women from expressing their views on certain issues.
100. Evelyn, interview with the author.
101. Brenda, interview with the author.
102. Walter, *Outsiders Inside*, p.256.
103. See, for instance, Hutchinson and O'Day, 'Gaelic Revival'.
104. John, interview with the author.
105. Brenda, interview with the author.
106. Quoted in Dunne, *Unconsidered People*, pp.108–9.
107. Victoria and Danny, interviews with the author.
108. Evelyn, interview with the author.
109. Fermanagh Association Minute Books, 1960, 1975 and 1981.
110. Fr McCabe, interview with the author.
111. Harrison, *Scattering*, pp.101, 134; *Irish Post*, 20 June 1981. See also Cumann na Poblachta, *A Salute to Pádraig Pearse* (n.d. [late 1970s]), Political Groups folder, Irish in Britain Archive. The Antrim Association sponsored this republican pamphlet.
112. 'Frank Dolan', *Irish Post*, 23 February 1974.
113. 'Frank Dolan', *Irish Post*, 14 April 1979.
114. Peter, interview with the author.
115. Ultan, interview with the author.
116. See http://www.politicsresources.net/area/uk/uktable.htm (accessed 19 August 2009).

117. Herbert, *Wearing of the Green*, p.155.

118. Note the setting upon the fringe Labour Committee on Ireland in 1980, which campaigned for Labour to break with the bipartisan policy and push for a united Ireland, which it succeeded in getting the party to do to a limited extent in 1981.

119. Letters page, *Irish Post*, 21 April 1979.

120. Fr Terence, interview with the author.

121. Fr Liam, interview with the author; Murphy, *Don't Wake Me at Doyle's*, p.372.

122. Danny, interview with the author.

123. Gerry, interview with the author.

124. Four Irish citizens were killed in the Birmingham bombings. For Irish and Irish descent people killed and injured in the Birmingham bombings, see Moran, *Irish Birmingham*, p.197.

125. Fr Terence, interview with the author.

126. Stephen, interview with the author.

127. Declan, interview with the author.

128. Robert, interview with the author.

129. Fr McCabe, interview with the author. Noraid is an Irish-American-run fund that has frequently been accused of channelling money to the IRA.

130. M.A.G. Ó Tuathaigh, 'Irish Historical "Revisionism": State of the Art of Ideological Project?', in Ciaran Brady (ed.), *Interpreting Irish History: The Debate on Historical Revisionism* (Dublin: Irish Academic Press, 1994), p.306.

131. Brenda, interview with the author.

132. David, interview with the author.

133. Letters page, *The Times*, 26 November 1974.

134. Appeared in the documentary 'Here to Stay', BBC Midlands Report, 1994.

135. Quoted in Dunne, *Unconsidered People*, p.50.

136. Danny and Peter, interviews with the author.

137. Declan and Robert, interviews with the author.

138. Quoted in Doyle, *History of The Irish Post*, p.24.

139. 'Frank Dolan', *Irish Post*, 6 February 1971.

140. 'Frank Dolan', *Irish Post*, 5 February 1972.

141. Ibid.

142. 'Frank Dolan', *Irish Post*, 12 February 1972.

143. 'Frank Dolan', *Irish Post*, 26 February 1972.

144. Fr Gilmore, interview with the author.

145. David, interview with the author.
146. 'Frank Dolan', *Irish Post*, 12 October 1974.
147. 'Frank Dolan', *Irish Post*, 7 December 1974.
148. 'Frank Dolan', *Irish Post*, 7 April 1979.
149. 'Frank Dolan', *Irish Post*, May–October 1981.
150. Poll in 'Frank Dolan', *Irish Post*, 29 January 1972.
151. *The Times*, 12 June 1974.
152. Letters page, *Irish Post*, 12 February 1972.
153. Letters page, *Irish Post*, 8 January 1972.
154. Letters page, *Irish Post*, 7 December 1974.
155. Letters page, *Irish Post*, May–October 1981.
156. Text of Act at http://cain.ulst.ac.uk/hmso/pta1974.htm (accessed 14 August 2009).
157. Paddy Hillyard, *Suspect Community: People's Experience of the Prevention of Terrorism Act in Britain* (London: Pluto Press, 1993).
158. Ibid, p.252.
159. Hickman and Walter, *Discrimination*, pp.125–8.
160. Dooley, *Choosing the Green*, p.115.
161. Herbert, *Wearing of the Green*, p.168.
162. *Irish Post*, 7 December 1974.
163. *Irish Post*, 17 September 1973.
164. *Irish Post*, 14 February 1974.
165. For example, see *Irish Post*, 26 February 1980, 1 March 1980, 21 April 1979.
166. *Irish Democrat*, September 1981.
167. *Troops Out: Journal of the Troops Out Movement* (Summer 1976), p.8; Socialist Worker's Party Pamphlet, *The Prevention of Terrorism Act: Legalised Terror* (c. mid-1970s).
168. IBRG, Lambeth, 'Seven Aims' (c. early 1980s).
169. Report of the London Irish Women's Conference, *Our Experience of Emigration* (London Irish Women's Centre, 1984), p.15.
170. Harrison, *Scattering*, p.150.
171. Ibid., p.150.
172. Hickman and Walter, *Discrimination*, p.40.
173. Hillyard, *Suspect Community*, p.5.
174. Ibid., pp.111–20.
175. Ibid., pp.34–67; Clarke, *No Faith*, pp.54–61.
176. Robert, interview with the author.
177. David and Peter, interviews with the author.
178. Fr McCabe, interview with the author. .

179. Declan, interview with the author.
180. Fr Terence, interview with the author.
181. Enda, interview with the author.
182. Patrick, interview with the author.
183. Ultan, interview with the author.
184. Diarmuid and Christopher, interviews with the author.
185. Diarmuid, Timothy and Christopher, interviews with the author.
186. Hickman and Walter, *Discrimination*, p.211.
187. Fr Gilmore, interview with the author.
188. Christopher and Ultan, interviews with the author.
189. Christopher, interview with the author.
190. Diarmuid, interview with the author.
191. Enda, interview with the author.
192. Peter and Timothy, interviews with the author.
193. Ciara, interview with the author.
194. Stephen, interview with the author.
195. Danny, interview with the author.
196. Brigid, interview with the author.
197. Declan, interview with the author.
198. Letters page, *Irish Post*, 9 January 1988.
199. Enda, interview with the author.
200. Colin Holmes, *John Bull's Island: Immigration and British Society, 1871–1971* (Basingstoke: Palgrave Macmillan, 1988), pp.252–3; Zigg Layton-Henry, *The Politics of Immigration, 'Race' and 'Race Relations' in Post-War Britain* (Oxford: Wiley-Blackwell, 1992), pp.33–4; Delaney, *Irish in Post-War Britain*, p.3.
201. There already exists a wide and comprehensive literature on this topic: See J. Kirkaldy, 'English Newspaper Images of Northern Ireland 1968–73: An Historical Study in Stereotypes and Prejudices' (unpublished PhD thesis, University of New South Wales, 1979); Sarah Morgan, 'The Contemporary Racialization of the Irish in Britain: An Investigation of Media Representations and Everyday Experience of Being Irish in Britain' (unpublished PhD thesis, University of North London, 1997), pp.50–67; Liz Curtis, *Nothing but the Same Old Story: The Roots of Anti-Irish Racism* (London: Information on Ireland, 1984); John Darby, *Dressed to Kill: Cartoonists and the Northern Ireland Conflict* (Belfast: Appletree, 1983).
202. Hickman and Walter, *Discrimination*, p.204; David Miller, *Don't Mention the War: Northern Ireland, Propaganda and the Media* (London: Pluto Press, 1994).

203. Delaney, *Irish in Post-War Britain*, pp.2, 125.
204. *Irish Times*, 7 February 2009.
205. Curtis, *Nothing* , p.83.
206. Geoff Robertson, *Reluctant Judas: The Life and Death of the Special Branch Informer, Kenneth Lennon* (London: Temple-Smith, 1976), p.5.
207. On benefits claims made in 1976, see Campaign for Free Speech on Ireland, *The British Media and Ireland: Truth, the First Casualty* (n.d. [1979?]), p.44. The Federation of Irish Societies campaigned against this and eventually won its case with the Press Council, although the paper still refused to apologize: see 'Daily Express Found Guilty', *Irish Post*, 26 August 1977. The Junor controversy was ongoing throughout late 1984 and early 1985 and *The Irish Post* campaigned for an apology: see, for example, *Irish Post*, 9 February 1985.
208. Harrison, *Scattering*, p.218; David, interview with the author.
209. Quoted in Elizabeth Wardle, 'The Effect of the Provisional IRA bombings in England on the Irish Community of London' (unpublished MA dissertation, NUI Galway, 2007), p.53.
210. 'London Irish Offer their Counsel of Despair', *The Times*, 10 August 1971.
211. 'Age Shows Up Differences in IRA Attitudes of the Irishmen in London', *The Times*, 29 November 1974.
212. Wardle, 'Effect', p.41.
213. 'Frank Dolan', *Irish Post*, 14 December 1974.
214. 'John Junor: Current Events', *Sunday Express*, 24 May 1981.
215. Darby, *Dressed to Kill*, p.59.
216. Quoted in Wardle, 'Effect', p.155.
217. Brendan Mulkere, Ultan and Stephen, interviews with the author.
218. Peter, interview with the author.
219. Harrison, *Scattering*, p.128.
220. Peter, David, Timothy and Robert, interviews with the author.
221. Fr McCabe, interview with the author.
222. Fr Terence, interview with the author.
223. Christopher, interview with the author.
224. Evelyn, interview with the author.
225. *Irish Post*, 23 November 1974.
226. Carlow Association Minute Book 1974.
227. *Irish Post*, 1 August 1981.
228. *Irish Post*, 3 October 1981.

229. Ciara, interview with the author.
230. Michael, interview with the author.
231. Quoted in Dunne, *Unconsidered People*, p.84.
232. All quotes from interviews with the author.
233. Eoin, interview with the author.
234. David, interview with the author.
235. Declan, interview with the author.
236. Ultan, interview with the author.
237. Fr McCabe, interview with the author.
238. Evelyn, interview with the author.
239. Eoin, interview with author.
240. Moran, *Irish Birmingham*, p.199; 'Here to Stay' documentary.
241. Letters page, *Irish Post*, 14 December 1974.
242. Oliver, interview with the author.
243. *Hansard*, House of Commons Debate, 11 December 1974, vol. 883, cc.518–64.
244. *The Times*, 23 November and 26 November 1974.
245. *Irish Post*, 11 March 1972.
246. David, interview with the author.
247. For example, Lennon, McAdam and O'Brien (eds), *Across the Water*, p.10.
248. Report of the London Irish Women's Conference, *Our Experience of Emigration*, pp.9, 23.
249. Ibid., pp.9–10, 12, 29.
250. Danny, interview with the author.
251. Diarmuid, interview with the author.
252. Edmund Leach, 'The Official Irish Jokesters', *New Society*, 20, 27 (December 1979), p.vii.
253. Fr Terence, interview with the author.
254. Robert, interview with the author.
255. For example, one attacking Irish jokes in the *Irish Post*, 28 June 1974, and a reply dismissing such worries on 22 July 1978.
256. Victoria, interview with the author.
257. Ryan, 'Who Do You Think You Are?', p.426; Walter, *Outsiders Inside*, p.82.
258. David, interview with the author.
259. Evelyn, interview with the author.
260. Keane, *Self-Portrait*, p.40.
261. Healy, *Grass Arena*, pp.2–4. It is acknowledged that Healy has perhaps felt alien in most environments during his troubled life.

262. Lydon, *No Irish, No Blacks,No Dogs*, p.13.
263. John and Brigid, interviews with the author.
264. Hickman and Walter, *Discrimination*, pp.125–8.
265. David, interview with the author.
266. *Irish Post*, 7 December 1974.
267. *Irish Post*, 21 December 1974.
268. *Irish Post*, 21 November 1987.
269. A smaller, religious parade did take place every year.
270. Documentary, 'Second-Generation Experience', Irish Video Project, 1984.
271. See John Nagle, ' "Everybody is Irish on St Paddy's": Ambivalence and Alterity at London's St Patrick's Day 2002', *Identities: Global Studies in Culture and Power*, 12, 4 (2005), pp.563–83.
272. John Nagle, *Multiculturalism's Double Bind: Creating Inclusivity, Cosmopolitanism and Difference* (Farnham: Ashgate, 2009), p.71.
273. Brendan Mulkere, interview with the author.

CHAPTER THREE

1. *Irish Times*, 6 October 2010.
2. Mary J. Hickman, Sarah Morgan and Bronwen Walter, *Second-Generation Irish People in Britain: A Demographic, Socio-Economic and Health Profile* (London: Irish Studies Centre, University of North London, 2001), pp.10, 11, 67.
3. Gerry, interview with the author.
4. Rory, interview with the author.
5. Enda, interview with the author.
6. SAS, 1971.
7. Tony Murray, 'Curious Streets: Diaspora, Displacement and Transgression in Desmond Hogan's London Irish Narratives', *Irish Studies Review*, 14, 2 (2006), p.245; Campbell, *Irish Blood, English Heart*, p.107.
8. Mangan, *Me and Mine*, pp.119, 128, 132, 143.
9. Enda, interview with the author.
10. Catherine, interview with the author.
11. Walsh, *Falling Angels*, pp.65–6.
12. Ibid., p.93.
13. Catherine, interview with the author.
14. Rory, interview with the author.
15. Anne, interview with the author.
16. Gerry, Joe and Patrick, interviews with the author.

17. M.J. Hickman, *Religion, Class and Identity: The State, the Catholic Church and Education of the Irish in Britain* (Avebury: Avebury Press, 1995).
18. Patrick and Gerry, interviews with the author.
19. Stephen, interview with the author.
20. Rory, interview with the author.
21. Patrick, interview with the author.
22. Lydon, *No Blacks, No Irish, No Dogs*, p.16.
23. George, interview with the author. Note that in this section, Gerry and Patrick attended the same school but Rory, Joe and John Lydon all attended different Catholic schools, as did George's 'Irish mates' and Stephen, the teacher.
24. Beatty, *From Post to Post*, p.100.
25. Brendan Mulkere, interview with the author.
26. 'Farewell to the Seventies', *Irish Post*, 23 February 1980.
27. 'Fleadh 1977', *Irish Post*, 9 July 1977.
28. 'Terry Bowler's Irish Dancing Scene', *Irish Post*, 12 January 1980.
29. 'Farewell to the Seventies', *Irish Post*, 23 February 1980.
30. Anne, interview with the author.
31. Orla, interview with the author.
32. 'Irish in England'; see reports on the festival in the *Irish Post*, 2 July, 9 July and 23 July 1977.
33. Barry, interview with the author.
34. Mary Allen, in 'Irish in England'; letters page, *Irish Post*, 13 August 1977 (actually from an Irishman from America who was impressed on a trip to Britain).
35. 'Irish in England'.
36. Paul, interview with the author.
37. Fr McCabe, interview with the author. *Comhaltas Ceoltóirí Éireann* (Gathering of Musicians of Ireland) is the main organizing body for traditional Irish music.
38. Campbell, *Irish Blood, English Heart*, p.76.
39. Keaney, *Don't Hang About*, p.95.
40. Catherine, interview with the author.
41. Gerry, interview with the author.
42. On 'authenticism' in the second generation, see Scully, 'Discourses of Authenticity', p.313.
43. Orla, interview with the author.
44. Anne, interview with the author.
45. Michael and Enda, interviews with the author.
46. 'Proud to be Irish', *Irish Post*, 10 October 1987.

47. Rory, interview with the author.
48. Campbell, *Irish Blood, English Heart*, pp.30–1.
49. Rory, interview with the author.
50. Michael, interview with the author.
51. Catherine, interview with the author.
52. Patrick, interview with the author.
53. Mary E. Malone and John P. Dooley, ' "Dwelling in Displacement": Meanings of "Community" and Sense of Community for two Generations of Irish People Living in North-West London', *Community, Work and Family*, 9, 1 (2006). pp.11–28.
54. Gerry, interview with the author.
55. Anne, interview with the author.
56. Catherine, Anne, Patrick and Enda all mentioned it being important to pass Irishness on. Gerry said it was not.
57. Walsh, *Falling Angels*, p.245.
58. Hornsby-Smith and Dale, 'Assimilation of Irish Immigrants', p.530.
59. Ibid., p.531.
60. Keaney, *Don't Hang About*, p.25; Rory, Patrick and Gerry, interviews with the author.
61. This is not to say that there is no class identity. It is noted that the current head of the GMB union, Paul Kenny, was born of two County Galway parents and brought up in west London.
62. Galway Association Minute Book 1967.
63. David, interview with the author.
64. 'Mixed up Kids', *Irish Post*, 23 December 1970.
65. Philip Ullah, 'Second-Generation Irish Youth: Identity and Ethnicity', *New Community* 12, 2 (1985), pp.310–20.
66. Mary Hickman, 'The Irish in Britain: Racism, Incorporation and Identity', *Irish Studies Review*, 10 (Spring 1995), p.18.
67. See summary of project results at http://www.londonmet.ac.uk/research-units/iset/projects/esrc-hidden-population.cfm (accessed 23 March 2012); Mary J. Hickman, 'Census Ethnic Categories and Second-Generation Identities: A Study of the Irish in England and Wales', *Journal of Ethnic and Migration Studies*, 37, 1 (2011), pp.79–97; Bronwen Walter, Sarah Morgan, Mary J. Hickman and Joseph Bradley, 'Family Stories, Public Silence: Irish Identity Construction Amongst the Second-Generation Irish in England', *Scottish Geographical Journal*, 118, 3 (2002), pp.201–17 .
68. Sean Campbell, 'Beyond "Plastic Paddy": A Re-Examination of the Second-Generation Irish in England', *Immigrants and Minorities*, 18, 2–3 (1999), p.273.

69. 'British' being more inclusive was mentioned by Fr Liam; 'European' was mentioned by Fr Liam and Gerry, interviews with the author.
70. All quotes from Patrick, interview with the author.
71. Dooley calls this 'The Great Passport Decision', in *Choosing the Green*, p.vii.
72. Michael Holmes and David Storey, 'Who are the Boys in Green? Irish Identity and Soccer in the Republic of Ireland', in Adrian Smith and Dilwyn Porter, *Sport and National Identity in the Post-War World* (London: Routledge, 2004), p.88.
73. On 'performing' ethnicity, see Rionach Casey, 'Community, Difference and Identity: The Case of the Irish in Sheffield', *Irish Geography*, 43, 3 (2010), p.215.
74. Rory and Patrick, interviews with the author. For a study of second-generation supporters, see Marcus Free, 'Tales From the Fifth Green Field: The Psychodynamics of Migration, Masculinity and National Identity Amongst Republic of Ireland Soccer Supporters in England', *Sport in Society*, 10, 3 (2007), pp.476–94.
75. Walter, *Outsiders Inside*, p.76.
76. Pete McCarthy, *The Road to McCarthy* (London: Hodder & Stoughton, 2002), p.33–4.
77. All quotes from Rory, interview with the author.
78. Campbell, *Irish Blood, English Heart*, pp.59, 71, for references to the term by the Pogues.
79. Catherine, interview with the author.
80. Walter et al., 'Family Stories', p.211.
81. All quotes by Enda, interview with the author.
82. Scully, 'Discourses of Authenticity', p.304.
83. Quotes from Kimberley, interview with the author.
84. Michael, interview with the author.
85. Rory, interview with the author.
86. Orla, Kimberley, Anne, Evelyn and Ciara, interviews with the author.
87. Kimberley, interview with the author.
88. 'Second-Generation Experience'
89. Rory, Patrick and Fr Liam, interviews with the author.
90. Mangan, *Me and Mine*, pp.13–14, 137.
91. Gerry, interview with the author.
92. Rory, interview with the author.
93. Maude Casey, *Over the Water* (London: Women's Press, 1987), pp.17–19.

94. Walter et al., 'Family Stories'.
95. Enda, interview with the author.
96. Joe, interview with the author.
97. Ibid.
98. Gerry, interview with the author.
99. Pete McCarthy, *McCarthy's Bar* (London: Hodder & Stoughton, 2000), pp.7–8; Mangan, *Me and Mine*, p.145; Lydon, *No Irish, No Blacks, No Dogs*, p.11.
100. Marella Buckley, 'Sitting on Your Politics: The Irish Among the British and the Women Among the Irish', in Jim MacLaughlin (ed.), *Location and Dislocation in Contemporary Irish Society: Emigration and Irish Identities* (Cork: Cork University Press, 1997), pp.111–12.
101. Patrick, interview with the author.
102. 'Second-Generation Experience'.
103. Orla and Anne, interviews with the author.
104. Anne, interview with the author.
105. 'Second-Generation Experience'.
106. Walsh, *Falling Angels*, p.113.
107. Keaney, *Don't Hang About*, p.13.
108. Casey, *Over the Water*, passim.
109. Michael, interview with the author.
110. Ullah, 'Second-Generation Irish Youth', pp.313–14.
111. Casey, *Over the Water*, pp.4, 38.
112. Ullah, 'Second-Generation Irish Youth', p.310.
113. 'Second-Generation Experience'.
114. Enda, interview with the author.
115. Catherine and Gerry, interviews with the author.
116. Orla and Enda, interviews with the author.
117. Enda, Patrick and Rory, interviews with the author.
118. Patrick, interview with the author.
119. Rory, interview with the author.
120. Catherine, interview with the author.
121. Fr Liam, interview with the author.
122. For example, 'Why Am I Treated as English?', *Irish Post*, 9 January 1988.
123. Marc Scully, ' "Plastic and Proud"? Discourses of Authenticity Among the Second-Generation Irish in England', *Psychology & Society*, 2, 2 (2009), pp.124–35.
124. Orla, interview with the author.
125. Enda, interview with the author.

126. Scully, 'Discourses of Authenticity', p.241.
127. Orla, interview with the author.
128. Mulhern, *Very Different County*, pp.67–87; John Healy, *The Grass Arena: An Autobiography* (London: Faber & Faber, 1988).
129. Gray, 'Curious Ethnicities', p.215; Mary Kells, ' "I'm Myself and Nobody Else": Gender and Ethnicity Among Young Middle-Class Irish Women in London', in Patrick O'Sullivan (ed.), *The Irish Worldwide: History, Heritage, Identity*, vol. 4, *Irish Women and Irish Migration* (Leicester: Leicester University Press, 1995), p.231.
130. 'Irish in England'.
131. Kimberley, interview with the author.
132. Gerry, interview with the author.
133. Free, 'Tales', p.485.
134. 'Irish in England'.
135. Michael, interview with the author.
136. Malone and Dooley, ' "Dwelling in Displacement" ', p.13.
137. Gerry, interview with the author.
138. Rory, interview with the author.
139. Catherine, interview with the author.
140. Gerry, interview with the author.
141. Enda, interview with the author.
142. Report of the London Irish Women's Conference, *Our Experience of Emigration*, p.19.

CHAPTER FOUR

1. Gray, 'From "Ethnicity" to "Diaspora"', pp.65–6.
2. Jim MacLaughlin, 'The New Vanishing Irish: Social Characteristics of "New Wave" Emigration', in MacLaughlin, *Location and Dislocation*, p.148; Breda Gray, *Women and the Irish Diaspora* (London: Routledge, 2004), p.8.
3. 'Federation Calls for Political Action', *London-Irish News and Advertiser*, 9 May 1987.
4. Kells, ' "I'm Myself and Nobody Else" ', p.232; Gray, *Women and the Irish Diaspora*, p.108.
5. Gray, *Women and the Irish Diaspora*, p.120.
6. Jack, interview with the author.
7. L. Curtis, J. O'Keefe, J. O'Brien and C. Keatinge, *Hearts and Minds/Anam agus Íntínn: The Cultural Life of London's Irish Community* (London: London Strategic Policy Unit, 1986), p.23.
8. 'London Hosts Irish Fanfare', *Irish Post*, 6 October 1979.

9. 'London Leads', *Irish Post*, 9 March 1985.
10. 'Proud to be Irish', *Irish Post*, 10 October 1987; 'Keeping a Heritage Alive', *Irish Post*, 21 November 1987.
11. 'Proud to be Irish', *Irish Post*, 10 October 1987. On McNally, see Nagle, *Multiculturalism's Double Bind*, pp.167–8.
12. 'Shock for History Centre', *Irish Post*, 2 May 1987; *Irish Studies in Britain*, 2 (Autumn–Winter 1981); 'Terence MacSwiney Memorial Lectures 1986' (London: GLC, 1986); www.bais.ac.uk/ (accessed 3 March 2012).
13. BAIS information booklet, 1986.
14. Brent Irish Advisory Service information leaflet, July 1979.
15. London Irish Women's Centre information leaflet, 1985; *Cara Annual Report 1986/7*, p.2.
16. Richard English, *Armed Struggle: A History of the IRA* (London: Macmillan, 2003), p.44.
17. Ed Moloney, *A Secret History of the IRA* (London: Penguin, 2002), p.209.
18. Tom Collins, *The Irish Hunger Strike* (Dublin: White Island Book, 1986), p.10.
19. 'Frank Dolan', *Irish Post*, 2 May, 9 May, 18 July 1981.
20. 'Frank Dolan', *Irish Post*, 25 July 1981.
21. For example, letters page, *Irish Post*, 30 May 1981.
22. Letters page, *Irish Post*, 23 May, 6 June 1981.
23. Stephen, interview with the author.
24. Brigid, interview with the author.
25. Enda, interview with the author.
26. Dooley, *Choosing the Green*, p.129.
27. All reported in just one issue, 'H-Blocks Vigil in Downing Street', *Irish Post*, 19 September 1981.
28. Diarmuid, Fr Gilmore and Christopher, interviews with the author.
29. *Irish Democrat*, 1981.
30. *Daily Express*, 27 April 1981.
31. Diarmuid, interview with the author; *Irish Times*, 26 May 1981; *Irish Post*, 30 May 1981.
32. *Irish Times* 27 April 1981.
33. Robert, interview with the author.
34. Letters page, *Irish Post*, 20 June 1981.
35. Letters page, *Irish Post*, 27 June 1981.
36. 'H Blocks challenge to Federation', *Irish Post*, 25 July 1981.

37. Letters page, *Irish Post*, 1 August 1981.

38. *Irish Democrat*, August 1981.

39. 'Frank Dolan', *Irish Post*, 5 September 1981.

40. 'Political Role the Primary Objective', *Irish Post*, 3 October 1981.

41. 'New Political Group Formed', *Irish Post*, 21 November 1981.

42. Doyle, *History of The Irish Post*, p.52.

43. Herbert, *Wearing of the Green*, p.178.

44. IBRG information leaflet c. mid-1980s.

45. For example, 'IBRG strengthens Fianna Fail Links', *Irish Post*, 2 March 1985 for talks with Brian Lenihan; 'Second Major Educational Conference', *Irish Post*, 9 February 1985.

46. Brendan Mulkere, interview with the author; *LIWC Tenth Anniversary Report 1996*, p.1; Rossiter, *Ireland's Hidden Diaspora*, p.114.

47. *Cáirde na nGael*, information leaflet c. mid-1980s.

48. Agenda, Irish Councillors' Meeting, 1988.

49. Letters page, *Irish Post*, 11 June 1988.

50. Letters page, *Irish Post*, 4 May 1988.

51. Letters page, *Irish Post*, 28 May 1988.

52. 'Guinness Ban', *Irish Post*, 12 December 1981.

53. Enda, interview with the author. Other interviewees gave similar criticisms but did not want to be quoted.

54. David, interview with the author.

55. Harrison, *Scattering*, p.150; David, interview with the author; *Irish Post*, 21 November 1981, 5 December 1981.

56. *London-Irish News and Advertiser*, 9 May 1987; *London-Irish News*, 19 September 1987.

57. Copy of CICA Statement, November 1981.

58. 'Irish in England'.

59. *Hearts and Minds*, London Strategic Policy Unit, p.23.

Bibliography

PRIMARY SOURCES

Archival Collections
The Archive of the Irish in Britain at London Metropolitan University.
British Library Sound Archive, London:
Noelle Egan, Hall Carpenter Collection
Anton Coyle, Reg Hall (Traditional Irish Music in Britain) Collection
John Hurley, Millennium Memory Bank
Des Cusack, Millennium Memory Bank.
HISTORYtalk, Kensington:
Irish Oral History Project transcripts.
Northern Ireland Political Collection, Linenhall Library, Belfast.
Private political pamphlet collection of an interviewee, Diarmuid.

Censuses
Census 1971, Country of Birth Tables (London, 1974).
Census 1971, England and Wales County Report, Greater London (London, 1973).
Census 1981, Country of Birth Tables (London, 1983).
Census of Population of Ireland, 1951 (Central Statistics Office Dublin, 1952).
Census of Population of Ireland, 1956 (Central Statistics Office Dublin, 1957).
Northern Ireland Census of population 1961, General Report (Belfast, 1964).
Small Area Statistics for Great Britain (http://casweb.mimas.ac.uk/).

Newspapers and Periodicals
Anti-Internment News
Ireland Socialist Review
Daily Express
Irish Democrat
Irish Post

Irish Studies in Britain
Irish Times
Labour and Ireland
London-Irish News and Advertiser
Rosc Catha (the organ of *Clann na hÉireann*)
Sunday Express
The Times

Printed Volumes of Interviews/Autobiography
Beatty, Tony, *From Post to Post: A Memoir* (Dublin: Currach Press, 2006).
Campaign for Free Speech on Ireland, The British Media and Ireland: Truth, The First Casualty (n. d. [1979?]).
Connolly Association, What is the Connolly Association? Constitution and Explanation (n. d. [1972]).
Dunne, Catherine, *An Unconsidered People: The Irish in London* (Dublin: New Island, 2003).
Healy, John, *The Grass Arena: An Autobiography* (London: Faber & Faber, 1988).
Holohan, Anne (ed.), *Working Lives: The Irish in Britain* (London: *The Irish Post*, 1995).
Keaney, Brian, *Don't Hang About* (Oxford: Oxford University Press, 1985).
Lennon, Mary, McAdam, Marie and O'Brien, Joanne (eds), *Across the Water: Irish Women's Lives in Britain* (London: Virago, 1988).
Lydon, John, with Keith and Kent Zimmerman, *Rotten: No Irish, No Blacks, No Dogs* (London: Hodder & Stoughton, 1992).
MacAmhlaigh, Donall, *An Irish Navvy: The Diary of an Exile*, translated from the Irish language original by Valentin Iremonger (London: Routledge & Kegan Paul, 1964).
Mangan, Anna May, *Me and Mine: A Warm-Hearted Memoir of a London Irish Family* (London: Virago, 2011).
Murphy, Maura, *Don't Wake Me at Doyle's* (London: Headline, 2004).
O'Donoghue, John, *In a Strange Land* (London: Batsford, 1958).
Schweitzer, Pam (ed.), *Across the Irish Sea: An Age Exchange Publication Based on Memories of London Irish Pensioners* (London: Age Exchange, 1989).
Wall, Rita (ed.), *Leading Lives: Irish Women in Britain* (Dublin: Attic, 1991).
Walsh, John, *The Falling Angels: An Irish Romance* (London: Flamingo, 1999).

SECONDARY SOURCES

Published Works

Anderson, Benedict, *Imagined Communities: Reflections on the Origin and Spread of Nationalism* (London: Verso 1983).

Arrowsmith, Aidan, 'Plastic Paddy: Negotiating Identity in Second Generation "Irish-English" Writing', *Irish Studies Review*, 8, 1 (2000), pp.35–43.

Arrowsmith, Aidan, 'Introduction: The Significance of Irishness', *Irish Studies Review*, 14, 2 (2006), pp.163–8.

Baddely, Alan, 'The Psychology of Remembering and Forgetting', in Thomas Butler (ed.), *Memory, History, Culture and the Mind* (Oxford: Blackwell, 1989), pp.33–60.

Belchem, John, 'Class, Creed and Country: The Irish Middle Class in Victorian Liverpool', in Roger Swift and Sheridan Gilley (eds), *The Irish in Victorian Britain: The Local Dimension* (Dublin: Four Courts Press, 1999), pp.190–211.

Buckley, Marella, 'Sitting on Your Politics: The Irish Among the British and the Women Among the Irish', in Jim MacLaughlin (ed.), *Location and Dislocation in Contemporary Irish Society: Emigration and Irish Identities* (Cork: Cork University Press, 1997), pp.94–132.

Campbell, Sean, 'Beyond "Plastic Paddy": A Re-Examination of the Second-Generation Irish in England', *Immigrants and Minorities*, 18, 2–3 (1999), pp.266–88.

Campbell, Sean, *Irish Blood, English Heart: Second-Generation Irish Musicians in England* (Cork: Cork University Press, 2011).

Casey, Maude, *Over the Waters* (London Women's Press, 1987).

Casey, Rionach, 'Community, Difference and Identity: The Case of the Irish in Sheffield', *Irish Geography*, 43, 3 (2010), pp.211–32.

Caulfield, Brendan and Bhat, Ashok, 'The Irish in Britain: Intermarriage and Fertility Levels, 1971–6', *New Community*, 9, 1 (1981), pp.73–83.

Clarke, Sr Sarah, *No Faith in the System: A Search for Justice* (Dublin: Mercier Press, 1995).

Courtney, Damien, 'A Quantification of Irish Migration with Particular Emphasis on the 1980s and 1990s', in Andy Bielenberg (ed.), *The Irish Diaspora* (Harlow: Pearson, 2000), pp.288–316.

Cowley, Ultan, *The Men Who Built Britain: A History of the Irish Navvy* (Dublin: Potters Yard Press, 2001).

Curtis, L., O'Keefe, J., O'Brien, J. and Keatinge, C., *Hearts and Minds/anam agus intinn: The Cultural Life of London's Irish Community* (London: London Strategic Policy Unit, 1986).

Curtis, Liz, *Nothing but the Same Old Story: The Roots of Anti-Irish Racism* (London: Information on Ireland, 1984).

Darby, John, *Dressed to Kill: Cartoonists and the Northern Ireland Conflict* (Belfast: Appletree, 1983).

Delaney, Enda, ' "Almost a Class of Helots in an Alien Land": The British State and Irish Immigration, 1921–45', *Immigrants & Minorities*, 18, 2–3 (1999), pp.240–65.

Delaney, Enda, *Demography, State and Society: Irish Migration to Britain, 1921–1971* (Liverpool: Liverpool University Press, 2000).

Delaney, Enda, 'Placing Postwar Irish Migration to Britain in a Comparative European Perspective, 1945–1981', in Bielenberg (ed.), *Irish Diaspora* (2000), pp.331–56.

Delaney, Enda, *The Irish in Post-War Britain* (Oxford: Oxford University Press, 2007).

Dooley, Brian, *Choosing the Green? Second-Generation Irish and the Cause of Ireland* (Belfast: Beyond the Pale, 2004).

Doyle, Martin (ed.), *A History of the Irish Post: The Voice of the Irish in Britain* (London: The Irish Post, 2000).

Drudy, P.J., 'Migration Between Ireland and Britain Since Independence', in P.J. Drudy (ed.), *Irish Studies 5: Ireland and Britain Since 1922* (Cambridge: Cambridge University Press, 1986), pp.107–24.

Dye, Ryan, 'Catholic Protectionism or Irish Nationalism? Religion and Politics in Liverpool, 1829–1845', *Journal of British Studies*, 40, 3 (2001), pp.357–390.

English, Richard, *Armed Struggle: A History of the IRA* (London: Macmillan, 2003).

Fielding, Stephen, *Class and Ethnicity: Irish Catholics in England, 1880–1939* (Buckingham: Open University Press, 1993).

Fitzpatrick, David, 'A Curious Middle Place: The Irish in Britain, 1871–1921', in Sheridan Gilley and Roger Swift (eds), *The Irish in Britain, 1815–1939* (Savage, MD: Barnes & Noble, 1989), pp.10–59.

Free, Marcus, 'Tales From the Fifth Green Field: The Psychodynamics of Migration, Masculinity and National Identity Amongst Republic of Ireland Soccer Supporters in England', *Sport in Society*, 10, 3 (2007), pp.476–94.

Gmelch, G., 'The Readjustment of Returned Migrants in the West of Ireland', in R. King, (ed.), *Return Migration and Regional Economic Problems* (London: Routledge, 1986), pp.152–85.

Gray, Breda, 'From "Ethnicity" to "Diaspora": 1980s Emigration and "Multicultural" London', in Bielenberg (ed.), *Irish Diaspora* (2000), pp.65–89.

Gray, Breda, *Women and the Irish Diaspora* (London: Routledge, 2004).

Gray, Breda, 'Curious Hybridities: Transnational Negotiations of Migrancy through Generation', *Irish Studies Review*, 14, 2 (2006), pp.207–23.

Greenslade, Liam, 'The Blackbird Calls in Grief: Colonialism, Health and Identity among Irish Immigrants in Britain', in Jim MacLaughlin (ed.), *Location and Dislocation in Contemporary Irish Society: Emigration and Irish Identities* (Cork: Cork University Press, 1997), pp.36–60.

Hannan, Damian F., 'Migration Motives and Migration Differentials Among the Irish Rural Youth', *Sociologia Ruralis*, 9, 3 (1969), pp.195–219.

Hansard, House of Commons Debate, 11 December 1974, vol. 883, cc. 518–64.

Harrison, Gerry, *The Scattering: A History of the London Irish Centre, 1954–2004* (London: London Irish Centre, 2004).

Harrison, Paul, 'Culture and Migration: The Irish English', *New Society*, 25, 272 (1973), pp.699–702.

Harte, Liam, 'Migrancy, Performativity and Autobiographical Identity', *Irish Studies Review*, 14, 2 (2006), pp.225–38.

Herbert, Michael, *The Wearing of the Green: A Political History of the Irish in Manchester* (London: Irish in Britain Representation Group, 2001).

Hickman, Mary, *Religion, Class and Identity: The State, the Catholic Church and Education of the Irish in Britain* (Avebury: Avebury Press, 1995).

Hickman, Mary, 'The Irish in Britain: Racism, Incorporation and Identity', *Irish Studies Review*, 10 (Spring 1995), pp.16–19.

Hickman, Mary, *The Irish Community in Britain: Myth or Reality?* Irish Studies Centre Occasional Papers Series, 8 (London: Irish Studies Centre, 1996).

Hickman, Mary J., 'Reconstructing Deconstructing "Race": British Political Discourses About the Irish in Britain', *Ethnic and Racial Studies*, 21, 2 (1998), pp.288–307.

Hickman, Mary J., *Alternative Historiographies of the Irish in Britain: A Critique of the Segregation/Assimilation Model*, in Roger Swift and Sheridan Gilley (eds), *The Irish in Victorian Britain: The Local Dimension* (Dublin: Four Courts Press, 1999), pp.236–53.

Hickman, Mary J., 'Census Ethnic Categories and Second-Generation Identities: A Study of the Irish in England and Wales,' *Journal of Ethnic and Migration Studies*, 37, 1 (2011), pp.79–97.

Hickman, Mary J. and Walter, Bronwen, *Discrimination and the Irish Community in Britain: A Report of Research Undertaken for the Commission for Racial Equality* (London: CRE, 1997).

Hickman, Mary J., Morgan, Sarah and Walter, Bronwen, *Second-Generation Irish People in Britain: A Demographic, Socio-Economic and Health Profile* (London: Irish Studies Centre, University of North London, 2001)

Hillyard, Paddy, *Suspect Community: People's Experience of the Prevention of Terrorism Act in Britain* (London: Pluto Press, 1993).

Holmes, Colin, *John Bull's Island: Immigration and British Society, 1871– 1971* (Basingstoke: Palgrave Macmillan, 1988).

Holmes, Michael, 'Symbols of National Identity and Sport: The Case of the Irish Football Team', *Irish Political Studies*, 9, 1 (1994), pp.81–98.

Holmes, Michael, and Storey, David, 'Who Are the Boys in Green? Irish Identity and Soccer in the Republic of Ireland', in Adrian Smith and Dilwyn Porter, *Sport and National Identity in the Post-War World* (London: Routledge, 2004), pp.88–104.

Hornsby-Smith, Michael P., and Dale, Angela, 'The Assimilation of Irish Immigrants in England', *British Journal of Sociology*, 39, 4 (1988), pp.519–44.

Hutchinson, John and O'Day, Alan, 'The Gaelic Revival in London, 1900–22: Limits of Ethnic Identity', in Roger Swift and Sheridan Gilley (eds), *The Irish in Victorian Britain: The Local Dimension* (Dublin: Four Courts Press, 1999), pp.254–76.

Jackson, Alvin, *Ireland 1798–1998* (Oxford: Blackwell, 1999).

Jackson, John, *Report on the Skibbereen Social Survey* (Dublin: Human Sciences Committee, 1967).

Jackson, John A., 'The Irish in Britain', in P.J. Drudy (ed.), *Irish Studies 5: Ireland and Britain Since 1922* (Cambridge: Cambridge University Press, 1986), pp.125–38.

Keane, John B., *Self-Portrait* (Dublin: Mercier Press, 1964).

Kells, Mary, 'Ethnicity in the 1990s: Irish Immigrants in London', in Ulrich Kockel (ed.), *Landscape, Heritage and Identity: Case Studies in Irish Ethnography* (Liverpool: Liverpool University Press, 1995), pp.223–36.

Kells, Mary, ' "I'm Myself and Nobody Else": Gender and Ethnicity Among Young Middle-Class Irish Women in London', in Patrick O'Sullivan (ed.), *The Irish Worldwide: History, Heritage, Identity*, vol. 4, *Irish Women and Irish Migration* (Leicester: Leicester University Press, 1995), pp.202–34.

Kelly, Kate and Tríona Nic Giolla Choille, 'Listening and Learning:

Experiences in an Emigrant Advice Agency', in Patrick O'Sullivan (ed.), *The Irish Worldwide: History, Heritage, Identity*, vol. 4, *Irish Women and Irish Migration*, pp.168–91.

Layton-Henry, Zigg, *The Politics of Immigration, 'Race' and 'Race Relations' in Post-War Britain* (Oxford: Wiley-Blackwell, 1992).

Leach, Edmund, 'The Official Irish Jokesters', *New Society* 20, 27 (December 1979), p.vii–ix.

Leavey, Gerard, Sembhi, Sati and Livingston, Gill, 'Older Irish Migrants Living in London: Identity, Loss and Return', *Journal of Ethnic and Migration Studies*, 30, 4, pp.763–79.

Lee, J. J., *Ireland 1912–1985: Politics and Society* (Cambridge: Cambridge University Press, 1989).

Lees, Lynn Hollen, *Exiles of Erin: Irish Migrants in Victorian London* (Manchester: Manchester University Press, 1979).

Light, Jr, Dale B., 'The Role of Irish-American Organisations in Assimilation and Community Formation', in P.J. Drudy (ed.), *Irish Studies 4: The Irish in America: Emigration, Assimilation and Impact* (Cambridge: Cambridge University Press, 1985), pp.113–41.

Lummis, Trevor, *Listening to History: The Authenticity of Oral Evidence* (London: Hutchinson Education, 1987).

Mac an Ghaill, Maírtín, 'What about the Lads? – Emigrants, Immigrants, Ethnics and Transnationals in Late 1990s Diaspora', in R. Lentin (ed.), *Emerging Irish Identities* (Dublin: Trinity College Dublin/ National Consultative Committee on Racism and Interculturalism, 2000), pp.40–9.

MacRaild, Donald M., *The Irish Diaspora in Britain, 1750–1939* (Basingstoke: Palgrave Macmillan, 2011).

Malone, Mary, 'The Health Experience of Irish People in a North West London "Community Saved" ', *Community, Work & Family*, 4, 2 (2001), pp.195–211.

Malone, Mary E., and Dooley, John P., ' "Dwelling in Displacement": Meanings of "Community" and Sense of Community for Two Generations of Irish People Living in North-West London', *Community, Work and Family*, 9, 1 (2006), pp.11–28.

McCarthy, Pete, *The Road to McCarthy* (London: Hodder & Stoughton, 2002).

McGovern, Mark, 'The "Craic" Market: Irish Theme Bars and the Commodification of Irishness in Contemporary Britain', *Irish Journal of Sociology*, 11, 2 (2002), pp.77–98.

McGowan, Brendan, *Taking the Boat: The Irish in Leeds, 1931–81* (Killala; self-published, 2009).

Miller, David, *Don't Mention the War: Northern Ireland, Propaganda and the Media* (London: Pluto Press, 1994).

Moran, James, *Irish Birmingham: A History* (Liverpool: Liverpool University Press, 2010).

Mulhern, Robert, *A Very Different County* (self-published, 2011).

Murray, Tony, 'Curious Streets: Diaspora, Displacement and Transgression in Desmond Hogan's London Irish Narratives', *Irish Studies Review*, 14, 2 (2006), pp.239–53.

Nagle, John, ' "Everybody is Irish on St Paddy's": Ambivalence and Alterity at London's St Patrick's Day 2002', *Identities: Global Studies in Culture and Power*, 12, 4 (2005), pp.563–83.

Nagle, John, *Multiculturalism's Double Bind: Creating Inclusivity, Cosmopolitanism and Difference* (Farnham: Ashgate, 2009).

Nickels, Henri C., Thomas, Lyn, Hickman, Mary J. and Silvestri, Sara, 'A Comparative Study of the Representations of "Suspect" Communities in Multi-Ethnic Britain and of Their Impact on Irish Communities and Muslim Communities – Mapping Newspaper Content', Working Paper 13 (London: Institute for the Study of European Transformations, 2009).

O'Connor, Kevin, *The Irish in Britain* (Dublin, 1972).

O'Day, Alan, 'Revising the Diaspora', in D. George Boyce and Alan O'Day (eds), *The Making of Modern Irish history: Revisionism and the Revisionist Controversy* (London: Routledge, 1996), pp.188–215.

O'Shea, Fr Kieran, *The Irish Emigrant Chaplaincy Scheme in Britain, 1957–82* (Naas, 1985).

Ó Tuathaigh, M.A.G., 'Irish Historical "Revisionism": State of the Art of Ideological Project?', in Ciaran Brady (ed.), *Interpreting Irish History: The Debate on Historical Revisionism* (Dublin: Irish Academic Press, 1994), pp.306–26.

Popoviciu, Liviu, Haywood, Chris and Mac an Ghaill, Máirtín, 'Migrating Masculinities: The Irish Diaspora in Britain', *Irish Studies Review*, 14, 2, (2006), pp.169–87.

Prince, Simon, *Northern Ireland's '68: Civil Rights, Global Revolt and the Origins of the Troubles* (Dublin: Irish Academic Press, 2007).

Purdie, Bob, *Politics in the Streets: The Origins of the Civil Rights Movement in Northern Ireland* (Belfast: Blackstaff Press, 1990).

Renwick, Ali, *Oliver's Army: A History of British Soldiers in Northern Ireland and Other Conflicts* hhttp://www.troopsoutmovement. com/ Ultansarmychap8.htm.

Robertson, Geoff, *Reluctant Judas: The Life and Death of the Special Branch Informer, Kenneth Lennon* (London: Temple-Smith, 1976).

Roseman, Mark, 'Surviving Memory: Truth and Memory in Holocaust Testimony', *Journal of Holocaust Education*, 8, 1 (1999), pp.1–20.

Rossiter, Ann, *Ireland's Hidden Diaspora: The 'Abortion Trail' and the Making of a London-Irish Underground, 1980–2000* (London: IASC, 2009).

Ryan, Liam, 'Irish Emigration to Britain Since World War II', in R. Kearney (ed.), *Migrations: The Irish at Home and Abroad* (Dublin: Wolfhound, 1990), pp.45–68.

Ryan, Louise, 'Who Do You Think You Are? Irish Nurses Encountering Ethnicity and Constructing Identity in Britain', *Ethnic and Racial Studies*, 30, 3, (2007), pp.416–38.

Scully, Marc, '"Plastic and Proud?", Discourses of Authenticity, Among the Second-Generation Irish in England', *Psychology & Society*, 2, 2 (2009), pp.124–35.

Smyth, Gerry, 'Who's the Greenest of Them All? Irishness and Popular Music', *Irish Studies Review*, 1, 2 (1992), pp.3–5.

Swift, Roger, 'The Historiography of the Irish in Nineteenth-Century Britain', in Patrick O'Sullivan (ed.), *The Irish Worldwide: History, Heritage and Identity*, vol. 2, *The Irish in the New Communities* (Leicester: Leicester University Press, 1997), pp.52–81.

Travers, Pauric, ' "There Was Nothing For Me There": Irish Female Emigration, 1922–71', in Patrick O'Sullivan (ed.), *The Irish Worldwide: History, Heritage, Identity*, vol. 4, *Irish Women and Irish Migration* (Leicester: Leicester University Press, 1995), pp.146–67.

Ullah, Philip, 'Second-Generation Irish Youth: Identity and Ethnicity', *New Community*, 12, 2 (1985), pp.310–20.

Walsh, James J. and McGrath, Fergus P., 'Identity, Coping Style, and Health Behaviour Among First Generation Irish Immigrants in England', *Psychology and Health*, 15 (2000), pp.467–82.

Walter, Bronwen, *Irish Women in London* (London: London Strategic Policy Unit, 1988).

Walter, Bronwen, 'Contemporary Irish Settlement in London: Women's Worlds, Men's Worlds', in Jim MacLaughlin (ed.), *Location and Dislocation in Contemporary Irish Society: Emigration and Irish identities* (Cork: Cork University Press, 1997), pp.61–94.

Walter, Bronwen, *Outsiders Inside: Whiteness, Place and Irish Women* (London: Routledge, 2001).

Walter, Bronwen, 'Voices in Other Ears: "Accents" and Identities of the First- and Second-Generation Irish in England', in Guido Rings and Anne Ife, *Neo-Colonial Mentalities in Contemporary Europe? Language and Discourse in the Construction of Identities* (Cambridge: Cambridge Scholars, 2008), pp.174–82.

Walter, Bronwen, Morgan, Sarah, Hickman, Mary J. and Bradley, Joseph, 'Family Stories, Public Silence: Irish Identity Construction Amongst the Second-Generation Irish in England', *Scottish Geographical Journal*, 118, 3 (2002), pp.201–17.

DISSERTATIONS/THESES

Graham, Paul M., 'The Effects of the Fatal Hunger Strike in the H-Blocks Long Kesh, on the Catholic/Nationalist Community' (unpublished MA thesis, Queen's University Belfast, 1983).
Hall, Reginald Richard, 'Irish Music and Dance in London, 1890–1970: A Socio-Cultural History' (unpublished PhD, University of Sussex, 1994).
Kirkaldy, J., 'English Newspaper Images of Northern Ireland 1968–73: An Historical Study in Stereotypes and Prejudices' (unpublished PhD thesis, University of New South Wales, 1979).
Maguire, Siobhán, 'The "Anti-Internment League": A Study of an Irish Political Organisation in 1970s Britain' (unpublished MA dissertation, University of North London, 1999).
Morgan, Sarah, 'The Contemporary Racialization of the Irish in Britain: An Investigation of Media Representations and Everyday Experience of Being Irish in Britain' (unpublished PhD thesis, University of North London, 1997).
Scully, Marc, 'Discourses of Authenticity and National Identity among the Irish Diaspora in England' (unpublished PhD thesis, Open University, 2010).
Wardle, Elizabeth, 'The Effect of the Provisional IRA Bombings in England on the Irish Community of London' (unpublished MA dissertation, National University of Ireland Galway, 2007).

DOCUMENTARIES AND FILMS

'Here to Stay', BBC Midlands Report, 1994.
'The Irish in England', Irish Video Project, first broadcast Channel 4, 1983.
The Irishmen: An Impression of Exile, BBC, 1964.
'Second-Generation Experience', Irish Video Project, 1984.

ELECTRONIC RESOURCES

Camden Council website: http://www.camden.gov.uk/ccm/content/council-and-democracy/who-represents-you/the-mayor-of-camden/file-storage/bookmark-of-mayors.en (accessed 15 August 2009).

Election results: http://www.politicsresources.net/area/uk/uktable.htm (accessed 19 August 2009).

Text of the PTA: http://cain.ulst.ac.uk/hmso/pta1974.htm (accessed 14 August 2009).

Index